IMMIGRANT AND ENTREPRENEUR

Max Kade German-American Research Institute Series

EDITED BY A. GREGG ROEBER

This series provides an outlet for books that reflect
the mission of the Penn State Max Kade Institute: to integrate
the history and culture of German-speakers in the Americas
with the major themes of early modern scholarship from
the sixteenth century to the early nineteenth century.

The Max Kade German-American Research Institute,
located on Penn State's campus (*http://www.maxkade.psu.edu/*),
was founded in 1993 thanks to a grant from the
Max Kade Foundation, New York. The directors of the
Penn State University Max Kade German American Research
Institute are Daniel Purdy and A. Gregg Roeber.

Immigrant and Entrepreneur

THE ATLANTIC WORLD OF CASPAR WISTAR, 1650–1750

Rosalind J. Beiler

THE PENNSYLVANIA STATE UNIVERSITY PRESS | UNIVERSITY PARK, PENNSYLVANIA

LIBRARY OF CONGRESS CATALOGING-IN-PUBLICATION DATA

Beiler, Rosalind J., 1961– .
Immigrant and entrepreneur : the Atlantic world of Caspar Wistar, 1650–1750 /
Rosalind J. Beiler.
p.   cm.—(Max Kade German-American research series)
Includes bibliographical references and index.
Summary: "Examines the life of 18th century German immigrant
and businessman Caspar Wistar. Reevaluates the modern understanding
of the entrepreneurial ideal and the immigrant experience
in the colonial era"—Provided by publisher.
ISBN 13: 978-0-271-03595-6 (pbk : alk. paper)
1. Wistar, Caspar, 1696–1752.
2. Germans—Pennsylvania—Philadelphia Region—Biography.
3. Immigrants—Pennsylvania—Philadelphia Region—Biography.
4. Merchants—Pennsylvania—Philadelphia Region—Biography.
5. Philadelphia Region (Pa.)—Biography.
6. Palatinate (Germany)—Biography.
7. Pennsylvania—Emigration and immigration—History—18th century.
8. Immigrants—Pennsylvania—History—18th century.
I. Title.

F158.9.G3B45 2008
974.8'1102092—dc22
2008005072

CONTENTS

MAPS, FIGURES, AND TABLES

Maps

Figures

Tables

for PAUL S. *and* ELSIE BEILER

PREFACE AND ACKNOWLEDGMENTS

When I began my research for this book, my intention was to undertake a comparative community study, not to write the story of one individual. Deeply influenced by historians writing about cultural transfer and adaptation from Great Britain to the American colonies, I wanted to examine similar processes among German-speaking immigrants.[1] I hoped to use Wistar's letters and family documents to link the people who lived and worked in Wistarburg, New Jersey, with their European home communities, but I discovered that there was little extant evidence for individuals at Wistarburg and that these people came from different regions. As I began to recover the Palatine context of Wistar's family, I was struck by the stark contrasts between his background there and what I knew about the British mid-Atlantic colonies. The more I learned about the world of his childhood, the more I was fascinated by how it shaped in unexpected ways the choices he made in America. The resulting book is, therefore, much more biographical than I originally intended but still reflects, I hope, my fascination with the forces that influence individual choices, which in turn create both change and continuity.

This book was also informed by questions that were giving rise to the new subfield of Atlantic history. When I first described Wistar's world as "transatlantic" in 1994, the term was not widely used. Nevertheless, my interest in the comparative project it implied was peaked by questions about how the people, ideas, and goods circulating between Europe, Africa, and the Americas were shaping

---

1. David G. Allen, *In English Ways: The Movement of Societies and the Transferal of English Local Law and Custom to Massachusetts Bay in the Seventeenth Century* (Chapel Hill: University of North Carolina Press, 1981); Ned Landsman, *Scotland and Its First American Colony, 1683–1765* (Princeton: Princeton University Press, 1985); David Cressy, *Coming Over: Migration and Communication Between England and New England in the Seventeenth Century* (Cambridge: Cambridge University Press, 1987); Jack Greene, *Pursuits of Happiness: The Social Development of Early Modern British Colonies and the Formation of American Culture* (Chapel Hill: University of North Carolina Press, 1988); David H. Fischer, *Albion's Seed: British Folkways in America* (New York: Oxford University Press, 1989); A. G. Roeber, "In German Ways? Problems and Potentials of Eighteenth-Century German Social and Emigration History," *William and Mary Quarterly* 44 (1987): 750–74.

events in North America. This book fits well into the field of Atlantic history that historians have begun to define and theorize in the past decade. To the extent that it tells the story of how Wistar's migration to Pennsylvania helped to create communities connected by the Atlantic, it has a "circum-Atlantic" focus. Through the lens of one individual's life, we catch glimpses of the Atlantic as, in David Armitage's phrase, a "zone of exchange and interchange, circulation and transmission," but in this case, that community extends beyond the rim of the ocean to the Neckar River valley.[2] At the same time, Wistar's story is "trans-Atlantic": it presents a comparison of social, political, and religious structures in the Palatinate and Pennsylvania, but from the perspective of an individual rather than the state.[3] Finally, Wistar's story allows us to view some of the integrative processes at work in the eighteenth-century Atlantic world.[4] For these reasons, I have chosen to describe Wistar's world as "Atlantic" rather than "transatlantic" in the title of this book.

During the fifteen years I have worked on this project, I have incurred numerous debts. I have had the good fortune to receive assistance from many archivists, librarians, historians, and friends. My research has been supported by grants from the German Historical Institute, the Fulbright Commission, the Philadelphia Center for Early American Studies (now the McNeil Center for Early American Studies), the Andrew J. Mellon Foundation, Winterthur Museum, the University of Central Florida, the Pennsylvania Historical and Museum Commission, and the Charles Warren Center for Studies in American History at Harvard University. In locating and reading historical documents, I received invaluable assistance from the staffs of historical repositories on both sides of the Atlantic. For their generous help, I wish to thank the archivists and librarians at the Historical Society of Pennsylvania; the Pennsylvania State Archives; the Library Company of Philadelphia; the New Jersey State Archives; the American Philosophical Society; the Salem County Historical Society, Salem, N.J.; Winterthur Museum; the Badisches Generallandesarchiv, Karlsruhe; and the Archiv des Evangelisches Oberkirchenrat, Karlsruhe. They served as excellent gatekeepers and guides to early modern Europe and America. I am also grateful to Eliza Childs for her meticulous and careful copyediting, to Erin Greb for her creative cartography, and to Kristin Peterson, editorial assistant at Penn State Press, for her generous help.

2. David Armitage, "Three Concepts of Atlantic History," in *The British Atlantic World, 1500–1800*, ed. David Armitage and Michael J. Braddick (New York: Palgrave Macmillan, 2002), 16.

3. Armitage, "Three Concepts," 18–21.

4. Bernard Bailyn, *Atlantic History: Concept and Contours* (Cambridge: Harvard University Press, 2005), 81–101.

I also wish to thank the many individuals who graciously listened, read, and responded as I tried to make sense of Wistar's world. Richard S. Dunn and Thomas M. Safley have been wonderful mentors from my earliest days as a graduate student to the present. Hartmut Lehmann, Hermann Wellenreuther, and Wolfgang von Hippel provided invaluable assistance in navigating German sources and archives. Liesl Schwind kindly shared her photographs of the village and her knowledge of Waldhilsbach's history and dialect with me. Arlene Palmer Schwind willingly passed on her extensive research on the United Glass Company. And Dr. Klaus Irmscher collaborated on efforts to trace the movements of glassmakers at Peterstal. I began to unravel some of the complexities of Wistar's land transactions with generous assistance from Joseph Foster, Craig Horle, and Jonathan Stayer. The lively exchanges among scholars in Wolfgang von Hippel's graduate seminar at the University of Mannheim in 1991–92, at the Philadelphia Center for Early American Studies from 1992 to 1994, and at the Charles Warren Center in 1997–98 provided wonderful intellectual communities in which to try out my arguments at very different points in the process. Carole Adams, Sean Adams, Bernard Bailyn, Steve Behrendt, Jon Butler, Richard Dunn, Aaron Fogleman, Gerry Friesen, Evan Haefeli, David Hancock, Susan Klepp, Wim Klooster, Mark Petersen, Dan Richter, Donna Rilling, Gregg Roeber, Tom Safley, Ian Steele, Marianne Wokeck, Janet Umble, and Hong Zhang read parts or all of the manuscript and gave valuable and constructive comments. The book is much stronger as a result of their insights; any shortcomings are solely my own.

A widely scattered group of friends and colleagues offered their support as my pursuit of Wistar's world spilled into my daily life. Whether they wanted to or not, they all became familiar with his world. Uwe, Antje, Inke, and Dörte Neundorf; Gudrun Retzer; Ingrid and Cetin Aydogan; the Schwehn family; the Sauer family; Nicola Hale, Ursula Lehmkuhl, Petra Dolata-Kreutzkamp, and Peter Busch created a home away from home during my extended stays in Germany. Their generous hospitality allowed me to mirror Wistar's cultural immersion in reverse in the twentieth century. Donna Rilling, Judy Ridner, Alison Isenberg, and Jane Merrit offered moral support and friendship as fellow graduate students and colleagues from our days in Philadelphia to the present. Susan Hunt and Pat Denault deserve special thanks for helping to make my year in Cambridge a delight. In Orlando, my colleagues in the History Department at the University of Central Florida have provided a collegial and nurturing environment that is truly a treasure in the academy. Richard Crepeau, Shirley Leckie, and Edmund Kallina have been model mentors, colleagues, and friends. Carole Gonzales and Nancy Rauscher have assisted me in more ways than I can ever recount. Without their daily help, I could not have completed this book.

Jake Ivey, Lindsay McNellis, and Derek Russell patiently assisted me with copy-editing. And to Paul and Linda Beiler, Janet and Ivan Umble, Donna Rilling, and Lisa Logan: thank you for your friendship, good humor, and constant belief that sooner or later Wistar would see the light of day.

Through the many years I have worked on this book, my family has provided unwavering encouragement. My sisters and brother and nieces and nephews have all listened patiently to endless stories (and lectures) about eighteenth-century characters and places. My parents, Paul S. and Elsie Beiler, have made amazing efforts to enter Wistar's world and my own. They endured trips to places they would not likely have chosen to visit, willingly stepped out of their comfort zones, and patiently explained my work to the many relatives and friends they see more often than I do. For their love and support and for always reminding me of the most important things in life, I am thankful.

BRKB	Bammental reformierte Kirchenbuch, Evangelisches Oberkirchenrat, Karlsruhe, Germany
EOK	Evangelisches Oberkirchenrat, Karlsruhe, Germany
GLA	Badisches Generallandesarchiv, Karlsruhe, Germany
HSP	Historical Society of Pennsylvania, Philadelphia
MPC	Samuel Hazard, ed. *Minutes of the Provincial Council of Pennsylvania from the Organization to the Termination of the Proprietary Government [Mar. 10, 1683–Sept. 27, 1775].* 10 vols. Philadelphia: Printed by J. Severns, 1851–52.
NgKKB	Neckargemünd katholische Kirchenbuch, Katholische Pfarramt, Goldene Anchor, Neckargemünd, Germany
NgLKB	Neckargemünd lutherische Kirchenbuch, EOK, Karlsruhe, Germany
NgRKB	Neckargemünd reformierte Kirchenbuch, EOK, Karlsruhe, Germany
NJA	New Jersey State Archives, Trenton, N.J.
NkRKB	Neunkirchen reformierte Kirchenbuch, EOK, Karlsruhe, Germany
PA Hist	*Pennsylvania History*
PMHB	*Pennsylvania Magazine of History and Biography*
PPOC	Penn Papers, Official Correspondence, HSP, Philadelphia
PSA	Pennsylvania State Archives, Harrisburg
Stadt- und Landkreise	Stadt- und Landkreise: Staatlichen Archivverwaltung Baden-Württemberg. *Die Stadt- und die Landkreise Heidelberg und Mannheim.* 4 vols. Die Stadt- und Landkreise in Baden-Württemberg. Karlsruhe: G. Braun GmbH, 1966–70.
Statutes at Large	Pennsylvania. *The Statutes at Large of Pennsylvania from 1682 to 1801.* [Harrisburg]: Clarence M. Bush, State Printer, 1896–1915.
Votes	Gertrude MacKinney and Charles F. Hoban, eds. *Pennsylvania Archives*, 8th ser. 8 vols. *Votes and Proceedings of the House of Representatives of the Province of Pennsylvania, 1682–1776.* [Harrisburg], 1931–35.
WMQ	*William and Mary Quarterly*
ZGO	*Zeitschrift die Geschichte des Oberrheins*

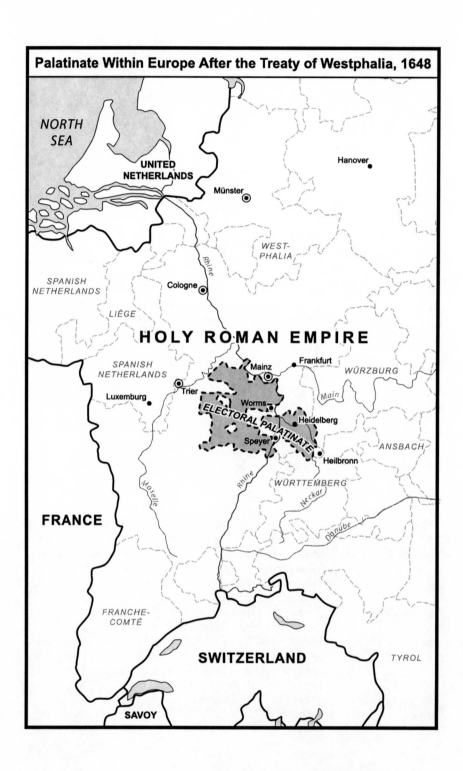

Palatinate Within Europe After the Treaty of Westphalia, 1648

NORTH SEA

UNITED NETHERLANDS

Hanover

Münster

WEST-PHALIA

SPANISH NETHERLANDS

LIÈGE

Rhine

Cologne

HOLY ROMAN EMPIRE

SPANISH NETHERLANDS

Trier

Luxemburg

Mainz

Frankfurt

WÜRZBURG

Main

Worms

ELECTORAL PALATINATE

Heidelberg

Speyer

ANSBACH

Heilbronn

Moselle

Rhine

WÜRTTEMBERG

Neckar

FRANCE

Danube

FRANCHE-COMTÉ

SWITZERLAND

TYROL

SAVOY

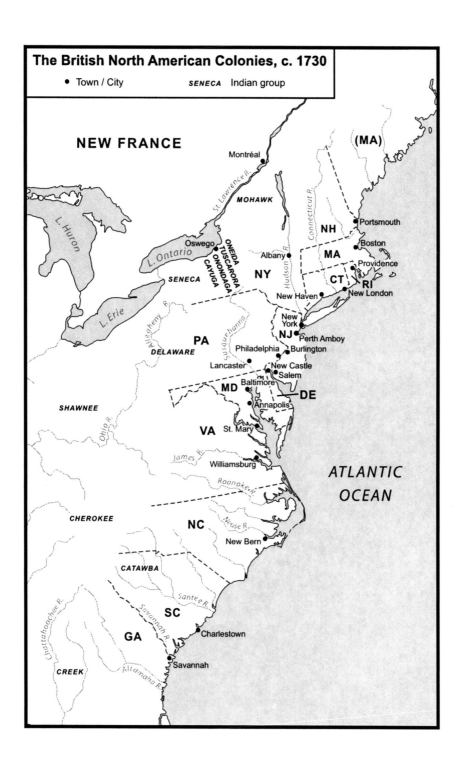

The British North American Colonies, c. 1730

- Town / City   *SENECA*   Indian group

NEW FRANCE

Montréal

L. Huron

MOHAWK

St. Lawrence R.

L. Ontario

Oswego

ONEIDA
TUSCARORA
ONONDAGA
CAYUGA

SENECA

L. Erie

Allegheny R.

Albany

Connecticut R.

(MA)

NH

Portsmouth

MA

Boston

Providence

NY

Hudson R.

CT

RI

New Haven

New London

New York

NJ

Perth Amboy

PA

DELAWARE

Susquehanna R.

Philadelphia

Burlington

Lancaster

New Castle

Salem

Baltimore

MD

DE

SHAWNEE

Ohio R.

Annapolis

VA

St. Mary

James R.

Williamsburg

ATLANTIC
OCEAN

Roanoke R.

CHEROKEE

NC

Neuse R.

New Bern

CATAWBA

Santee R.

Chattahoochee R.

Savannah R.

SC

GA

Charlestown

CREEK

Altamaha R.

Savannah

Introduction

In the 1740s, Caspar Wistar (1696–1752) sat down at his walnut desk in the little front room beneath the stairs to pen his memoirs. By then he was a successful, wealthy Quaker entrepreneur at the peak of his career. Wistar lived with his wife, Catharine, and their six children and seven servants in a comfortably furnished three-story brick house on High Street in Philadelphia. On the same property, he carried out his brass-button-making business, which by 1752 included four servant-apprentices and was valued at 676 Pennsylvania pounds.[1] Wistar sold hardware, dry goods, and glass out of his shop a few blocks away.[2] He ran another "country store" at Wistarburg, the village that had grown up around his United Glass Company in Salem County, New Jersey.[3] He also owned several "plantations" and numerous large tracts of land in Philadelphia, Bucks, and Lancaster counties.[4] By all accounts, Wistar had joined the elite among Philadelphia's Anglo-American Quaker community.

Wistar's life in the 1740s contrasted sharply with the humble beginnings he described in his memoir, "A Short Report of Caspar Wistar." The oldest son of a forester, or hunter, he was born in the Palatinate near Heidelberg, in what is today Germany. The electorate of the Palatinate was an early modern state that encompassed land on the east and west sides of the Rhine River and was headed by the elector Palatine. As a forester, Wistar's father was a government official, appointed by the elector to monitor the state's natural resources. According to his autobiographical account, Wistar had grown up in a "small, wretched village or country town," which was too poor to afford a schoolmaster. Indeed, his own scrawl of phonetically written Waldhilsbach dialect attests to the rudimentary nature of his education. The people in his village made their living primarily from farming and from potter's clay, which they dug from the ground and

1. "Inventory of the Goods and Chattels of Caspar Wistar, Apr. 4, 1752," Wistar Family Papers, HSP; Philadelphia County Wills, bk. I, 493, microfilm copy, HSP; Philadelphia County Deeds, G-4, 361–65, microfilm copy, HSP; Richard Wistar Davids, *The Wistar Family: A Genealogy of the Descendants of Caspar Wistar, Emigrant in 1717* (Philadelphia, 1896).
2. Receipt Book of Caspar Wistar, 1747–84, Am .941, HSP.
3. Caspar Wistar, Account Book G, 1743–69, Wistar Family Papers, HSP.
4. Philadelphia County Wills, bk. I, 493, microfilm copy, HSP.

carted an hour through the woods to the neighboring market town.[5] The image Wistar painted of his impoverished European childhood stood in stark relief to the tremendous wealth of his later life.

Wistar's description of his arrival in Pennsylvania reinforced this image of poverty. He claimed that he stepped onto Philadelphia's docks with only ninepence to his name, wandered the city's streets because he could not afford a meal at an inn, and used his remaining money to purchase a loaf of bread. Desperate for funds, he took a job hauling ashes in a wheelbarrow for a soap-maker named John Bearde.[6] Wistar's imagery is very familiar to twenty-first-century Americans; it has an uncanny similarity to the story his neighbor and contemporary Benjamin Franklin told in his own autobiography, written some twenty years later. Franklin's portrayal of his destitute arrival in Philadelphia and rise to prominence through hard work is the picture we associate today with the self-made American man.[7]

Wistar's six-page memoir ends abruptly two years after his arrival in Pennsylvania and does not include his interpretation of his success. Nevertheless, contemporaries and family members frequently commented on his career. In 1750, Pennsylvania's governor cited Wistar's meteoric rise to wealth when discussing the potential problems of German-speaking immigrants receiving the franchise before they understood the rights of English men. "Caspar Wistar, whom I remember wheeling ashes about this Town," he wrote, "is now worth sixty thousand pounds."[8] The author of his obituary likewise attested to his "unaccountable worldly riches."[9] Wistar's descendants perpetuated this image of a young man who began life in America with few resources but who through courage, hard work, and independence amassed a fortune.[10]

5. "Ein kortzer Bericht von Caspar Wistar" (hereafter "Short Report"), [n.d.], Wistar Family Papers, HSP. All translations are by the author unless otherwise specified.
6. Ibid.
7. The two men arrived in Philadelphia within six years of one another; throughout most of the 1730s and 1740s, they lived within a block or two of one another. Franklin's Junto often met at the Indian King Tavern across the street from Wistar's home. At the same time he was writing his autobiography, Wistar's glassmakers were fashioning custom-ordered glass "electrical" tubes for Franklin's experiments. Arlene Palmer, "The Wistarburg Glassworks of Colonial New Jersey" (master's thesis, University of Delaware, 1973), 122–23; 145–60. See the foldout map of Franklin's Philadelphia, 1723–76, in Leonard Labaree, ed., The Papers of Benjamin Franklin (New Haven: Yale University Press, 1960), vol. 2. I have found no evidence that Wistar's "Short Report" was ever published or that Franklin knew of its existence. Nevertheless, both present themselves as self-made men. For a discussion of eighteenth-century autobiography, see Susan E. Klepp and Billy G. Smith, eds., The Infortunate: The Voyage and Adventures of William Moraley (University Park: The Pennsylvania State University Press, 1992), 14–20. See also Vincent Carretta, Equiano the African: Biography of a Self-Made Man (Athens: University of Georgia Press, 2005), xiii.
8. Governor James Hamilton to Thomas Penn, Sept. 24, 1750, PPOC, 5:55, HSP.
9. Christopher Sauer, obituary for Caspar Wistar, Apr. 1, 1752, Pennsylvania Berichte oder Sammlung wichtiger Nachrichten aus dem Natur- und Kirchen-Reich, HSP.
10. Wistar's comment on his education—that he did not concern himself much with it—suggests an alternative image to the hard-working self-made man his descendants promoted. "Short Report,"

Indeed, Wistar's rise to wealth was astonishing and unusual. At a time when Philadelphia's elite men held property with an average value of 24,000 Pennsylvania pounds, Wistar's net worth, 60,000 pounds, was considerably more.[11] He represented the potential opportunity the British American colonies furnished Anglo-American men. He embodied the eighteenth-century masculine American ideal of the self-made man—the ideal that "associated manhood with individualism, materialism, and an entrepreneurial spirit."[12] Wistar was clearly referencing this construction of himself when he described his near-penniless arrival in Pennsylvania, and his contemporaries would have recognized it immediately.

Nevertheless, Wistar's "Short Report" included another construction of himself that contemporaries and descendants failed to comment on so frequently. This second theme emerges in his description of the heart-wrenching and emotional experience of leaving home. When he decided to migrate to the British colonies, he supposedly acted against the wishes of his parents, his master, other family members, and friends. Pennsylvania, according to Wistar, was not well known then "so that it was thought one would never be heard from again, much less seen again." His renunciation of his parents, his decision to travel to an unknown land, and the thought of leaving behind everything he knew elicited "sadness, and heavy hearts and crying and tears" from Wistar and his family.[13]

At the time he recorded his story, sometime between 1743 and 1752, Wistar was likely writing for his six living children, who had been born in Pennsylvania and who had no firsthand knowledge of his European world.[14] They would have

---

Wistar Family Papers, HSP. Catharine Morris Brown, "Interesting Records of the Wistar Family," 1879, Wistar Family File, Salem County Historical Society, Salem, N.J.; poem by Susan Stevenson, in Jones Wister, *Jones Wister's Reminiscences* (Philadelphia: J. B. Lippincott, 1920), 4–6; Robert C. Moon, *The Morris Family of Philadelphia: Descendants of Anthony Morris* (Philadelphia, 1898), 1:356–66; Caspar Wistar Haines, *Some Notes Concerning Caspar Wistar (Immigrant) and on the Origin of the Wistar and Wister Families* ([Philadelphia], 1926); Isaac Jones Wistar, *Autobiography of Isaac Jones Wistar, 1827–1905* (Philadelphia, 1914).

11. Thomas Doerflinger, *A Vigorous Spirit of Enterprise: Merchants and Economic Development in Revolutionary Philadelphia* (New York: W. W. Norton, 1987), 126–34.

12. Mark E. Kann, *A Republic of Men: The American Founders, Gendered Language, and Patriarchal Politics* (New York: New York University Press, 1998), 5–16, quote on 14. Kann argues that there were multiple masculine ideals in eighteenth-century America and that the self-made man managed to use characteristics of other ideals for commercial purposes. See also Anthony E. Rotundo, *American Manhood: Transformations in Masculinity from the Revolution to the Modern Era* (New York: Basic Books, 1993), 17–20; Michael S. Kimmel, *Manhood in America: A Cultural History* (New York: Free Press, 1996), 45; Richard Bushman, *The Refinement of America: Persons, Houses, Cities* (New York: Random House, 1992), 402–3.

13. "Short Report," Wistar Family Papers, HSP.

14. Wistar does not address his "Short Report" to anyone in particular; however, the stories he includes have been passed down from one generation to the next either through Wistar's "Short Report" or orally. See especially Brown, "Interesting Records," which records the stories Thomas

identified immediately the dramatic contrast between their father's supposed childhood poverty and his American wealth. Wistar wanted them also to understand what it was like to be an immigrant. The narrative he began conveyed the difficulties of leaving home and arriving in a foreign land without the support of family, friends, connections, or money.

The dual construction Wistar referenced in his autobiography—the self-made man and the immigrant—signals the strength of his story for modern readers. Wistar complicates our understanding of the entrepreneurial ideal that has come to dominate modern American identity. Historians writing about colonial America point to the ways inexpensive land and a high demand for labor supplied many free, eighteenth-century Americans with relatively open opportunities for success.[15] At the same time, a growing Atlantic economy increasingly drew colonists into a commercial world that reached far beyond local markets. The integration of the colonies into transatlantic economic networks provided new possibilities for merchants and other enterprising individuals.[16] All of these factors created a society with an incredible capacity for flexibility and creativity.

Wistar's life exemplifies this space for maneuvering within colonial American society. Deeply influenced by his family's struggle to succeed in the Palatinate, Wistar aggressively pursued wealth in the British colonies. In Waldhilsbach, neighbors actively opposed Wistar's father when he used political influence to gain access to limited resources. The son lacked language skills, social connections, political rights, and financial resources when he arrived in Pennsylvania, but these limits were easier to overcome. His status as a foreigner denied him

---

Wistar, Wistar's grandson, shared with his daughter Mary Wistar Brown in 1838, which were later written down by Mary's own daughter (Catharine Morris Brown) in 1879. Many of the details she recorded match those in "Short Report." I have dated Wistar's "Short Report" through internal evidence. His mother, about whom he wrote in the past tense, died in 1743. Her two brothers, about whom Wistar wrote in the present tense, were still alive at Wistar's death in 1752.

15. Bernard Bailyn, *The Peopling of British North America: An Introduction* (New York: Random House, 1986); *Voyagers to the West: A Passage in the Peopling of America on the Eve of the Revolution* (New York: Random House, 1986); Gary Nash, *Urban Crucible: Social Change, Political Consciousness, and the Origins of the American Revolution* (Cambridge: Harvard University Press, 1978); Jon Butler, *Becoming America: The Revolution Before 1776* (Cambridge: Harvard University Press, 2000).

16. John J. McCusker and Russell Menard, *The Economy of North America, 1607–1789* (Chapel Hill: University of North Carolina Press, 1985); Doerflinger, *Vigorous Spirit;* David Hancock, *Citizens of the World: London Merchants and the Integration of the British Atlantic Community, 1735–1785* (Cambridge: Cambridge University Press, 1995); T. H. Breen and Timothy Hall, "Structuring Provincial Imagination: The Rhetoric and Experience of Social Change in Eighteenth-Century New England," *American Historical Review* 103 (1998): 1411–39; Claudia Schnurmann, *Atlantische Welten: Engländer und Niederländer im amerikanisch-atlantischen Raum, 1648–1713* (Cologne: Bölau Verlag, 1998); Nuala Zahedieh, "Economy," in *The British Atlantic World, 1500–1800,* ed. David Armitage and Michael J. Braddick (New York: Palgrave Macmillan, 2002), 51–68; Timothy H. Breen, *The Marketplace of Revolution: How Consumer Politics Shaped American Independence* (New York: Oxford University Press, 2004).

access to government offices, so he sought to improve his profits as a private entrepreneur. A high demand for labor and inexpensive land provided Wistar with new opportunities, just as they did for many other early eighteenth-century Anglo-American colonists. He became a successful brass button maker, invested in an iron furnace, and established a glass manufactory—all ways in which he could address the growing American demand for manufactured goods. And, Wistar speculated heavily in land, the activity most critical to the development of his tremendous wealth.

Wistar's success was not a foregone conclusion, however; readily available land and labor possibilities did not automatically lead to wealth. Instead he had to learn how to use his ethnic and religious identity and his European knowledge and skills as forms of "capital." By becoming a Quaker, Wistar joined the dominant political group in Philadelphia and gained a solid reputation and access to commercial networks. He then employed his ethnic identity and his knowledge of Palatine society to fashion a position as a mediator among the growing numbers of German-speaking immigrants arriving in the colony. He sold them land and culturally specific merchandise that he imported from Europe. He also capitalized on knowledge from his hunting apprenticeship by importing European rifles specially modified for American consumers. Recognizing a demand in the colonial market for glass, Wistar drew from his experience with the Palatinate's forestry administration and his European trade connections to establish a glass manufactory. In each instance, Wistar's success was not solely a result of "liberating" American circumstances. Instead, his European background offered new forms of capital—knowledge and ethnic identity—that he invested creatively and effectively. Wistar's story, therefore, furnishes us with a more complex image of the entrepreneurial ideal as it began to emerge in the eighteenth century.

Wistar also complicates our understanding of immigrant experience in early America. He was one of roughly 100,000 German-speaking immigrants to arrive in the colonies between 1683 and 1776.[17] He crossed the Atlantic in 1717, in the early years of significant migration from the German territories to British

---

17. These immigrants, however, made up only 16 percent of all those who left the Rhine Valley. The large majority of people moving out of the region went to Hungary, Prussia, and what is today Poland, Russia, and Spain. Georg Fertig, *Lokales Leben, atlantische Welt: Die Entscheidung zur Auswanderung vom Rhein nach Nordamerika im 18. Jahrhundert* (Osnabrück: Universitätsverlag Rasch, 2000), 69–80. See also Marianne Wokeck, *Trade in Strangers: The Beginnings of Mass Migration to North America* (University Park: The Pennsylvania State University Press, 1999), 37–58; A. Gregg Roeber, *Palatines, Liberty and Property: German Lutherans in Colonial British America* (Baltimore: Johns Hopkins University Press, 1993; 1998), 98; Aaron S. Fogleman, "Progress and Possibilities in Migration Studies: The Contributions of Werner Hacker to the Study of Early German Migration to Pennsylvania," *Pennsylvania History* 56 (1989): 318–29; and "Migrations to the Thirteen British North American Colonies, 1700–1775: New Estimates," *Journal of Interdisciplinary History* 22 (1992): 691–709.

North America. Beginning in 1727, immigrant ships landed at Philadelphia with increasing frequency, peaking in the period between 1749 and 1754. Although family and kin groups who brought some financial resources dominated the early years of this migration, by its peak the newcomers were increasingly young, single men and women who arrived as indentured servants.[18]

Wistar was not a typical German-speaking immigrant. In contrast to his shipmates and to many who came in the 1720s, he arrived in Pennsylvania as a twenty-one-year-old single man with no connections to family or friends in the colony.[19] In spite of the poverty he described in writing about his European background, he had sufficient money to pay for his journey; he did not arrive as an indentured servant as was the case for many young people migrating in the 1740s and 1750s.[20] Wistar also was exceptional in his role as a cultural mediator. Certainly other German immigrants rose to positions of leadership in their communities. But they tended to be clergy who maintained their links to institutional European networks or agents who created secular trade connections beginning in the 1740s after travel between the colonies and the southwestern German territories was regularized.[21] Few of the early immigrants who arrived without family or institutional ties to others in Pennsylvania managed to fashion such positions of prominence, and few immigrants (or other British colonists, for that matter) obtained a similar level of wealth.

Nevertheless, by understanding why Wistar was exceptional, what distinguished his career path from that of other German-speaking immigrants, we catch glimpses of an evolving, interactive German-Atlantic world that was interwoven with the larger British Empire. Historians studying German-speaking immigrants have painted a vivid picture of people, traditions, ideas, and commodities traveling back and forth between the southwestern German territories

18. Wokeck, *Trade in Strangers*, 37–58.

19. Mark Häberlein, "Communication and Group Interaction Among German Migrants to Colonial Pennsylvania: The Case of Baden Durlach," in *In Search of Peace and Prosperity: New German Settlements in Eighteenth-Century Europe and America*, ed. Hartmut Lehmann, Hermann Wellenreuther, and Renate Wilson (University Park: The Pennsylvania State University Press, 2000), 158–59; Wolfgang von Hippel, *Auswanderung aus Südwestdeutschland: studien zur württembergischen Auswanderung und Auswanderungspolitik im 18. und 19. Jahrhundert* (Stuttgart: Klett-Cotta, 1984) and Hans Ulrich Pfister, *Die Auswanderung aus dem Knonauer Amt, 1648–1750: Ihr Ausmaß, ihre Strukturen und ihre Bedingungen* (Zurich: H. Rohr, 1987).

20. Wokeck, *Trade in Strangers*, 37–58. See also Richard S. Dunn, "Servants and Slaves: The Recruitment and Employment of Labor," in *Colonial British America: Essays in the New History of the Early Modern Era*, ed. Jack P. Greene and J. R. Pole (Baltimore: Johns Hopkins University Press, 1984), 157–94, for a good overview of indentured servitude in the British colonies.

21. Roeber, *Palatines*, 113–32; Häberlein, "Communication," 162–66; Thomas Müller-Bahlke, "Communication at Risk: The Beginnings of the Halle Correspondence with the Pennsylvania Lutherans," in *In Search of Peace*, ed. Lehmann, Wellenreuther, and Wilson, 138–55.

and North America. Some have outlined the rise of a regular transportation system or the emergence of specific trade networks in the eighteenth century.[22] Others have studied the influence of European political and religious traditions in American circumstances.[23] Still others have examined particular migrations, either from or to a specific locale.[24] Each has contributed to our knowledge of an eighteenth-century German-Atlantic world.

Wistar illustrates the emergence of this world in its early stages. He established ties to his home region in the late 1720s, as the transportation system that was bringing growing numbers of immigrants to the British colonies was beginning to evolve but before the institutional networks of the Lutheran Halle Pietists, German Reformed, or Moravian churches were in place. By the 1750s, people with connections to these more formalized institutional networks were mediating German American experiences.[25] Wistar provides us with an opportunity to see this kind of mediation early on.

Wistar also broadens our understanding of the German-Atlantic world by illustrating how it functioned for individuals who operated largely outside of the more formal networks. His communication channels were flexible and fluid rather than tied to any particular institution or group. In the 1730s, he relied on participants in the emerging immigrant transportation system, dominated

22. Wokeck, *Trade in Strangers;* Renate Wilson, *Pious Traders in Medicine: A German Pharmaceutical Network in Eighteenth-Century North America* (University Park: The Pennsylvania State University Press, 2000).

23. A. Gregg Roeber, "The Origin and Transfer of German American Concepts of Property and Inheritance," *Perspectives in American History,* n.s., 3 (1986); "'The Origin of Whatever Is Not English Among Us': The Dutch-Speaking and the German-Speaking Peoples of Colonial British America," in *Strangers Within the Realm: Cultural Margins of the First British Empire,* ed. Bernard Bailyn and Philip D. Morgan (Chapel Hill: University of North Carolina Press, 1991); Roeber, *Palatines;* Aaron S. Fogleman, *Hopeful Journeys: German Immigration, Settlement, and Political Culture in Colonial America, 1717–1775* (Philadelphia: University of Pennsylvania Press, 1996); Thomas J. Müller, *Kirche zwischen zwei Welten: Die Obrigkeitsproblematik bei Heinrich Melchior Mühlenberg und die Kirchengründung der deutschen Lutheraner in Pennsylvania* (Stuttgart: Franz Steiner Verlag, 1994).

24. George F. Jones, *The Georgia Dutch: From the Rhine and Danube to the Savannah, 1733–1783* (Athens: University of Georgia Press, 1992); Mark Häberlein, *Vom Oberrhein zum Susquehanna: Studien zur badischen Auswanderung nach Pennsylvania im 18. Jahrhundert* (Stuttgart: W. Kohlhammer Verlag, 1993); Susanne M. Rolland, "From the Rhine to the Catawba: A Study of Eighteenth-Century Germanic Migration and Adaptation" (Ph.D. diss., Emory University, 1991); Fertig, *Lokales Leben;* Philip Otterness, *Becoming German: The 1709 Palatine Migration to New York* (Ithaca: Cornell University Press, 2004); Elizabeth Sommer, *Serving Two Masters: Moravian Brethren in Germany and North Carolina, 1727–1801* (Lexington: University Press of Kentucky, 2000).

25. Roeber, *Palatines,* 113–32; Wilson, *Pious Traders,* 99–156; Müller-Bahlke, "Communication as Risk," 139–55; Fogleman, *Hopeful Journeys,* 100–126; Charles H. Glatfelter, *Pastors and People: German Lutheran and Reformed Churches in the Pennsylvania Field, 1717–1793,* vol. 2, *The History* (Breinigsville, Pa.: Pennsylvania German Society, 1981), 3–133; Kate Carté Engel, "'Commerce That the Lord could Sanctify and Bless': Moravian Participation in Transatlantic Trade, 1740–1760," Working paper no. 03009, International Seminar on the History of the Atlantic World, Harvard University, August 2003.

by London and Philadelphia merchant firms, to carry letters between him and family members in the Neckar Valley. He drew bills of exchange on English Quakers to pay for his land and purchased merchandise for his store from English wholesalers as well as business associates in Krefeld and Neckargemünd. And he used people connected to European Mennonite communication networks to find immigrants willing to transport his imported goods with their household belongings. As an immigrant without family or religious ties to specific German-Atlantic networks, Wistar fashioned contacts with a diverse group of individuals who were integrated into other more formalized German and British commercial and religious networks.

Wistar's life, therefore, demonstrates the process through which immigrants uprooted and transplanted themselves to new places. For Wistar, this process included some Anglicization. He did not completely resist acculturation; he learned to speak English and figured out how to take advantage of the British colonial legal system. Yet he ultimately did not become prominent and wealthy because he abandoned his Palatine heritage; instead, he exploited his cultural background and his connections in both the British and German-Atlantic worlds as fully as possible.

Thus, in this book I portray the processes at work in the eighteenth century by examining the life and times of one man. It is not a traditional biography. Wistar was only twenty-one years old when he migrated to Pennsylvania in 1717; there is little historical evidence specifically related to him in the European archives. The only documents locating him in the Palatinate are the records of his baptism and those noting his role as a baptismal sponsor.[26] But the world of his childhood can be filled in by reconstructing the history of his family for the two generations that preceded him. On the American side, a collection of family and business correspondence allows us to hear snatches of Wistar's voice, but that evidence is also sporadic at best. Copybooks of his letters survive for 1731 to 1737, and occasional letters from Georg Friederich Hölzer, his associate in Neckargemünd, provide details on his life from 1732 to 1744. Many of Wistar's activities can be reconstructed only through public records and the words of his contemporaries. Each chapter opens with Wistar's voice—his own construction of himself through his autobiography, letters, or public records—to give readers a sense of the man through his own words. Nevertheless, this book is as much about Wistar's surroundings and the worlds he and his fellow immigrants inhabited as it is about him. It begins some forty years before his birth in 1696 and ends with his death in 1752.

26. Feb. 19, 1696, BRKB; Jan. 30, 1711, NgLKB, 1699–1760 and 1700–1769, EOK.

This book is divided into two parts. The first four chapters outline Wistar's Palatine world. He was the son of a forester who worked for the elector. His family's position as part of the government bureaucracy shaped almost every aspect of the young man's life: it supplied their income, established their standing within the village social hierarchy, and determined their religious affiliation. The first three chapters examine the family's economic, social, and religious background. In Chapter 4, I discuss the communication networks that funneled information about the colonies to Wistar's home region and illustrate the opportunities he may have perceived in the British colonies.

The second half of this book is about Wistar's American world. In Chapter 5, I examine the ways Wistar adapted his father's strategies to establish professional and family networks in his new home. Having secured his reputation, Wistar set out to turn Pennsylvania's abundant resources into assets through land speculation and trade. In Chapter 6, I trace Wistar's investments in real estate, which provided financial rewards beyond the imagination of a Palatine immigrant. His purchases allowed him to secure his children's economic future in a way his father never managed to do for him. In Chapter 7, I outline the transatlantic trade networks Wistar developed as a merchant. His connections spanned two continents and provided him with social status and a leadership position among the colony's German-speaking settlers. In Chapter 8, I examine Wistar's United Glass Company in Salem County, New Jersey, as a microcosm of integration and adaptation that happened throughout the British colonies as immigrants transferred their knowledge and technology to America's diverse economy.

The reconstruction of Wistar's world complicates our understanding of both the entrepreneurial ideal and the immigrant experience in early eighteenth-century British North America. His story, while exceptional, allows us to observe the ways some immigrants were able to capitalize on their European experience to fashion new lives for themselves in the British colonies. At the same time, Wistar provides a vantage point on the interactive nature of the emerging German-Atlantic world. He demonstrates the potential for individuals to create their own communication and trade channels by relying on a variety of other more formal networks. These connections facilitated the flow of information and goods in both directions across the Atlantic. His story is one example of the ways some immigrants became cultural mediators, in this case between the German and Anglo-American worlds. The experiences of Caspar Wistar offer an important illustration of the processes by which the British colonies increased in diversity and simultaneously were integrated into the broader Atlantic world.

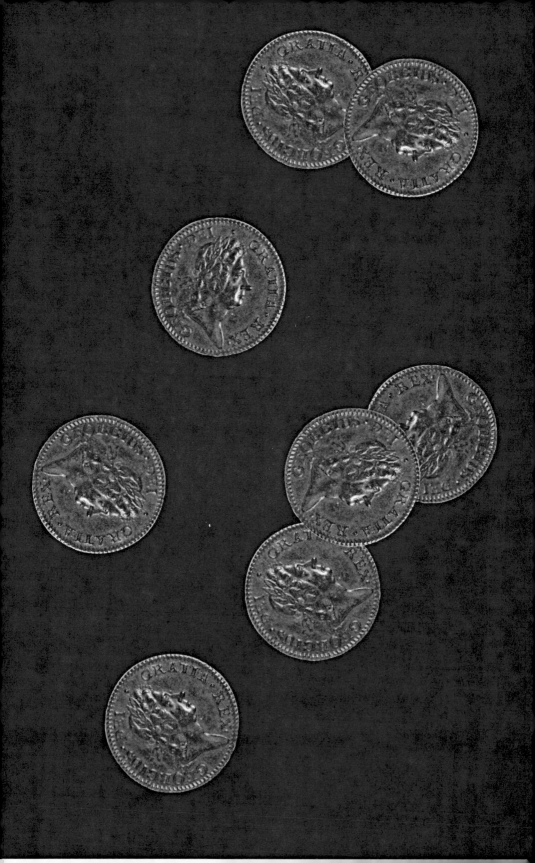

PART I

Wistar's Palatine World

[My] fatherland and the place where I was born is as follows: where the biggest forest in the world is and remains, in the Palatinate, two hours from Heidelberg in the mountains. . . . My parents their names were as follows: my father's name was [Hans] Caspar Wistar, hunter there, and [he] was born in Mospacher Ambt, the place was called Neunkirchen and his father's name was Andres Wüster, he was also a hunter there and my mother was born in [Wald]Hilspach and her name was Anna Catharina Miller and [she] has 2 brothers living there. . . . I worked as a hunter and fowler until I was 14 or 15 years old because my father was a hunter. After that I went to the chief hunter, Georg Michael Förster, at Bruchhausen, and served him for four years as a hunter's apprentice.

—CASPAR WISTAR, "A Short Report"

CHAPTER 1

Men in the Middle
FORESTERS AND HUNTERS IN THE EARLY MODERN PALATINATE

Caspar Wistar opened his autobiography with the most salient image from his childhood: the forest. Virtually every aspect of his life in the Palatinate was interwoven with his family's position as hunters and foresters—government employees appointed to protect the ruling family's natural resources.[1] The heavily wooded hills provided revenue for Wistar's village, and they supplied his family's income and established its social standing within Amt Dilsberg (a government jurisdiction roughly equivalent in size and function to a colonial Pennsylvania county). Long after he had moved to America and became a button maker and a merchant, Wistar continued to identify his origins and early years with the forest.

The process through which Wistar adapted to his American environment began on the other side of the Atlantic. In his home region, as in America, forests were the primary source of commodities for everyday life. Timber provided the construction material for buildings, fences, tools, and ships. Wood also furnished heat for homes and energy for the industries that made soap, charcoal, potash, and glass—all enterprises that consumed significant amounts of timber. On both continents, people relied heavily on the forests' natural resources.

Institutionalized conflicts over their use, however, distinguished Palatine forests from those in the British colonies. On one hand, the elector (the ruler of the territory) viewed forests as potential sources of income for the state. At the end of the Thirty Years' War, the government's financial resources were depleted. Consequently, state and local officials carefully defined the jurisdiction controlling each plot of woodland and drew precise boundaries to ensure efficient use of its commodities. The ruling family subsidized glass-making, charcoal-making, and iron-making enterprises on state-held lands to generate revenue for the

---

1. Because foresters frequently assisted with royal hunts and were often trained by master hunters, villagers frequently referred to them as hunters. Wistar's father and grandfather were always listed as foresters in the official department records but are frequently referred to as hunters in court and village documents. For a more detailed discussion of the differences, see Rosalind J. Beiler, "The Transatlantic World of Caspar Wistar: From Germany to America in the Eighteenth-Century" (Ph.D. diss., University of Pennsylvania, 1994), 29–32.

realm. By the end of the seventeenth century, ruling electors had built extensive bureaucracies of foresters and hunters to police the well-organized tracts of land they were trying to monopolize.

On the other hand, villagers resisted encroaching state authority and sought to retain traditional rights to commonly held meadows and woods. Forests provided timber and grazing land for small hamlets in a world where capital and property increasingly determined wealth. Villagers could sell the timber from their woods or rent village meadows to fund community projects, pay tithes and taxes, or hire a cowherd or shepherd. For Palatine peasants, using local forests for the common interests of the village became even more pressing in the aftermath of the devastating wars at the end of the seventeenth century.[2]

Caught between these competing interests was the class of foresters and hunters to which Wistar's family belonged. As government officials, foresters depended on the state for their livelihoods and thus owed the elector their loyalty. But they also belonged to villages struggling to survive the effects of war and growing government bureaucracies.

This world of conflicted loyalties profoundly influenced the young Wistar in two important ways. First, he inherited from his father and grandfather an ability to maneuver between competing and disparate interest groups, as each group struggled for control of resources and commodities. Pennsylvania offered Wistar no career as a forester; in comparison to the Palatinate, the colony had virtually no bureaucracy. The Penns' agents attempted to protect the family's interests, but they did not have the financial and human means to do so. Nevertheless, Pennsylvanians still competed for control of the land. In his new home Wistar relied on the skills he learned in his father's household and as a hunter's apprentice—the skills of a mediator between local and government interests—to get ahead.

Second, the image of well-ordered Palatine forests filled with marketable commodities shaped Wistar's American enterprises. He knew from his background and training the potential for profit that Pennsylvania's "wilderness" offered. His investments in an iron furnace, a glass manufactory, and thousands of acres of "undeveloped" land all reflected his training as a forester. Each one fit the blueprint in his head for turning the "wilderness" into a mart.[3] The world of the Palatine forester and hunter, therefore, furnishes the best starting point for understanding Wistar's transatlantic experience.

2. For a discussion of similar prince vs. peasant contests in the Kraichgau, see Fogleman, *Hopeful Journeys*, 42–60.

3. William Cronon, *Changes in the Land: Indians, Colonists, and the Ecology of New England* (New York: Hill and Wang, 1983).

In 1653, Andreas Wüster (1627–92), Caspar Wistar's grandfather, applied to the elector of the Palatinate for the vacant position of forester for Neunkirchen.[4] Most likely the son of a forester, Wüster had already served for one year at the elector's hunting lodge in Bruchhausen as an arms bearer during the elector's hunts. The twenty-six-year-old huntsman believed he had "carried himself in such a manner that [he] hoped in all truth no one could register a complaint against him."[5] Wüster was hired for the position and moved with his wife to Neunkirchen, where he began his career as a forester.[6]

Wüster joined the forestry administration shortly after the signing of the Treaty of Westphalia in 1648 and as the Palatinate was beginning to recover from the Thirty Years' War. Karl Ludwig (1648–80), the reigning elector, began instituting policies to repopulate devastated villages, foster manufacture and trade, and restore his family's depleted revenues. Evolving ideas about the role of the state in economic growth encouraged an active promotion of trade and manufacturing.[7] The resources of the forests were an important part of his program. By constructing fiscal policies that focused on necessity and economic development rather than creating a luxurious court, Karl Ludwig hoped to restore prosperity to the Palatinate. Simultaneously, the elector also tried to extend and increase his power. Like many other European political rulers, his response to the Thirty Years' War was to engage in a process of state-building. To expand his political influence, Karl Ludwig increased the bureaucracy of government officials who were connected to him through a labyrinth of obligations and duties.[8]

The bureaucracy Wüster joined, therefore, was expanding. Traditionally, the highest level of government officials in the Palatinate consisted of a few noble courtiers who advised the elector in legal and fiscal matters. The most important advisors were in residence in the castle at Heidelberg. They constituted three

4. Wistar/Wister is the anglicized version of Wüster. American descendants of Caspar Wüster have adopted Wistar; those of his brother Johannes Wüster spell their name Wister. I have retained the original German spelling when referring to European family members and have used the American spellings for those who emigrated.

5. Petition of Andreas Wüster, Feb. 12, 1663, GLA 77/1865.

6. Apr. 23, 1663, GLA 77/1865. Andreas Wüster and his wife Anna baptized nine children between 1665 and 1687 in the Reformed Church at Neunkirchen. See NkRKB, EOK.

7. "Cameralism," the German mercantilist school of thought, was founded in the 1670s and 1680s by J. J. Becher, who proposed establishing commercial colleges to promote trade and manufacturing. "Neue Impulse innerhalb des Faches Wirtschafts- und Sozialgeschichte: Alte Themen, Neue Akzente," in *Frühe Neuzeit*, ed. Annette Völker-Rasor (Munich: Oldenbourg Verlag, 2006); Richard Gawthrop, *Pietism and the Making of Eighteenth-Century Prussia* (Cambridge: Cambridge University Press, 1993), 26–33.

8. Hajo Holborn, *A History of Modern Germany, 1648–1840* (Princeton: Princeton University Press, 1964), 42–50. See Wolfgang Reinhard, *Geschichte der Staatsgewalt: Eine vergleichende Verfassungsgeschichte Europas von den Anfängen bis zur Gegenwart* (Munich: Verlag C. H. Beck, 2002), 125–209, for the process of state-building in a broader European context.

administrative bodies: the advisory council (*Hofrat*), the elector's legal court (*Hofgericht*), and the exchequer's court or treasury (*Rechenkammer*).[9] A second tier of officials lived in the outlying villages and represented the elector's interests within their local regions. They held positions in the forestry and hunting administration, the church consistory, and the war department, each of which was accountable to the exchequer's court. In addition, small geographic regions were organized into local districts (*Ämter*), which were headed by a district administrator or district secretary. Drawn from among the elites and well-educated classes of Palatine society, government officials usually inherited their positions.[10]

As a forester, Wüster operated at the bottom of the second level of government. In the mid-seventeenth century, the forestry department consisted of a master hunter, three master foresters (one for regions on each side of the Rhine and one for Amt Simmern), and a group of foresters, hunters, fowlers, and rabbit wardens. The department's primary responsibility was to administer the Palatinate's natural resources, a task that fell into two general categories: forestry and hunting. Foresters were to insure that the elector and his subjects had access to a continuous supply of timber. They also protected and supplied the game that furnished the elector's kitchen and provided him and his court with a favorite form of leisure, hunting.

Wüster's tasks as a forester brought him into daily contact with the forest itself. He, along with the rabbit wardens and fowlers, answered to a master forester and had a number of duties. First and foremost, Wüster had to insure that no one took timber without permission and that cleared tracts were replanted. Second, he was responsible for fencing in and protecting the deer within his jurisdiction and for reporting anyone caught poaching. And finally, like other officials in the forestry administration, he could be called upon to assist in the elector's hunts. Consequently, he and other foresters often were referred to as "hunters" by their neighbors, though as part of his position Wüster swore not to take any wood or game for himself or to bargain with anyone for the same.[11]

During Wüster's tenure as the forester for Neunkirchen, Karl Ludwig's economic reforms resulted in decreased salaries for government officials.[12] Wüster

9. This organizational structure is constructed from government records in GLA, Abt. 77. See also Meinrad Schaab, *Geschichte der Kurpfalz*, vol. 2, *Neuzeit* (Stuttgart: W. Kohlhammer Verlag, 1992), 87–88, and *Stadt- und Landkreise*, vol. 1, *Allgemeiner Teil* (Karlsruhe, 1966), 241–43.

10. Rüdiger Lenz, *Kellerei und Unteramt Dilsberg: Entwicklung einer regionalen Verwaltungsinstanz im Rahmen der kurpfälzischen Territorialpolitik am unteren Neckar* (Stuttgart: W. Kohlhammer Verlag, 1989); Christine van den Heuvel, *Beamtenschaft und Territorialstaat: Behördenentwicklung und Sozialstruktur der Beamtenschaft im Hochstift Osnabrück, 1550–1800* (Osnabrück: Kommissionsverlag H. Th. Wenner, 1984).

11. Commission letters of Heinrich Dillinger, forester from Gaiberg, May 22, 1688, GLA 229/30951. In addition to his responsibilities, Wüster and other foresters often supervised apprentices (*Knechte* or *Junge*) who lived and worked with them and for whose education they were responsible.

12. Schaab, *Geschichte der Kurpfalz*, 2:34–36, 138–40.

was clearly affected by the elector's policies. In 1669, when the department eliminated a vacant forester's position to cut costs, Wüster and a colleague divided the former forester's jurisdiction.[13] For six years the two men received no reimbursement for their additional responsibilities. Only in 1675 was the salary of the former position split between Wüster and the other forester.[14]

In spite of temporary setbacks, Wüster ultimately benefited from the changes begun under Karl Ludwig. The elector's reforms soon began to yield positive economic results, and the region showed signs of recovery. As it did so, the elector added new layers of officials to assume the daily decisions of government, and higher positions became sinecures. One result of this policy was an increase in the number of officials who did not belong to the nobility. Jurists and lawyers began to replace noblemen as the elector's primary advisors while commoners and people with specific qualifications filled lower-level offices. This new class of professional officials operated beside or in place of traditional aristocratic government servants.[15]

Wüster belonged to the rising class of professional bureaucrats produced by the elector's policies. In 1680, after sixteen years of service, he petitioned his employer for a raise in salary. Wüster claimed that during his tenure as a forester, he had delivered as much food to the court's kitchen as five or six of his fellow foresters combined (he cited the kitchen's accounts as proof). He also argued that he had been instrumental in improving the government's stock of game. During the elector's recent hunt, forty deer had been shot within Wüster's region. He believed, however, that his success in balancing the contradictory demands of hunter and forester was being poorly rewarded. The law had recently changed, and Wüster was no longer permitted to supply his own household with meat from the forest. At the same time, fiscal reforms had eliminated the commission money that he previously received for the game he shot and from which he had maintained his family. Wüster, who had to feed and clothe six children and a servant on 18 *Gulden* (roughly £2 sterling) and 12 *Malters* of wheat annually, could no longer support his household.[16]

That same year, Wüster's superior, Master Hunter Eberhard Friederich von Venningen, highly recommended him to the exchequer's court; nevertheless, his petition languished. During the summer of 1680 Karl Ludwig died.[17] The following year Wüster successfully petitioned the new elector for the position of chief forester (*Oberförster*). His promotion brought a significant raise in salary

13. Sept. 16, Oct. 26, and Nov. 23, 1669, GLA 77/1865.
14. June 28, July 17, July 28, 1675, GLA 77/1865.
15. Lenz, *Kellerei und Unteramt Dilsberg*, 101–4; *Stadt- und Landkreise*, 1:241–43.
16. Mar. 28, 1680, GLA 77/1865.
17. May 30, 1680, GLA 77/1865.

to match his new responsibilities. Von Venningen suggested that a salary of 60 *Gulden* (£6 sterling), 20 *Malters* of wheat, 25 *Malters* of oats, 6 *Ohm* of wine, and traveling money was appropriate. Wüster was awarded even more; he received 90 *Gulden* (£9 sterling) in addition to the recommended amount of wheat, oats, wine, and traveling money.[18]

Wüster's promotion was indicative of the momentum with which Karl Ludwig's successor, Karl (1680–85), expanded his government. In contrast to his father's tight control over state finances, Karl nearly doubled the court's expenditures from 70,000 to 130,000 *Gulden*. In spite of continued financial difficulties, he added new positions and levels to the government, increased salaries, maintained a standing army, and instituted a more elaborate court culture than his predecessor.[19]

As a chief forester, Wüster gained considerable responsibility and prestige. He was commissioned to oversee the "woods, parks, game preserves, hunting grounds, fisheries, etc." in the Dilsberg, Mosbach, and Boxberg districts and to "direct and encourage" the foresters in his region to "justly protect, ride through, and frequent" the same. Wüster's three districts were in the southernmost region of the Odenwald and the most heavily forested areas surrounding Heidelberg. The chief forester patrolled the forests frequently to note their condition and to insure that no one cut timber, hunted, or fished without the written permission of the forestry department or the exchequer's court. Wüster's administrative duties consisted of filing commission letters (letters patent or contracts) for the foresters in his district, submitting accounts of timber sold, and reporting any infringements on the elector's realm from neighboring rulers. Finally, Wüster, in contrast to the other two chief foresters, kept the elector's kitchen supplied with small and large game. This extra assignment most likely resulted from the proximity of his jurisdiction to the castle at Heidelberg. His added responsibilities brought him a higher annual salary than those of the other chief foresters in the department.[20]

Wüster's promotion was a part of the bureaucratic expansion and professionalization of Karl's administration. As a chief forester (*Oberförster*), his tasks were interchangeable with those of a master forester (*Forstmeister*). Whereas three master foresters previously had overseen Palatine forests, now three new chief foresters joined them, carving the administrative regions into six smaller jurisdictions. Although their duties varied little, chief foresters were promoted from the ranks of foresters because of their special abilities and knowledge, while master foresters usually inherited their positions.[21]

18. Jan. 8, Feb. 2, and Feb. 5, 1681, GLA 77/1865.

19. Schaab, *Geschichte der Kurpfalz*, 2:143–44.

20. Feb. 3 and Feb. 4, 1681, GLA 77/1865.

21. 1707, GLA 77/1182; Hans Hausrath, "Zur Geschichte der kurpfälzischen Forstorganisation," in *Forstwissenschaftliches Centralblatt*, ed. Hermann von Fürst (Berlin: Verlagsbuchhandlung Paul Parey, 1908), 451.

The addition of new professional positions to the forestry department signaled the government's increasing attempts to raise revenue from its natural
resources.[22] Between 1680 and 1700, the electors of the Palatinate gradually
assumed rights and privileges to personal and communal property that had previously belonged to individuals or villages. For example, the forestry law of 1687
stated that no individual was allowed to take lumber out of his own forests without the prior approval of the local government officials and the appraisal of a
carpenter. Furthermore, village councils (*Gemeinde*) were required to obtain the
approval of the forestry department before cutting timber from their communal
forests.[23]

Village leaders soon contested the government's encroachments, and several
court cases illustrate the kinds of disputes the new law created. In one instance,
the forestry department sued the village of Gaiberg, a village in Wüster's jurisdiction, for selling wood from its communal forest without proper authoriza-
tion. Village leaders reported that they had received sufficient approval from the
forester and his son. They also pleaded innocent to charges that they should have
sought the permission of a master forester, arguing that the sale took place prior
to the law of 1687.[24] In another case, the chief hunter imposed fines against several villages for grazing cattle in newly seeded forests and hunting grounds.[25]

In addition to usurping his subjects' rights to the land, the elector monopolized the symbolic capital of the hunt. He began to eliminate traditional hunting
privileges that had belonged to the nobility and government officials. Palatine
electors had denied their subjects hunting privileges for generations. Nevertheless, many government officials belonged to noble families that had won special
rights. When the elector began to encroach on their hunting privileges, they
fought back. One official submitted an extensive defense to the local administration, arguing that he should be permitted to enjoy hunting rights.[26]

By the end of the seventeenth century, hunting had evolved into elaborately
staged events that required an entourage of assistants. Hunters drove large herds
of wild game through a labyrinth of trails to a festively decorated spot where
the elector and his company, often other dignitaries and visiting officials, shot at
their prey. On such occasions, Wüster and his fellow foresters participated in the

22. Christof Dipper, *Deutsche Geschichte, 1648–1789* (Frankfurt: Suhrkamp, 1991), 208–23.

23. Joachim Allmann, *Der Wald in der frühen Neuzeit. Eine mentalitäts- und sozialgeschichtliche Untersuchung am Beispiel des Pfälzer Raumes, 1500–1800* (Berlin: Duncker and Humblot, 1989), 112. The term *Gemeinde* is difficult to translate into English. For a good discussion of its meaning in the early modern period, see Bob Scribner, "Communities and the Nature of Power," in *Germany: A New Social and Economic History*, vol. 1, *1450–1630*, ed. Bob Scribner (London: Arnold, 1996), 294–98.

24. Sept. 12, 1687, GLA 61/5463.

25. May 26, 1689, GLA 61/5463. See also May 18, 1690, GLA 61/9861.

26. Sept. 27, 1686, Jan. 1, Aug. 11, 1687, GLA 145/183.

FIG. 1 Deer hunt at Neckargemünd, 1758. Courtesy of the Kurpfälzisches Museum, Heidelberg.

staged hunts. Only those with sufficient capital and personnel could prove their importance through these grand displays.[27]

Foresters and hunters were caught in the middle of this contest for control of natural resources and symbolic capital. Men like Wüster, who owed their rise in status to the elector's expanding authority, lived in villages with strong traditions of local autonomy and control. Like Wüster—who had moved from Crailsheim, a city in Württemberg, first to Bruchhausen and then to Neunkirchen—foresters were often outsiders who were trying to establish their reputations with their neighbors. At the same time, they owed their increased economic security, and thus some of their loyalty, to the elector's government. At no time was their position in the middle more evident than during war, as forestry officials attempted to mediate between disparate interests in an environment of shrinking resources.

War brought wrenching changes to the Palatinate following the death of Elector Karl in 1685. Because Karl died without a male heir, Philipp Wilhelm (1685–90)

27. Hans Wilhelm Eckardt, *Herrschaftliche Jagd, bäuerliche Not, und burgerliche Kritik: Zur Geschichte der fürstlichen und adligen Jagd Privilegien, vornehmlich im südwestdeutschen Raum* (Göttingen: Vandenhoeck and Reprecht, 1976); *Stadt- und Landkreise*, 1:313–15. Two paintings depicting royal hunts in the mid-eighteenth century are in the Kurpfälzisches Museum der Stadt, Heidelberg.

of Neuburg, the Catholic duke of Jülich and Berg, succeeded him as the elector. In response to Philipp Wilhelm's succession, Louis XIV of France claimed some of Karl's property on behalf of the duchess of Orleans, Karl's sister and Louis's sister-in-law. French troops seized Phillipsburg in 1688 and raided towns in the Neckar Valley, including Eberbach, Dilsberg, Neckargemünd, Heidelberg, and Mannheim. The following year the Holy Roman Empire declared war on France, prompting Louis to pull his troops out of the Neckar and Rhine valleys. In their retreat, the French destroyed whatever might have proven useful to their enemies; they bombed castles, burned towns, murdered villagers, and plundered livestock and crops. The war that followed devastated the region surrounding the Neckar Valley.[28]

War had tremendous consequences for Wüster and the forestry department. Not only did French troops raze the government seat, the castle at Heidelberg, they also destroyed the forests. In the wake of their retreat, the Holy Roman Empire's army further depleted the few remaining resources to supply its troops. In the forestry department, the war decreased the number of positions, lowered salaries, and increased demands for natural resources. Almost immediately hostilities threatened the jobs of foresters and hunters.[29] The government consolidated positions, vacant slots remained empty, and the treasury withdrew both salaries and benefits. Soon after the war began, Wüster and the master forester from Heidelberg received orders to report any reduction in oats that the department could make without diminishing the foresters' abilities to carry out their duties.[30]

Shortages of revenue were not the only threat to the department. Preoccupation with war meant that the elector spent less time hunting. When Eberhard Friederich von Venningen, the chief master of the hunt, wanted to hire a new secretary, the exchequer's court declined his request "because hunting is exercised so seldom now and it is necessary to reduce costs as much as possible because of the bad times."[31] Nevertheless, the department's arms bearers still worked hard to protect the hunting grounds, increasingly "in danger to their bodies and lives." Von Venningen confirmed that they had faced great difficulty "protecting the hunting grounds from total destruction, not only because of the French troubles but also because of the daily increase in soldiers [in the region]." He warned that if the elector wanted to enjoy "some recreation" when he arrived,

28. John Gagliardo, *Germany Under the Old Regime, 1600–1790* (London: Longman, 1991), 252–70; *Stadt- und Landkreise*, 1:358–59.

29. "Verzeichnüs Aller Ober- und Unterbeambten, so in hießigem Oberambt Heydelberg vor der letztern ao. 1688 Vorgangenen reduction gestanden . . . ," [c. 1688], GLA 145/45.

30. Jan. 10, 1692, GLA 61/9862.

31. Mar. 9, 1690, GLA 61/9861.

FIG. 2 Heidelberg, view from the north, 1620. Courtesy of the Kurpfälzisches Museum, Heidelberg.

he should, "as encouragement," give several of the hunters some money, wine, or provisions from their lapsed salaries.[32]

A lack of funds frequently left foresters without pay and increased temptations to embezzle government funds. One chief forester, who had not received his salary for four years, petitioned to receive 60 *Gulden* (£6 sterling). The exchequer's court ruled in his favor since he had delivered 281 *Gulden* in forest taxes to the military garrison. Court officials feared that "if he sees that he will not be permitted to flourish on his salary, he will dip into the taxes himself and pay himself from them."[33]

The war also increased the strain on natural resources. Since early modern Palatines used timber in every aspect of daily life, the tensions between extracting and preserving trees increased in periods of conflict. Wüster was particularly active in one special use of wood during the war—building palisades or stockades. In 1689, French troops besieged the castle at Heidelberg and then withdrew down the Neckar, plundering and burning eleven villages as they went. They returned later that year, attacking Heidelberg once again. The following year the elector's defenses managed to withstand another French attack, but in 1693 the Heidelberg castle and the city were destroyed.[34] Because of his region's proximity to Heidelberg, Wüster frequently floated lumber for building fortifications up the Neckar River. With the war's destruction, however, he claimed his region was one of the few with remaining stands of timber. By 1690, he knew of "no other place nearby where one could find [timber for] stockades because the woods in the Neckar Valley had been so ruined through cutting palisades."[35]

32. Apr. 1, 1691, GLA 77/1738.
33. Sept. 13, 1692, GLA 61/9864.
34. *Stadt- und Landkreise*, 1:358–59.
35. May 18, 1690, GLA 61/9861.

Nevertheless, Wüster continued to deliver wood for stockades for several more years.[36]

Wüster's actions were at the heart of the competing interests within the elector's government. Wüster insisted that he did not know where to find any more wood for stockades. The chief hunter, who previously had argued that charcoal burners were destroying timber in the elector's hunting grounds, suggested that a ban on charcoal-making in Heidelberg would yield more than enough wood for buildings and fortifications. Charcoal, however, was critical for the region's glass- and iron-making industries, from which the government also gained revenues. The elector's advisors thought "that all kinds of artisans, who need charcoal for their work, would be greatly hindered" by a ban.[37] Consequently, the exchequer's court ordered Wüster and other foresters to police the woods more diligently and to insure the charcoal burners cut only legal timber.

Increased demands for timber during war also placed Wüster and other foresters at the center of conflicts between the elector's government and villagers. Village councils frequently sold timber to fund community projects. In the mid-seventeenth century, wood merchants from Holland began to purchase timber in the Rhine and Neckar valleys for building ships; by 1690, the market was entering its peak period.[38] Wüster and other chief foresters oversaw these sales. With permission from the exchequer's court, they determined whether or not wood should be cut, decided which trees to fell, and collected taxes and fees on timber sales.[39]

During the war, competition for communal timber heightened. In 1692, for example, the exchequer's court refused to allow Schrießheim to sell wood to a Dutch wood merchant "because the government needed lumber in the near future for its own building projects."[40] When the master forester reported that the oak trees the village wanted to sell were inappropriate for building, however, the exchequer's court relented because Schrießheim would "receive the help that money from the sale will bring."[41] Since foresters received commission money for each stand of wood they sold, the master forester was serving his own interests (as well as the villagers') when he convinced the exchequer's court to approve the sale.[42]

---

36. May 29, Sept. 13, 1691, GLA 61/9862; June 4, 1692, GLA 61/9864. After her husband's death in July 1692, Wüster's widow petitioned the *Hofcammer* to receive the rest of Wüster's commission money for the palisades he had floated down the river the previous year; Sept. 25, 1692, GLA 61/9864.

37. May 18, 1690, GLA 61/9861.

38. Documents throughout GLA 61/9862 and 229/82943, II; Dietrich Ebeling, *Der Holländerholzhandel in den Rheinlanden* (Stuttgart: Franz Steiner Verlag, 1992).

39. June 13, July 28, 1691, GLA 61/9862; May 3, 1692, GLA 61/9864. For Andreas Wüster's participation in selling wood, see May 21, June 2, 1691, GLA 61/9862.

40. May 6, 1692, GLA 61/9864.

41. June 4, 1692, GLA 61/9864.

42. Hausrath, "Kurpfälzischen Forstorganisation," 460–65.

Villages also paid the elector a tax from each sale of timber, which helped to fund the foresters' salaries. In June 1692, Wüster submitted receipts for 480 *Gulden,* 57 *Kreuzer;* 94 *Malters* of buckwheat; 62 *Malters* of wheat; and 9 *Malters* of field oats in taxes paid on wood sales. The exchequer's court ordered that the foresters'"lapsed salaries" should be paid from the collected taxes.[43] Thus Wüster and other foresters negotiated a fine balance between their own interests, those of the villages in their jurisdiction, and the elector's.

Poaching disputes also placed foresters and hunters in the middle of competing interests. In July 1689, Hans Mosselbach, one of Wüster's former foresters, was arrested and questioned on charges of poaching after a search through his house revealed preserved venison. In 1688 and 1689, when the French seized and then plundered and burned villages south of the Neckar, villagers sought shelter in the woods. Upon questioning, Mosselbach readily admitted that "during the last French commotion, he shot a deer." He claimed, however, that he had done so "at the bidding of the current forester [from Gaiberg]."[44] Mosselbach also killed another small deer "out of need and poverty, for the enemy recently had plundered [his property] completely and [he] had nothing with which to feed himself and his children."[45]

In spite of the fact that it was made a capital offence in 1687, poaching had become widespread throughout the region as a result of war.[46] Mosselbach "heard shots everywhere, morning and evening." Villagers from the Kirchheimer and Leimen districts shot wild game for food, as did those from Waldhilsbach and the Kohlwald. In fact, Mosselbach claimed, the villagers in Gauangelloch "even hunted with their dogs."[47] Villagers elsewhere echoed Mosselbach, admitting to shooting "wild swine at different times out of necessity and so that the people there could live."[48] Throughout Amt Dilsberg peasants turned poachers as they struggled to survive during the French invasion.

43. June 24, 1692, GLA 61/9864.
44. July 6, 1689, GLA 61/5463.
45. Ibid.
46. European laws against poaching became harsher throughout the seventeenth and eighteenth centuries as rulers attempted to reserve greater hunting privileges for themselves; Johann Keiper, *Pfälzische Forst- und Jagdgeschichte mit einem forstlichen und geschichtlichen Übersichtskärtchen* (Speyer: Pfälzische Gesellschaft zur Förderung der Wissenschaften, 1930), 192–99. Erich Bauer notes in *Der Soonwald: Auf den Spuren des Jägers aus Kurpfalz* (Stuttgart, DRW-Verlag, 1974), 121, that laws in the eighteenth century were stronger than previous laws but in comparison to other European principalities, the Palatine punishments were always relatively mild. Eckhardt, *Herrschaftliche Jagd*, 128–41, also claims that punishments became harsher in the seventeenth and eighteenth centuries. But he portrays the punishment more harshly than Bauer by emphasizing that in the Palatinate poaching became a capital offense. For a comparison to England's hunting codes, see E. P. Thompson, *Whigs and Hunters: The Origin of the Black Act* (New York: Pantheon, 1975).
47. July 6, 1689, GLA 61/5463.
48. Sept. 24, 1689, GLA 61/5463.

The combination of war and harsher punishments for poaching placed the foresters in a difficult position. On one hand, they represented the elector and his interests; their first loyalties were to him. Their contracts obliged them to uphold the law that made poaching a capital offence. On the other hand, they, along with their neighbors, suffered hunger, which could push them to endorse poaching. One forester allegedly argued that "it would be no sin [to kill one deer], for then we would receive something to eat."[49] When faced with the starvation of the people around them, foresters were forced to confront their divided loyalties.

The conflicts surrounding poaching during the war illustrate the kinds of problems that arose as the elector attempted to consolidate his power. Such centralization of control required the loyalty of a growing bureaucracy, but the very nature of the bureaucracy—professionalized commoners with newly raised economic status—constantly threatened that process as the bureaucrats continued to identify with their friends and neighbors.

In July 1692, a few years before Wistar the immigrant was born, his grandfather, Andreas Wüster, died.[50] The elder Wüster had taken advantage of the expanded bureaucracy fostered by a long period of recovery. He had advanced to a higher rank because of his knowledge and proven ability rather than because of his birth and education. By demonstrating his loyalty to the elector, he had achieved an economic status that was equivalent to that of the traditional master forester.[51]

Just as Wüster's promotion to chief forester for Neunkirchen reflects the professionalization and upward mobility of government officials with specific knowledge and skills, so too the circumstances surrounding his death illustrate the tenuous nature of advancement. Wüster died in the midst of war, when funds were short. When Anna Wüster, his wife, applied for a widow's pension, the elector's advisors claimed that "the widow's pension is not generally granted to such servants but is reserved for the elector's councilors." They added, however, that "some money has been granted through a special dispensation to a few foresters' widows, whose husbands have served a long time and who have carried themselves well."[52] Wüster's service earned his widow and children 5 *Reichstaler* and 2 *Malters* of wheat as a one-time dispensation.[53]

49. July 6, 1689, GLA 61/5463. There is no surviving evidence to indicate that these men were sentenced to death. Losch was no longer alive in 1706, but Hanß Martin Beck, who admitted to killing wild swine, was alive that same year. See the religious census taken in 1706, GLA 61/5479.

50. NkRKB, EOK.

51. In June 1692, shortly before his death, the *Hofcammer* ordered that the same instructions should be sent to the *Oberförster* from Neunkirchen as those sent to the *Forstmeisters.* June 17, 1692, GLA 61/9864.

52. Sept. 27, 1692, GLA 61/9864.

53. Jan. 5, 1693, GLA 61/9864.

When Anna Wüster received the reward for her husband's service, she most likely lost all rights to her husband's position. As a chief forester, Wüster did not automatically receive the privilege of passing his job on to his children. Upon his death, the exchequer's court investigated whether Wüster's son, Hans Caspar Wüster, or his son-in-law was prepared to serve as a forester for Neunkirchen. Neither stayed in Neunkirchen, however. His son-in-law became the forester of Sinsheim; his oldest son, Hans Caspar Wüster, moved to Gaiberg, where he replaced a forester who had recently died. The younger Wüster's experience as a forester and his constant struggle to affirm his social status, as we shall see, illustrate the tenuous position of foresters as the Palatinate's government attempted once again to recover from war.[54]

---

54. On January 28, 1694, Nicklaus Krauß was the chief forester for Neunkirchen, and Hans Caspar Wüster was listed as the forester for Neunkirchen who had moved away. NkRKB, EOK.

I was born . . . in a small, poor village or town that lies one hour from Neckargemünd,
called [Wald]hilsbach, in Amt Dilsberg. The people in the village subsist primarily from
potter's clay which they dig from the earth and carry in large quantities to a small city,
that lies along a river called the Neckar and whose name is Neckargemünd. . . .

I, Caspar Wistar, was born in the year of 1696 on the third day of February. I was
raised there without much education because the village was small and poor and did
not have the means to support a schoolmaster and because, at the same time, I did not
concern myself with my education.

—CASPAR WISTAR, "A Short Report"

CHAPTER 2

Individual Pursuits Versus the Common Good
THE CONSTRAINTS OF VILLAGE LIFE IN WALDHILSBACH

Looking back on his youth from the vantage point of a fifty-year-old Philadelphia merchant, Wistar remembered his home village as a place of poverty and limited opportunity. As the owner of a three-story brick dwelling and thousands of acres of Pennsylvania land, he saw the world he had left behind as one filled with constraints. And, indeed, the contrast was startling.

Waldhilsbach was a small hamlet with dwindling resources where Wistar's father and his contemporaries competed for wealth, social status, and power through virulent political discourse carried out in public village spaces. Conflicts over property and power became inextricably linked with issues of honor and reputation. Shaped by the *mentalité* of the era, contenders often argued that their opponents sought personal advancement at the expense of the community, each party using such rhetoric to improve his own individual position of authority. Government officials were particularly prone to such arguments because the growing bureaucracy offered new avenues to wealth. But villagers also used the same discourse to combat the state's encroachment on their community's resources.

Like his neighbors and contemporaries, Wistar's father seized every chance he had to secure a better future for his children. To do so, he was forced to maneuver within competing sets of interests. As a forester, he owed the elector his loyalty and service. But at the same time, he lived in Waldhilsbach, where the villagers, in the form of the *Gemeinde* (the legal organization of full citizens in the village), sought to protect the interests of the whole community.[1] Wistar's father also competed for wealth and power with individual neighbors and other government officials, all of whom were striving to improve their own economic, social, and political positions.

Wistar likely was influenced by his father's participation in these political disputes and his maneuvering among competing interests. The poverty of Waldhilsbach and his family's struggle to get ahead informed the young man's choices as he set out to establish himself in Pennsylvania. At the very least, his childhood

1. Scribner, "Communities," 294–309.

memories reveal why he and other German-speaking immigrants viewed Penn's colony as "the best poor man's country." Clearly, early eighteenth-century Pennsylvania society was more fluid and flexible than that of the Palatinate. Wistar must have gained invaluable experience from observing his father's struggle in the multifaceted contest for profit and gain in the face of limited opportunity.

The more important legacy that Wistar's father left the young man, however, was his persistence in his efforts to secure his place in Waldhilsbach. He arrived in the tight-knit village as an outsider—a man without family connections—who represented the elector's interests. The strategies he chose for establishing himself included marriage to the daughter of the hamlet's local government official, a man who belonged to the appropriate church and possessed well-established kinship networks. He also sought the patronage of those with political power. His attempts to become an insider, to create social connections and economic security in his new home, foreshadow the young immigrant's choices twenty-some years later on the other side of the Atlantic.

Visiting the area surrounding Waldhilsbach today, one readily imagines the place Wistar wrote of in his autobiography. Dark forests thickly blanket the rolling hills in the region. Walking up the steep slope to the castle in Heidelberg and beyond it to the peak of the Königstühl, a view of the old city, the seat of government in Wistar's Palatinate, and the Neckar Valley opens up below. To the south, through the labyrinth of trails that lead into the densely forested hills, is the district that Wistar's father oversaw.[2] Hans Caspar Wüster not only patrolled the use of timber and the hunting of wildlife on the property belonging to the government, he also directed and approved the way village communities within his district used their own resources. He and his sons knew intimately the many paths that crisscrossed the wooded hills south of Heidelberg.

A mile or so deeper into the woods, the towering trees suddenly give way to a clearing and a small cluster of buildings known as the Kohlhoff. Here one of Wistar's uncles lived and worked as a charcoal burner; he watched over the smoldering fire that transformed cords of wood into high-energy fuel.[3] Wistar's father monitored how much timber the charcoal burners used to insure that they did not destroy too much of the forest and its wildlife.[4] Ties between the forester and charcoal burners were understandably close, if not always harmonious.

2. His district was bounded by Rohrbach, Königstühl, and Neckargemünd to the north, the Elsenz River to the east, Zuzenhausen, Dielsheim, and Wiesloch to the south, and Wiesloch, Nußloch, and Rohrbach to the west. Foresters' contracts, Feb. 22, 1652, and May 22, 1688, GLA 229/30951.

3. BRKB, EOK. Hans Peter Müller was a brother of Anna Catharina Müller, Wistar's mother.

4. *Chur-Fürstlicher Pfaltz Forst- und Wald- auch Weid-werks Jagd- und Fischerey- Ordnung* (Heidelberg: Hof u. Universitäts Buchdrucker, Johann Meyer, 1711).

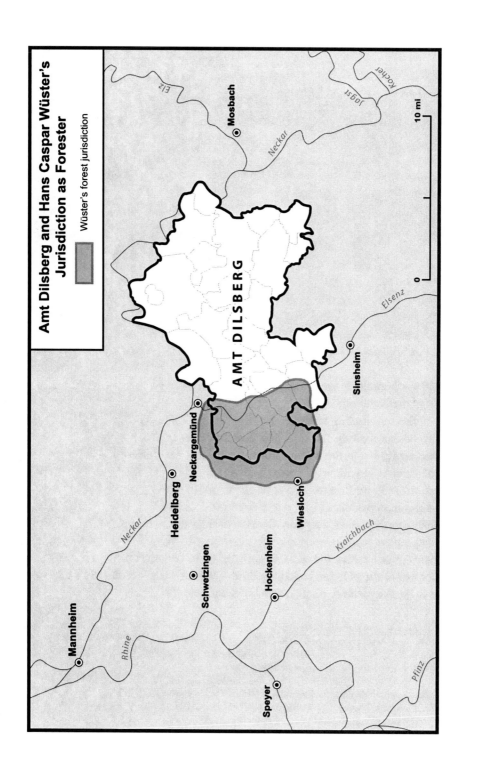

Amt Dilsberg and Hans Caspar Wüster's Jurisdiction as Forester

Wüster's forest jurisdiction

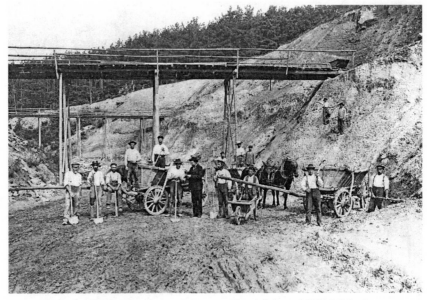

FIG. 3 Clay pits, Waldhilsbach, 1915. Courtesy of Liesl Schwind, Waldhilsbach.

Wistar himself, at age fifteen, was godparent to the son of a charcoal burner from the Kohlhoff.[5]

The trail leading from the Kohlhoff to Waldhilsbach twists and turns for several miles along the bubbling Forellenbach (trout stream) through thick stands of trees. In the seventeenth and eighteenth centuries the area was called the Streitwald (contested forest) and was one of Waldhilsbach's few common resources. In contrast to some of its neighbors, the village owned a small amount of common woodland.[6] At the edge of the Streitwald, the forest opens into a shallow valley. There, hugging the edge of the woods on the eastern side of the road, are the sites of the old clay pits mentioned by Wistar in his autobiography.[7] During his lifetime, the clay soil provided an important source of income for a number of the villagers, including some of Wistar's extended family, who carted it to Neckargemünd, where it was fashioned into ceramic jugs.[8]

5. Jan. 30, 1711, NgLKB, EOK.

6. *Stadt- und Landkreise*, vol. 2, *Die Stadt Heidelberg und die Gemeinden des Landkreises Heidelberg* (Karlsruhe, 1968), 950–51. Julius Schmidt, *Chronik von Gaiberg-Waldhilsbach. Zugleich ein Beitrag Pfälzer Kirchengeschichte* (Heidelberg, 1901), 118–19.

7. I wish to thank Mrs. Liesl Schwind, Waldhilsbach, for identifying the sites and buildings in the following description. For brief histories of Waldhilsbach's families, see Günther Wüst, *Waldhilsbach: Ein Beitrag zur Ortsgeschichte* (Neckargemünd: Druckerei Odenwälder, 2000), 379–404.

8. Wistar, "Short Report," Wistar Family Papers, HSP; June 10, 1717, GLA 61/5469; *Stadt- und Landkreise*, 2:954.

Just beyond the clay pits, nestled among the trees that line the valley, the houses of Waldhilsbach cluster together, surrounded by orchards and rolling meadows. The road from the Kohlhof forms the main thoroughfare, which cuts southeast through the village. In 1706, twelve households were scattered along the road (see Table 1). Hans Nicolas Müller's widow, three sons, and a son-in-law made up more than one-third of the households and over one-half of the permanent citizens (*Bürger*) in the village. Andreas Ziegler and Bernhard Ganßhorn represented another complex, interwoven kinship network that included families in two neighboring villages. The remaining permanent citizens in Waldhilsbach belonged to two households headed by Martin Schmidt and Jacob Fertig. Together, these nine households and three additional families of temporary inhabitants (*Beisaßen*) constituted the core of villagers who lived along the road from the Kohlhoff.[9]

A decade later, the number of households in Waldhilsbach had grown from twelve to sixteen (see Table 1). Hans Nicolas Müller's widow had died and another son, along with Jacob Fertig and two of the temporary inhabitants, had moved away. Throughout the decade, nine new families, many of whom came from the neighboring villages of Gaiberg and Bammental, established households. Andreas Bauer, one of the temporary inhabitants from 1706, had become a permanent resident and one new temporary inhabitant had joined the community. As the number of permanent residents grew, common land became more scarce and new houses pushed farther south along the main road through town.[10]

At the northeast entrance to the village, just beyond the sites of the old clay pits, Kapellenweg (Chapel Way) turns off to the east; the name of the street is the only remaining sign of the hamlet's old chapel. When Wistar was a child, only the ruins of the chapel, destroyed by the Swedes during the Thirty Years' War, remained. Nevertheless, the ruins and the property on which the chapel stood continued to prove a point of contention throughout the period.[11] In the absence of their own church, the Reformed inhabitants of Waldhilsbach traveled to Gaiberg or Bammental to baptize their children and bury their dead while the Lutheran and Catholic parishioners attended church in Neckargemünd.[12]

9. "Verzeichnus der sambdtliche Inwohner zu Dilsperg waß religion die selben sein," 1706, GLA 61/5479 (hereafter "Religionsverzeichnis," 1706).

10. "Register über die Bedienten u. Untertanen, die im Oktober 1716 zu Weinheim, Wiesloch u. Leimen gehuldigt haben, auch zu Schönau, Neckargemünd, in den Centen Schriesheim u. Kirchheim, Kellerei Waldeck u. Amt Dilsberg," 1716, GLA 145/292 (hereafter "Register," 1716); *Stadt- und Landkreise*, 2:948–50.

11. Schmidt, *Chronik*, 68–72; Feb. 14, 1713, GLA 61/5467; Wüst, *Waldhilsbach*, 263–67. The discussion in Chapter 3 relates how the religious policies of the Palatine government resulted in a diversity of confessional affiliation and complex property disputes.

12. *Stadt- und Landkreise*, 2:952; Wüst, *Waldhilsbach*, 331–44. In 1706, there were three Catholic households in Waldhilsbach with a total of fifteen members. The Lutheran and Reformed congregants

TABLE 1 Heads of Households in Waldhilsbach

1706 (12 households)	1716 (16 households)	1736 (21 households)
Andreas Ziegler	Andreas Ziegler	——
		Martin Ziegler
Bernhard Ganßhorn	Bernhard Ganßhorn	Bernhard Ganßhorn
		H. Adam Ganßhorn
		G. Heinrich Haffner
H. Nicolas Müller (W)	——	——
Wendell Müller	——	——
Adam Müller	Adam Müller	Adam Müller
		Andreas Bollack
Nicolas Müller	Nicolas Müller	Nicolas Müller
		Georg Müller
		H. Heinrich Bollack
H. Caspar Wüster	H. Caspar Wüster	H. Caspar Wüster (W)
Martin Schmidt	Martin Schmidt	——
Jacob Fertig	——	——
Andreas Bauer (B)	Andreas Bauer	——
Jacob Weithofen (B)	——	——
Caspar Pechder (B)	——	——
	Georg Rauch	——
	Leonhard Kellerman	Leonard Kellerman
	Hans Wolf Beck	Wolf Beck
		Hans Georg Beck
	Georg Meyer	Georg Meyer
	David Ruckmesser	——
	H. Mich. Abendschein	H. Mich. Abendschein
	H. Georg Funck	H. Georg Funck
	Lorentz Bödenheimer	——
	Georg Wiedemann (B)	Georg Wittemann (W)
		H. Adam Braun
		Johannes Krone
		Mattias Pleyller
		Jakob Bär (W)

Sources: "Religionsverzeichnis," 1706, GLA 61/5479; "Register," 1716, GLA 145/292; Schmidt, *Chronik*, 129.
Note: (W) = widow of. (B) = *Beisitzer* (temporary inhabitant). Children are listed under their father or father-in-law.

Kapellenweg gives way to Schulweg (School Way) toward the southwest. Waldhilsbach did not have its own school in the early eighteenth century. Instead, the village children walked to Gaiberg or Neckargemünd, depending on their religious affiliation, to receive their formal education. In 1709, the Reformed Church sent a teacher to Gaiberg, where Wistar's friend Georg Müller donated land for a school building.[13] Children who belonged to Lutheran or Catholic households had to walk one hour to Neckargemünd to attend classes. Although Wistar claims he did not receive much education, he did attend class in Neckargemünd at least often enough to learn to read and write. It was here that he became friends with Georg Friederich Hölzer, who became his business associate later in life.[14]

At the end of Schulweg an old tavern overlooks the main street and the small "square" at the center of town. During Wistar's lifetime, Andreas Ziegler and his family ran the local tavern or inn.[15] Since the hamlet had no town hall, the community transacted much of its business, including town meetings and court sessions, at the tavern. The village magistrate, justice, and the district administrator formed the civil court that settled disputes on court days. Ziegler's house also functioned as a social center in the village where the latest news was exchanged, official orders were read, and villagers gathered to drink and eat. Thus, Ziegler's tavern played a central role in the public cultural space of early modern Waldhilsbach.

Farther down the valley a small street turns east off of the main road. Along this street, tucked behind fruit trees, stands the Müller house and barn. The Müllers were an old family in Waldhilsbach. Wistar's mother, Anna Catharina, was the daughter of Hans Nicolas Müller, the village magistrate at the end of the seventeenth century, and his wife Barbara.[16] Müller also had served as an elder in the Reformed congregation, and he had been the overseer of the poor before he became Waldhilsbach's magistrate.[17]

Just beyond the Müller house at the corner of the road to Bammental and the Totenweg (Way of the Dead) is the Forsthaus (forester's house). Here, according

---

were not as easily divided into households because of intermarriage across confessional bounds. Four of the village households were exclusively Reformed, two were exclusively Lutheran, and the remaining three were headed by mixed marriages. "Religionsverzeichnis," 1706, GLA 61/5479. Further discussion of the religious diversity in Waldhilsbach can be found in Chapter 3.

13. Wistar, "Short Report," Wistar Family Papers, HSP; Schmidt, *Chronik*, 92–102.

14. *Stadt- und Landkreise*, 1:298–303; Wistar, "Short Report," Wistar Family Papers, HSP; Georg Friederich Hölzer, Neckargemünd, to Caspar Wistar, Philadelphia, Feb. 23, 1742, Wistar Family Papers, HSP.

15. Nov. 25, 1719, GLA 61/5471.

16. BRKB, EOK.

17. Schmidt, *Chronik*, 75; BRKB, EOK.

FIG. 4 Forsthaus, Waldhilsbach, c. 1913. Wistar's parents lived here when he was a small child. Courtesy of Liesl Schwind, Waldhilsbach.

to family tradition, Wistar was born.[18] Although village records indicate that his parents lived in the Müller house for a number of years after their marriage and at the time of his birth, they moved to the Forsthaus sometime prior to his emigration.[19] Today the half-timbered barn is gone and the house has been altered almost beyond recognition. Nevertheless, from its interior, the original structure is still clearly defined by the low, bowed beams that support the upper floors.[20]

The location of the forester's house at the community's periphery replicates the position of Wistar's father within village society. He was an outsider, trying to secure a place in his new home. His forestry tasks also turned his attention outward, away from life in the hamlet. His house stood at the intersection of two roads leading to neighboring villages. Traveling southwest, the Totenweg was the main route to Gaiberg; to the southeast, the road from the village continued on to Bammental.[21] Since the district that Wistar's father oversaw lay

18. Robert C. Moon, *The Morris Family of Philadelphia: Descendants of Anthony Morris,* vol. 1 (Philadelphia, 1898), 356–57.

19. In a court case from 1718, Wüster noted that he had lived in the house of his father-in-law many years previously. Sept. 17, 1718, GLA 61/5470. For the changes made on the property, see photos belonging to Mrs. Liesl Schwind. Davids, *Wistar Family,* 5, comments on the prominence of the house in the village.

20. I wish to thank Mr. and Mrs. Edgar Hoffmann, the owners of the Forsthaus in 1992, for generously opening their home to me.

21. The Totenweg received its name because it was the path that the Reformed parishioners in Waldhilsbach used to carry their dead to the cemetery in neighboring Gaiberg. Personal communication with Mrs. Liesl Schwind, Sept. 1992.

Çruss aus Waldhilsbach

Der Æppelwei soll lebe,
Der Salzweck danebe!
Der Kand'käs und die Worscht,
Prosit merr hawwe Dorscht.

FIG. 5 Gruss aus Waldhilsbach, c. 1902. Courtesy of Liesl Schwind, Waldhilsbach.

largely to the south of Waldhilsbach, the location of the forester's house on the southern periphery of the hamlet provided the best access to his jurisdiction.

Just as the Forsthaus stands at the nexus of routes to neighboring villages, so Wüster often stood at the intersection of competing interests. Wistar's father was the state's link to Waldhilsbach and the rich resources of the surrounding forests. But he was also a full citizen of the village. If he did not balance the preservation of village resources with his forestry tasks, his neighbors could make his life miserable. The forester's ability to maintain an equilibrium between preserving his loyalty to the elector's government, protecting his neighbors' interests, and pursuing his own advancement proved a difficult struggle.

Wistar's father, Hans Caspar Wüster (1671–1726), began his career as an outsider. Born in Neunkirchen in 1671, he moved to Waldhilsbach in spring 1695, following the death of Johann Henrich Dillinger, the forester for Gaiberg. In a brawl with the magistrate from Bammental, fought over who had the right to harvest wild fruit, Dillinger had suffered broken ribs and a serious face injury. He died on March 10, 1695, perhaps as a result of his injuries.[22] Dillinger's problems demonstrate the conflicts foresters faced as they negotiated between their own

22. Apr. 5, 1671; NkRKB, EOK; Jan. 28, 1694, GLA 61/5463. For Dillinger, see July 6 and Aug. 28, 1694, GLA 61/5463; BRKB, EOK.

interests, those of their neighbors, and those of their employer. Village struggles for resources, authority, and honor more often than not turned violent. The daily tasks of a forester could be, at best, difficult; at worst, deadly.

Wüster replaced Dillinger as the forester for Gaiberg early in 1695 and shortly thereafter he married Anna Catharina Müller.[23] The young couple's marriage helped to secure Wüster's position at the top of the hamlet's society because Müller's father held one of the most prestigious offices in the village: the magistrate. By the end of the seventeenth century the magistrate's position was an appointed government office. As magistrate, Müller chaired the village court and worked under the mayor of Meckesheim as the government's representative in the community. He also acted as the hamlet's attorney before the district, regional, and state courts. The magistrate's tasks included carrying out government orders, overseeing compulsory service the village owed the state, collecting village tithes and taxes, settling property and minor civil disputes (with the help of the justices of the court), and determining how the village used its common land. Although he received only a minimal salary, Müller's office rewarded him with lucrative fees, perquisites, and elevated social status.[24] In a hamlet the size of Waldhilsbach, the magistrate was the most powerful man.

The union of Wüster and Anna Catharina Müller was typical of the choices made by people of their rank and position. Foresters, like magistrates, pastors, and school teachers, belonged to a class of government officials who intermarried and created a complex web of social and kinship relationships. When Wüster arrived in Waldhilsbach, Müller was the only other appointed government official in the village; thus, Anna Catharina was an appropriate choice for marriage. Furthermore, the Müllers had lived in the hamlet for generations, and they made up a significant portion of the village population (five of seven households in 1706). They offered Wüster numerous family connections that enhanced his reputation within his new community and, perhaps unknown to him, linked him to age-old animosities.[25]

23. According to the NkRKB, Hans Caspar Wüster and Anna Catharina Müller married on July 20, 1695. In the BRKB they are recorded as having married on August 18, 1695. As the marriage was performed in Gaiberg by the minister of the Bammental Reformed Church, his record is most likely more accurate.

24. *Stadt- und Landkreise,* 1:270–71; Lenz, *Kellerei und Unteramt Dilsberg,* 33; Günther Wüst, *Bammental: Geschichte einer Elsenztalgemeinde* (Heidelberg: Heidelberger Verlagsanstalt, 1983), 255; GLA 145/45. A *Schultheiß* normally held the top magisterial position in Palatine towns. In Waldhilsbach, the *Anwald* was equivalent to a *Schultheiß.* David W. Sabean, in *Power in the Blood: Popular Culture and Village Discourse in Early Modern Germany* (Cambridge: Cambridge University Press, 1984), 12–20, outlines similar relationships between government officials and villagers in early modern Württemberg.

25. Church records demonstrate kinship networks for people with similar occupations and social status. For example, two children of Hans Wendel Mosselbach, the forester for Gaiberg in the 1670s, married the children of the magistrate for Gaiberg; BRKB. For other examples, see the marriages of Bernhard Ganßhorn and Andreas Ziegler, below; BRKB, NkRKB, NgLKB, and NgRKB, EOK.

During his first decade as the forester in Waldhilsbach, Wüster lived peacefully with his neighbors. He and his wife spent several years in the Müller household, which must have eased Wüster's entrance into village relationships. Their oldest son, Caspar Wistar, was born a half-year after their marriage and was baptized in the Reformed Church at Bammental.[26] Caspar's baptismal sponsors reflect Wüster's transition to his new home: one was from Neunkirchen and one was Anna Catharina's sister from Waldhilsbach. Over the next decade, however, the couple sought patronage connections within the area immediately surrounding the village. The Schäfers, merchants at Neckargemünd, and the Lemlers, peasant proprietors at Gauangelloch, sponsored most of the baptisms of their remaining children.[27] By 1706, Wüster and his wife had moved into their own dwelling and established a household that included five children, a male servant, and a female servant.[28]

The Wüsters simultaneously became patrons within the village. Between 1703 and 1706, they were baptismal sponsors for three of Hans Bernhard Ganßhorn's children, two of whom were namesakes. Ganßhorn, who was the son of the justice from the neighboring town, had married the daughter of the justice in Waldhilsbach in 1695. Within several years he had taken over the judicial responsibilities of his father-in-law.[29] Justices, or members of the court, shared the magistrate's social and political status. Comparable to justices of the peace in colonial British America, members of the court resolved minor disputes and property issues within the village on special court days held four times annually. The number of justices varied from one town to another; for most of Wistar's childhood, Ganßhorn was the only justice in Waldhilsbach.[30] Therefore, Ganßhorn's choice of Wüster and Anna Catharina (the magistrate's daughter) as baptismal sponsors for his children reinforced connections between him and the Müllers and simultaneously affirmed Wüster's social status in the village.

In addition to fostering alliances with the Ganßhorns, Wüster strengthened his social position by making connections to patrons in the district government.

26. It was not unusual during the period for young women to be pregnant when they married. See David W. Sabean, *Property, Production, and Family in Neckarhausen, 1700–1870* (Cambridge: Cambridge University Press, 1990), 329–34.

27. BRKB and NgRKB, EOK; Wüst, *Bammental,* 471. Connections between the Schäfers and the Wüsters continued throughout Wistar's lifetime, if somewhat indirectly. Justi Schäfer's daughter married Johannes Leonard, the father of Rosina Coecilia and father-in-law of Georg Friederich Hölzer. Hölzer was a schoolmate of Wistar's and his business associate after he migrated to Pennsylvania.

28. "Religionsverzeichnis," 1706, GLA 61/5479.

29. BRKB, EOK. Ganßhorn is listed as the justice in Waldhilsbach, Mar. 12, 1706, GLA 61/5465.

30. Within Amt Dilsberg the terms *Gericht* and *Rat* were used interchangeably; I have translated them both as "justice." At court sessions, village citizens submitted notice of any dispute that had occurred since the previous court day. The *Anwald* (magistrate) and *Gericht* determined the outcome of the disputes and collected fines. *Stadt- und Landkreise,* 1:270–71; Wüst, *Bammental,* 256–58.

As a forester, Wüster was one of seven secular government officials for Amt Dilsberg, which was under the regional government at Heidelberg.[31] At the top of the pyramid was the district commissioner for Dilsberg, who held a vote on the elector's advisory council.[32] Directly under him was Johann Georg Kauffman, the district administrator, who also claimed two additional government positions: the mayor of Meckesheim and the tax administrator for Amt Dilsberg. Through his combined offices, Kauffmann held oversight of the district's day-to-day administrative, fiscal, and judicial operations.[33] Wüster communicated regularly with Kauffman who, as the mayor of Meckesheim, also appointed magistrates. By the end of Wüster's first decade in Waldhilsbach, his father-in-law was aging and the promise of holding the most powerful position in the village seemed imminent.[34]

There was, however, a second contender for Müller's position. Nine years Wüster's senior, Andreas Ziegler was the son of the village magistrate who had preceded Müller. In fact, throughout the seventeenth and early eighteenth centuries, the office rotated between the two families.[35] In 1681, Ziegler married the daughter of neighboring Wiesenbach's justice. By the time Wüster arrived in Waldhilsbach in 1695, Ziegler was a permanent citizen and had a growing family. Thus, a decade later both Ziegler and Wüster were well-established and potential candidates for the magistrate's office.[36] The competition between the two men for power and honor illustrates the constraints Wüster faced as he sought to secure his place in the village.

The year 1705 proved to be a pivotal point in the public careers of the two men. Perhaps because Müller was becoming infirm or perhaps in anticipation of transferring his office to his successor, the district government licensed Wüster

31. "Register," 1716, GLA 145/292.

32. Lenz, *Kellerei und Unteramt Dilsberg*, 96–104; Ludwig Häusser, *Geschichte der Rheinischen Pfalz nach ihren politischen, kirchlichen, u. literarischen Verhältnissen*, vol. 2 (Heidelberg: J. C. B. Mohr, 1845), 840–41; Roeber, *Palatines*, 79.

33. When Kauffmann obtained the three positions in the 1670s and 1680s, the mayor's position, which had been an elective office, became a part of the elector's appointed administration. The office of the mayor of Meckesheim (*reisige Schultheiß von Meckesheim*) evolved from the earl of Meckesheim Hundred (*Zentgraff von Meckesheim*). He supervised the magistrates (*Anwälder*) from the villages in the Meckesheim Hundred, which owed no allegiance to the nobility. Those villages that included subjects of the nobility had their own mayors (*Schultheißen*). The Meckesheim and Stüber Hundreds were subdivisions of Amt Dilsberg. Lenz, *Kellerei und Unteramt Dilsberg*, 120–21. The career of Kauffmann is described throughout Lenz's study, but see especially pages 100–102, 104–5, 110–11, 214–23.

34. Lenz, *Kellerei und Unteramt Dilsberg*, 32–34, 221. At the same time, Wüster had not yet received his official letters patent or contract for his position as forester. Oct. 28, 1706, GLA 145/50.

35. BRKB, EOK.

36. BRKB, EOK; Oct. 31, 1684, GLA 61/5479; Nov. 25, 1719, GLA 61/5471.

as a temporary or deputy magistrate.[37] Ziegler clearly thought he was the better candidate for the position. Signs of the struggle between the two men first
appeared when Wüster appealed to the district court for help in defending his
reputation. He claimed Ziegler had assaulted his honor and character in public
by accusing Wüster of "trying to win the favor of the district administrator so
that the same would be indulgent with him."[38] In addition, Ziegler allegedly
had mocked his abilities as acting magistrate. "Because he had no intention of
letting these charges against him stand, especially since the entire community
had heard them," Wüster sought recourse at the district court.[39]

   Like so many of the disputes in Waldhilsbach, arguments surrounding reputation and privilege were inseparable from attempts to obtain money, resources,
and political power. Wüster's accusations of slander were rooted in a particular
incident: Ziegler had refused to pay his full share of the cowherd's salary because,
he argued, he had kept his cows at home for fourteen days. Wüster, as the temporary magistrate and with the other villagers' consent, pressed Ziegler to con-
tribute his portion since failure to do so would burden his neighbors with extra
costs.[40] Ziegler, infuriated that the forester had won the support of the community at his expense, retaliated with public verbal accusations against Wüster. He
recognized that Wüster was using his temporary position to increase his political influence within Waldhilsbach. Since he hoped to win the office for himself,
Ziegler needed to convince his neighbors and the district administrator that
Wüster was incapable of the job. By claiming that the forester failed to understand the magistrate's tasks and blindly followed his superiors' orders, Ziegler
implied that Wüster would not act to protect village interests from government
encroachments.[41]

   Retaining the balance of power within village relationships required delicate
diplomacy. A good magistrate needed both a respectable character and connections with higher government officials. Because Wüster's forestry position tied
him to regional public servants, Ziegler attacked his character; he accused the
forester of repeatedly bribing Kauffman to win his indulgence. Wüster probably
had sought Kauffman's favor given his influence and power; bribery and favoritism were becoming more prevalent as the bureaucracy expanded. Kauffman, as
the mayor of Meckesheim, actually appointed magistrates. Furthermore, Wüster
chose to file his complaint against Ziegler with the district court, which meant

   37. Jan. 9, 1705, GLA 61/5465. According to testimony heard in the dispute, Wüster was granted a
license by the *Obereinnehmer* Schlichter (a government official at the regional level).
   38. Jan. 9, 1705, GLA 61/5465.
   39. Ibid.
   40. Ibid.
   41. Ibid.

Kauffman would hear the dispute. He likely expected the district administrator's patronage to swing the outcome in his favor. Such connections could benefit the whole village if Wüster exploited them for the commonweal. Ziegler's accusations, however, implied that Wüster would use them only for his personal benefit.[42]

Ziegler's charges evolved, at least in part, from the rising tensions between Palatine foresters and villagers. Following the end of war in 1697, the forestry department expanded rapidly and its members gained significant salary increases and new perquisites. Foresters frequently quarreled with their neighbors over "personal freedoms" and tax exemptions as they flaunted their growing social and economic status. On several occasions the head of the department succeeded in gaining the elector's protection of the foresters' rights.[43] It is not surprising, therefore, that Ziegler, when asked if he had any formal accusations against Wüster, claimed that "he knew of nothing against him, except one thing alone, that he should not raise himself above the others." He predicted that just as the hunter was "held accountable by the forestry department," so the subjects of Waldhilsbach would hold him responsible for his actions as a village official. Wüster's position as forester continued to make his allegiance to his neighbors suspect.[44]

Some time between 1706, when Müller died, and 1712, Ziegler not only succeeded in disqualifying Wüster from becoming Waldhilsbach's next magistrate, he managed to obtain the office for himself.[45] That did not end the competition for power, however; the struggle between the two men resurfaced again in 1712. After failing to succeed his father-in-law, Wüster turned to real estate investment to improve his economic position. His attempt to purchase land fueled old antagonisms as issues regarding the private use of resources became inextricably intertwined with public duty and official authority. To secure his land purchase, Wüster needed Ziegler and Ganßhorn, as the magistrate and justice, to notarize the sale at the village court. But Wüster claimed that "because the magistrate and others had possession of these [properties], none of them wanted to acknowledge [his purchase] officially."[46] Ziegler was now the one gaining personally from his position as magistrate, and Wüster charged him with profiteering and dishonesty.

42. Ibid. Testimony in a 1701 court case revealed that Wüster had accepted a bribe when he encountered a man illegally carrying a gun through the forest. Nov. 9, 1701, GLA 77/1818. For the rise of favoritism, see Lenz, *Kellerei und Unteramt Dilsberg*, 96–104.

43. Beiler, "Transatlantic," 53–71.

44. The outcome of the case remains unknown because the regional records for Oberamt Heidelberg, where Wüster's case was heard, are no longer extant for 1705.

45. Müller was buried June 20, 1706; BRKB, EOK.

46. Aug. 4, 1712, GLA 61/5467. For a discussion of confusing property claims that followed the Thirty Years' War, see Wüst, *Waldhilsbach*, 283–84

In addition, Wüster brought a slander suit against Ziegler. The magistrate's response highlights how important reputation and honor were for local political influence and economic gain. During a legal process, and in front of Kauffman and the magistrates from three neighboring villages, Wüster taunted Ziegler by asking him if he was going to read a legal document "line by line." As a fellow government official and his peer, Wüster embarrassed the magistrate by implying he did not know how to perform his job properly. Ziegler, in a fit of anger, blurted out that Wüster "was driving the subjects out of the village with his actions," implying that Wüster's attempts to undermine his authority and buy up property were causing his neighbors to suffer. Ziegler warned the forester that he was "also a subject [in the village] and would be driven out in like manner."[47]

Later the same evening, Wüster entered Ziegler's house and insulted him in front of several neighbors. During the dispute, Wüster "declared [Ziegler] to be a public rogue and added that he would not be the magistrate for another fourteen days."[48] Ziegler retorted that if he were removed from the magistrate's office, no one would be willing to buy the position—it brought so few perquisites. But if Wüster's office as forester were "auctioned, it could easily be bid up to 100 *Gulden*" owing to its more lucrative nature.[49] Since "no one among the villagers wanted to lay a hand on [Wüster]," Ziegler called his son Tobias, who (with the help of Ziegler's wife) "threw him out of the house by his hair."[50]

Wüster obviously aspired to more than magisterial remuneration; he also craved the influence and power of the position. Ziegler had abused his power to prevent Wüster from purchasing property. In response Wüster tried to convince Ziegler's peers and the villagers that he was incompetent for his office, just as Ziegler had done to him six years earlier. He used a public occasion to present a magisterial critique of Ziegler's activities: he performed his official duties poorly. Ziegler responded with a village critique of Wüster: he was hurting his neighbors' interests.

By this point, the villagers wisely refused to interfere in the dispute between the two government servants. They may have been siding with Wüster in the conflict since they refused to lay a hand on him. More likely, however, they were wary of Wüster as a forester and generally savvy about staying out of disputes with superiors. In 1709, a new series of laws had increased foresters' power to punish poachers. Several foresters had won the backing of high government officials and the elector himself in a couple of lengthy disputes with village

47. Aug. 4, 1712, GLA 61/5467.
48. Ibid.
49. Ibid.
50. Ibid.

magistrates.[51] In any event, Kauffmann, who needed to keep Ziegler as a potential ally, determined that the dispute was clearly "undertaken in idle drink," fined
each party, and ordered them not to hurt each other again.[52] Neither man succeeded in recruiting support from the villagers or Kauffmann, but they both
used public political discourse to keep the other from obtaining additional economic and social status.

Six months later, however, family members and villagers did choose sides
in the Wüster-Ziegler feud. Nicolas Müller, Wüster's brother-in-law, claimed
that Ziegler sold property that did not belong to him but rather to the old
ruined chapel, therefore to the government.[53] Müller claimed Ziegler was hurting his neighbors when he accused the magistrate of being "a thief and a rogue
who betrayed the entire village." When Ziegler tried to defend himself, Müller,
his brothers, and Wüster, with the approval of virtually the entire community,
attacked the magistrate, "ripping his hair from his head and his clothes from his
body" like "wild people."[54]

Wüster continued Müller's allegations that Ziegler had embezzled what
rightfully belonged to the government. He accused the magistrate of omitting
from the accounts village taxes that he had collected in 1712 and 1713. The money
had disappeared and Wüster accused Ziegler of having pocketed it. The magistrate countered that he had used the money to build a house for the village
herdsman, a project intended for the common good of the community. Kauffmann, his patience with the people from Waldhilsbach stretched thin, ordered
an investigation and "earnestly instructed" Ziegler and the villagers "to bear better witness thereto and in everything to do no harm, or the authorities would
levy fines against them."[55] He had not yet determined whether Ziegler was at
fault or if the villagers were in collusion with him in withholding money from
the government.

By 1716, the entire community believed that Ziegler had placed his own
interests above his obligations to the village. They discovered that Ziegler had
pocketed a portion of the tax receipts to pay his own debts.[56] Ziegler had also
used his authority to gain for himself exclusive usage rights to meadow land that
the community badly needed, and he did so, it seemed, by intentionally ignoring
the instructions of the villagers to bid sufficiently to secure its use. In the past,

51. Aug. 30, 1700, through Jan. 15, 1701, GLA 77/1818.
52. Aug. 4, 1712, GLA 61/5467.
53. Feb. 14, 1713, GLA 61/5467; Schmidt, *Chronik*, 68–72.
54. Feb. 14, 1713, GLA 61/5467.
55. Ibid.
56. May 10, 1715, GLA 61/5468. The district administrator's review of the accounts revealed that the
money was missing and he ordered Ziegler to submit it immediately.

the village had rented the meadow from the City of Heidelberg for common use in exchange for performing compulsory labor (*Frohndienst*) in the form of delivering the game shot in the city's forest to the castle. Ziegler failed to bid high enough to rent the meadow for the village but managed to secure it for his own personal use. As the magistrate, he claimed exemption from compulsory labor, which then fell to the villagers. Since Ziegler had not fulfilled his commission, the community requested relief from the mandatory work. In addition, they asked the district court to instruct the magistrate "to represent the community better in its affairs and not to stand himself before the light; otherwise they would be forced to sell their humble houses and clear out of the little hamlet."[57]

Ziegler attempted to diffuse blame by implicating Wüster, the other government official in the village responsible for the use of common property. But Kauffman supported the villagers and reprimanded Ziegler. He ordered the magistrate, since his actions "strive against Christian love and all justice," to refrain from "taking prohibited advantage" of his position.[58] Ziegler's neighbors hindered his attempts to use the perks of his position for his individual benefit. They did so by soliciting the support of the government—his employer and the source of his special status. As magistrate, Ziegler suffered from the same constraints he had predicted in 1705 Wüster would face if he became the village magistrate.

Like many other government officials of his period, Ziegler used and abused his power at the expense of the villagers. As a result, Wüster succeeded in using a village critique—claiming that Ziegler's actions were hurting the community—to gain support from his neighbors in his long-standing feud with Ziegler. Nevertheless, Wüster was also a government official whose allegiance his neighbors constantly scrutinized. If they concurred that Ziegler was a self-seeking, corrupt magistrate, they also regarded Wüster as equally suspect. The forester, therefore, faced constraints not only from individuals like Ziegler but also from the community of Waldhilsbach as a whole.

In 1716, a change in power threatened Wüster's forestry position. Karl Philipp (1716–42), the new elector, ordered severe reforms that led to salary freezes and massive cuts in the forestry department, reminiscent of the cuts during the lifetime of Wüster's father.[59] Faced with a diminished income and the prospect of losing his position altogether, Wüster increased his efforts to secure his family's

57. Sept. 29, 1715, GLA 61/5468.
58. Ibid.
59. 1716–19, GLA 77/1738.

political and social status in Waldhilsbach. The villagers, meanwhile, perceived that his position within the government was weakening and used the opportunity to gain more freedom from the state's interference in their daily lives. To that end, the community sued Wüster in 1718. The charges concerned ways Wüster maximized opportunities for individual gain at the expense of his neighbors. Upon closer examination, however, issues of individual gain were linked inseparably to his position as a government official.

One set of charges against Wüster revolved around property and privileges. The villagers argued, for instance, that Wüster claimed too much of the communal property for his own use. He already had four cleared fields and was trying to claim another piece of land. In doing so, Wüster denied the poor of the village their nourishment. Furthermore, Wüster's neighbors claimed he took away opportunities for them to earn money by hoarding all of the carting jobs for himself. Finally, he purchased two parcels of land, which included an assessment of mandatory carting service for the government, but he insisted he was exempt from such service. As a result, the villagers had to perform the tasks.[60] In each case, Wüster used the privileges of his forestry position for personal gain. By arguing that he was abusing his power at their expense, the villagers engaged in political discourse intended to erode government interference.

A second set of issues concerned Wüster's refusal to submit to the appropriate authority. The villagers claimed, for instance, that Wüster had ripped out some of the fencing around the communal field. As a result, his neighbors were forced to protect the field from wild game. When Ziegler, as the village magistrate, ordered him to repair the fence, Wüster slandered him with "unrepeatable words." At another time, the forester responded to an order from the regional government by saying that "no one except for the chief master of the hunt could give him orders."[61] Clearly the forester believed he answered to a higher authority than the regional government. By questioning his interpretation, Wüster's neighbors sought to minimize the central government's power within the village.[62]

In their final set of complaints, Wüster's neighbors argued that his position as a forester was oppressing them. They insisted he created more work for them by making his permanent residence in Waldhilsbach rather than in Gaiberg, where his predecessors had lived. Since his home was in Waldhilsbach, Wüster's neighbors had to help him deliver game to the elector's court more frequently

60. Sept. 17, 1718, GLA 61/5470. For previous cases concerning exemptions for mandatory government service, see Nov. 5, 13, 19, 1700; Dec. 5, 1700; Jan. 15, 1701; Aug. 6, 1701; Sept. 1, 1701; Nov. 1, 9, 1701; Feb. 20, 1706; Mar. 1, 1706; GLA 61/5470.

61. Sept. 17, 1718, GLA 61/5470.

62. In a similar power struggle between a forester and the village of Sandhausen in 1700, the higher authorities decided in favor of the forester. GLA 77/1818.

than other subjects in Wüster's jurisdiction.[63] In this instance, the community explicitly argued against the central government's presence in their village.

Waldhilsbach's residents did not succeed in removing Wüster from the hamlet or in stripping him of his government position. The organizational and monetary problems that wracked the forestry department were ending at precisely the time the villagers attempted to take advantage of them. In the months preceding their case, the head of the forestry department died and his replacement revised the stringent cutbacks he had planned.[64] Ludwig Anton von Hack, whom Ziegler called "a hunter's friend," managed to secure enough support among the elector's advisors to keep most of the positions in the forestry administration.[65] Consequently, the district administrator referred the villagers' complaints to the vice chief master of the hunt.

Wüster managed to retain his forestry position, but his struggle to secure his family's social status in Waldhilsbach continued beyond his death in 1726. As Wüster's mother had done, Anna Catharina sought the perquisites due a forester's widow; she requested the personal freedom and exemptions from compulsory government service that her husband had enjoyed. In addition, she asked for the four *Malters* of wheat the previous forester's widow had received annually. More telling, however, Wüster's widow sought some sort of recompense for "the strong persecution" she suffered from her neighbors because "her son, who apprenticed as a hunter, converted to the Catholic religion."[66] When her request seemed in jeopardy, she appealed directly to the elector. She insisted that her husband, through his loyal service to the government, had made enemies in the village of Waldhilsbach. Anna Catharina implored him to continue Wüster's benefits, so that "at least [I] will be freed from the torment of the farmers in this place, who hate me like poison and do not know how they can torture me enough."[67]

By 1729, Anna Catharina had no children left in the village to support her. Her sons Caspar and Johannes, who might have inherited their father's position, emigrated to Pennsylvania, leaving her Catholic son, Johann Ludwig, next in line. Upon completing his apprenticeship, he took a forestry job in Amt Simmern, on the other side of the Rhine.[68] In 1719, Maria Barbara married Johan Georg Bauer, a miller from the neighboring town of Meckesheim. After his death, she eventually moved from Meckesheim with her second husband, Johan Georg Hütner,

---

63. Sept. 17, 1718, GLA 61/5470.
64. 1716–18, GLA 77/1738 and 77/1805.
65. Nov. 25, 1719, GLA 61/5471; Mar. 26, 1715, GLA 77/1805.
66. Feb. 28, 1729, GLA 77/1738.
67. 1729, GLA 77/1738.
68. Georg Friederich Hölzer, Neckargemünd, to Caspar Wistar, Philadelphia, Feb. 20, 1740; June 1, 1740; June 16, 1741; Feb. 23, 1742; Wistar Family Papers, HSP. Johannes migrated in 1727; Ralph B.

their two children, and those from her first marriage, to Pennsylvania.[69] Dorothea converted to Catholicism and in 1720 married Johannes Ganßhorn, who may have been the son of Bammental's justice. They disappear from the village records.[70] The same year, Anna Barbara married Johannes Epler, a farmer from Gaiberg whose family had lived there for several generations. They migrated with Maria Barbara and her family to Pennsylvania in 1737.[71] And Albertina, the youngest living daughter, converted to Catholicism and in 1722 married Johannes Ulm from Langenbrücken, a town near the city of Karlsruhe.[72]

Wüster's widow continued to struggle for survival in the village. Eventually the Wüster house (Forsthaus) was sold at auction.[73] In 1729, Ziegler and the local justice indicted the widow's hired man, Hans Adam Braun, for stealing wood from the Streitwald. Braun claimed the widow had directed him to cut the timber; she maintained one of the foresters had given it to her, but the magistrate and justice produced evidence to the contrary and fined her for taking the wood.[74]

The widow's plight did not improve. It seemed Anna Catharina constantly fought to keep what meager resources remained. After her house sold, she moved in with Braun, her hired man, and his family. Evidently she loaned him money, but Braun was in such deep financial trouble that the widow nearly became liable for his debt. In 1740, Braun traded properties with Leonhard Kellerman, the magistrate who succeeded Ziegler, to alleviate his indebtedness. Anna Catharina managed to retain her right to live in the house, but Kellerman wanted her out and tried several times to convince the widow to move in with her son Johann Ludwig in Amt Simmern.[75] Her son also borrowed money from

Strassburger and William Hinke, eds., *Pennsylvania German Pioneers: A Publication of the Original Lists of Arrivals in the Port of Philadelphia from 1727 to 1808*, vol. 1, *1727–1775* (Norristown, Pa., 1934; repr. Baltimore: Genealogical Publishing, 1980), 7 (pagination from 1980 reprint).

69. Their marriage, the baptisms of their children, and his death are recorded in the Bammental and Meckesheim Reformed Church records. Annette R. Burgert, *Eighteenth-Century Emigrants from German-Speaking Lands to North America*, vol. 1, *The Northern Kraichgau* (Breinigsville, Pa.: Pennsylvania German Society, 1983), 184. See also Caspar Wistar, Philadelphia, to Georg Friederich Hölzer, Nov. 10, 1735, Wistar Family Papers, HSP.

70. Ganßhorn was a common name in Bammental and the surrounding areas. The Johannes Ganßhorn whose marriage to Dorothea in 1720 is recorded in the Neckargemünd Catholic Church records may have been the son of Hans Georg and Veronica (Berger) Ganßhorn who was baptized in 1693 in Bammental; NgKKB, BRKB, EOK. Dorothea died sometime before November 1736. Caspar Wistar, Philadelphia, to Baltasar Langhaer, Krefeld, Nov. 25, 1736, Wistar Family Papers, HSP.

71. Epler family records are recorded in the Bammental Reformed Church records. Burgert, *Eighteenth-Century Emigrants*, 1:103–4.

72. International Genealogical Index, Church of the Latter-Day Saints.

73. Mar. 3, 1729, GLA 61/5474.

74. Apr. 22, 1729, GLA 61/5474.

75. Georg Friederich Hölzer, Neckargemünd, to Caspar Wistar, Philadelphia, Feb. 20, 1740; June 1, 1740; June 16, 1741; Feb. 23, 1742, Wistar Family Papers, HSP.

the widow for a building project. When she died in 1743, Anna Catharina left her "very modest legacy" to be divided equally among her four daughters or their descendants. She believed her two sons in Pennsylvania had been "richly blessed by God" and would, "out of love for their needier siblings," give up their shares in her estate. She considered the unpaid loan she had made to Johann Ludwig his inheritance. And, in recognition of all the help the Braun family had given her during her widowhood, she pardoned him from the debt he owed her.[76]

Anna Catharina's "very modest legacy" and the exodus of her children from Waldhilsbach suggest that Wüster had failed to achieve a secure place for his family in the village. Each of his sons sought to earn a living elsewhere. With the possible exception of Dorothea, none of his daughters married local men who belonged to the family's class of government officials. And, in spite of his marriage into a well-established kinship network, Wüster's children all (again, with the possible exception of Dorothea) moved out of the immediate area.

Hans Caspar Wüster's legacy, therefore, was the constant struggle to negotiate with competing interests for control of the meager resources available in Waldhilsbach. Whether fighting for privilege, honor, income, or property, he and his contemporaries tried to wield public discourse to their own advantage. Wüster's individual initiatives, however, met constraints at every turn. At different times, Ziegler and the village used legal and political institutions to keep his acquisitive behavior in check. Wistar, the immigrant, was ten years old when his father's feud with Ziegler first began. As a young man, he must have watched with frustration while the elder Wüster fought unsuccessfully to obtain an adequate subsistence for his growing family. The constant bickering, conflicts, and claustrophobia of village life and his father's apparent inability to find a firm place in local hierarchies encouraged him to seek better opportunities elsewhere and informed his subsequent actions in Pennsylvania.

Despite his father's failure, however, the young man also inherited a set of strategies for establishing his place as an outsider in new circumstances. As his father had done, Wistar sought the patronage of government officials and those in positions of power. He curried the favor of Pennsylvania's Quaker politicians and merchants and sought to serve the interests of its proprietary family when doing so promised to provide him with profits. Wistar, like his father, also chose a marriage partner whose family shared his social status. His father-in-law was a well-established justice of the peace and prominent landowner in Germantown. And Wistar, like his father and grandfather, adapted his religious identity when doing so promised to aid in securing his status within his new community.

76. Testament of Catharina Wüsterin, Jan. 21, 1743, Wistar Family Papers, HSP.

MY DEARLY BELOVED MOTHER, BROTHER AND SISTERS, AND OTHER GOOD FRIENDS:

In greeting you, I wish you all the peace and comfort of God in your souls, which peace can strengthen you in all of your present burdens and misery, which at this present time will be very great where you are. . . . So, my dear friends, [I] want to wish from the bottom of my soul that I, with you, and you, with me, [might] examine our hearts with our minds and consult with ourselves with the light that through Christ shines in us and in the world and see what has taken charge in our hearts. If God is in us with his love, then it will not remain unknown to us, for his love will awaken sighs and love for God and his work in our hearts, and will repel us every time from our willfulness and self love and our own strength and . . . teach us that we are nothing and that God is everything in everything.

—CASPAR WISTAR to his family, November 10, 1735

CHAPTER 3

Contested Identities
RELIGIOUS AFFILIATION AND DIVERSITY IN THE PALATINATE

At the time Wistar penned these words of encouragement to his widowed mother, siblings, and friends in 1735, troops had invaded the Rhine Valley. He had received no news from his European friends or family for more than a year. As the silence from home grew longer, the language of Wistar's correspondence became more spiritual and apocalyptic. The less he knew about their safety, the more he encouraged family and friends to turn to God during "these end times."[1]

Wistar's spiritual language masks the complex religious identities of the people to whom he wrote. By 1735, Wistar's father had died and been buried at the Lutheran Church in Neckargemünd.[2] His mother belonged to the Reformed congregation, in which Wistar had been baptized.[3] Of his siblings remaining in Europe, two sisters, who had been baptized in the Lutheran congregation, belonged to local Reformed churches, and his other two sisters and one brother had converted to Catholicism. His brother John, who arrived in Pennsylvania in 1727, flirted with joining several of the radical Pietist groups in the colony, whereas Wistar became a member of the Society of Friends shortly after his migration.[4] Wistar's family was unusually diverse at a time when most European families belonged to a single church and when confessional allegiances were critical.

This surprising diversity evolved from the complex religious history of the early modern Palatinate and the changing relations between the church and the state. Beginning with the Peace of Augsburg in 1555, the religious policy in the Holy Roman Empire was *cuius regio, eius religio* (the ruler's religion is the religion of the land). As a result, the Palatinate witnessed a change in its official religion

1. Caspar Wistar, Philadelphia, to Georg Friederich Hölzer, Neckargemünd, June 19, 1734; Caspar Wistar, Philadelphia, to Andreas Weynert and Jan van Emrath, Krefeld, Nov. 6, 1734; Caspar Wistar, Philadelphia, to Georg Friederich Hölzer, Neckargemünd, Nov. 7, 1734; Caspar Wistar, Philadelphia, to Georg Friederich Hölzer, Neckargemünd, Nov. 10, 1735, Wistar Family Papers, HSP.

2. NgLKB, EOK.

3. Georg Friederich Hölzer, Neckargemünd, to Caspar Wistar, Philadelphia, May 27, 1743, Wistar Family Papers, HSP.

4. NgLKB; BRKB; NgKKB, EOK.

eight times between 1550 and 1700 as electors from different confessions assumed power.[5] Nevertheless, until 1685, the Palatinate engaged in what historians of early modern German history have called "confessionalization"—the process through which political and religious authorities encouraged a single religious identity among their subjects.[6] In the Palatinate (as in most other German territories), everyone belonged to and practiced the sacraments in the official church, regardless of their beliefs. Thus, under Karl Ludwig, Lutheran and Catholic parishioners had to baptize their children and marry in the Reformed Church.

Political changes at the end of the seventeenth century, however, ended the dominance of a single official church. Beginning in the late 1680s, the Catholic, Reformed, and Lutheran churches were all legally recognized in the Palatinate. Theoretically, new religious policies allowed individuals to worship and receive the sacraments in the church of their choice. Ironically, official religious toleration led to increased conflict at the local level as clergy from the three churches competed with one another and with villagers for church property, fees, and souls. The new policies also revealed a religious diversity within villages and families that previously had been subsumed under the umbrella of a single official confession. Those belonging to "mixed marriages"—families produced by couples with more than one religious identity—faced new decisions about where to baptize their children and how to educate them.

The religious identity of Wistar's family reflects the complex shifts in policy and the ways that they affected government officials and their families. Confessional allegiance continued to play a critical role in early modern European political, economic, and constitutional issues. Religious identity was particularly important for members of the bureaucracy trying to negotiate their positions

---

5. Donald Durnbaugh, *European Origins of the Brethren* (Elgin, Ill.: Brethren Press, 1958), 30; Schaab, *Geschichte der Kurpfalz*, 2: chaps. 2–17; *Stadt- und Landkreise*, 1:282–87.

6. For recent assessments of the "confessionalization" paradigm, see Ute Lotz-Heumann, "The Concept of 'Confessionalization': A Historiographical Paradigm in Dispute," *Memoria y Civilizacion* 4 (2001): 93–114, and Thomas Kaufmann, "Einleitung," in *Interkonfessionalität-Transkonfessionalität-binnenkonfessionelle Pluralität: Neue Forschungen zur Konfessionalisierungsthese*, ed. Kaspar von Greyerz, Manfred Jakubowski-Tiessen, Thomas Kaufmann, and Hartmut Lehmann (Gütersloh: Mohn, 2002), 9–15. For some classic examples of confessionalization studies, see Wolfgang Reinhard, "Zwang zur Konfessionalisierung? Prolegomena zu einer theorie des konfessionellen Zeitalters," *Zeitschrift für hisorische Forschung* 10 (1983): 257–77; Ernst Walter Zeeden, *Konfessionsbildung* (Stuttgart, 1985); Heinz Schilling, ed., *Die reformierte Konfessionalisierung in Deutschland—Das Problem der "Zweiten Reformation"* (Gütersloh: Mohn, 1986); Wolfgang Reinhard, "Reformation, Counter-Reformation, and the Early Modern State: A Reassessment," *Catholic Historical Review* 75 (1989): 383–404; R. Po-Chia Hsia, *Social Discipline in the Reformation: Central Europe, 1550–1750* (London: Routledge, 1989); H.-Ch. Rublack, ed., *Die lutherische Konfessionalisierung in Deutschland* (Gütersloh: Mohn, 1992); Heinz Schilling, "Konfessionelle und politische Identität," *Nationale und ethnische Minderheiten und regionale Identitäten in Mittelalter und Neuzeit*, ed., A. Czacharowski (Thorn, 1994), 103–23; Wolfgang Reinhard and Heinz Schilling, eds., *Die katholische Konfessionalisierung* (Munster and Gütersloh, 1995).

during periods of political change and war. Thus Wistar's grandfather and father, although Lutherans, baptized and educated their children in the Reformed Church until the Lutheran Church received official status in 1698. From then on, however, Wistar's father and mother were considered a "mixed marriage" and continued so until their deaths. Their children were baptized and educated by both the Reformed and Lutheran churches and several of them converted to Catholicism.

His family's response to their Palatine circumstances shaped Wistar's reaction to religious conditions in Pennsylvania. William Penn's province, like the Palatinate, was well known for its religious toleration and diversity. Penn intended his colony to be a haven for religious exiles, and in its early years it was a magnet for a wide variety of dissenters as well as those from state churches. Although Pennsylvania never had an official, tax-supported church, the Society of Friends held political and economic power in the early colony. For Wistar, the colony's religious diversity posed no obstructions to pursuing his goals. Accustomed to dealing with people holding a variety of religious identities, he transacted business with people from all religious faiths. Perhaps more important, like his grandfather and father before him, Wistar understood the importance of the appropriate religious affiliation for establishing himself in new local social and economic hierarchies. By joining the Quaker meeting, he became a part of the dominant political and economic group in the colony. He applied the Palatine strategies that he carried with him to his new Pennsylvania circumstances.

When Andreas Wüster, Wistar's grandfather, became a Palatine forester in 1653, he followed the pattern of confessional allegiance that had dominated the Palatinate for nearly a century: he performed the sacraments in the church of the elector. Although likely raised in a Lutheran family, Wüster began to baptize his children in the Reformed Church.[7] By this time, officials and other subjects had grown accustomed to changing their religious identities as electors converted or were succeeded by rulers belonging to a different church. Outward identity, however, did not necessarily conform to personal belief. One government official noted in 1640, when the official church was Catholic, that the large number of Protestants who obeyed orders to attend Mass on Sundays indicated public support for the Catholic Church. "Nevertheless, barely one-third of [the subjects] are Catholic in reality and in their hearts."[8] Inhabitants of the Palatinate became

7. Wüster moved to the Palatinate from Crailsheim, a town in Württemberg, where the Lutheran Church was the state church in the seventeenth century. Feb.12, 1663, GLA 77/1865. For the baptisms of his children, see NkRKB, vol. 2, 1657–1705, EOK.

8. Report of the Heidelberger Regierung to Maximilian von Bayern as quoted in Meinrad Schaab, "Die Wiederherstellung des Katholizismus in der Kurpfalz im 17. und 18. Jahrhundert," *ZGO* 114 (1966): 153.

adept at participating in the rituals and practice of one confession while retaining the beliefs of another.

This disjuncture between religious affiliation and personal belief became more visible during the reign of Karl Ludwig (r. 1648–80), a Calvinist who became the elector of the Palatinate at the end of the Thirty Years' War.[9] The Treaty of Westphalia specified that all property belonging to the state church prior to the war went to the Reformed Church and that the elector determined the religion of the land. As a young man, Karl Ludwig had studied in the Netherlands, where he became acquainted with religious toleration in theory and practice. Consequently, he restored the Reformed Church to its official position, but he also established policies intended to promote religious toleration.[10]

Karl Ludwig's methods encouraged freedom of conscience through several formal means. Shortly after he became the elector, he reached accommodations with Catholic and Lutheran leaders permitting their congregants to practice their religious beliefs and to hold public office. The agreements allowed the two churches to hold private worship services, but the law required parishioners to have their baptisms, marriages, and burials performed and recorded in the Reformed Church, that is, the state church.[11] The government also permitted many of the Lutheran nobility, who owned land in the Palatinate, to control the churches in their villages.[12] In particular, the landed gentry in the Meckesheimer and Stüber Zent (two of the administrative regions that belonged to Amt Dilsberg) hired their own pastors and designated village tithes. As a result, Lutheran congregations continued to flourish even though the Reformed Church was the official church.[13]

Wüster's family demonstrates the disjunction between religious affiliation and belief that continued under Karl Ludwig's rule. He and his wife Anna baptized

9. For examples of the complex ways confessional allegiances shaped political and religious circumstances following the Thirty Years' War, see W. R. Ward, *The Protestant Evangelical Awakening* (Cambridge: Cambridge University Press, 1992), 1–53; Richard Gawthrop, *Pietism and the Making of Eighteenth-Century Prussia* (Cambridge: Cambridge University Press, 1993), 14–35.

10. Gustav Adolf Benrath, "Die konfessionellen Unionsbestrebungen des Kurfürsten Karl Ludwig von der Pfalz," *ZGO* 116 (1968): 188–90; Häusser, *Geschichte*; Alfred Hans, *Die Kurpfälzische Religionsdeklaration von 1705: Ihre Entstehung und Bedeutung für das Zusammenleben der drei im Reich tolerierten Konfessionen* (Mainz: Selbstverlag der Gessellschaft für mittelrheinische Kirchengeschichte, 1973), 11–12; Schaab, *Geschichte der Kurpfalz*, 2:238–40. For the broader context of religious toleration, see Joachim Whaley, "A Tolerant Society? Religious Toleration in the Holy Roman Empire, 1648–1806," in *Toleration in Enlightenment Europe*, eds. Ole Peter Grell and Roy Porter (Cambridge: Cambridge University Press, 2000), 175–95.

11. Schaab, "Die Wiederherstellung des Katholizismus," 154.

12. For the complex shifts in the privileges held by the petty nobility in this region, see *Stadt- und Landkreise*, 1:232–33; Lenz, *Kellerei*, 27–43.

13. Schaab, *Geschichte der Kurpfalz*, 2:138–40; Häusser, *Geschichte*, 595–608; Günther Wüst, *1000 Jahre Neckargemünd, 988–1988: Beiträge zur Geschichte einer Neckartalgemeinde* (Neckargemünd, 1988), 397; *Stadt- und Landkreise*, 1:285.

nine children in the Neunkirchen Reformed Church between 1665 and 1687 (see Appendix 1). Hans Caspar Wüster, Wistar's father, was the oldest son. Although the baptisms occurred in the Reformed Church, at least one Lutheran parishioner sponsored each child's baptism. In several cases, Lutheran clergy from towns belonging to Lutheran nobility served as godparents.[14] During Andreas Wüster's lifetime, his family conformed to the law that required affiliation with the official Reformed Church while they retained their Lutheran beliefs.

In addition to the accords signed with Lutheran and Catholic Church leaders, Karl Ludwig invited sectarian groups, for example, French Huguenots and Swiss Anabaptists (later called Mennonites), to settle in the Palatinate. In exchange for helping to repopulate areas devastated by war, he offered them the freedom to practice their own religious beliefs. A group of Quakers also won limited recognition after William Penn, who traveled down the Rhine in 1677, wrote to Karl Ludwig to request official toleration. The government invited these immigrant groups into the Palatinate, but it granted them only a limited category of citizenship, which placed them on the periphery of village social and economic life.[15]

While Karl Ludwig created policies promoting religious diversity, he also worked to establish religious unity at the local level. One of his more controversial (and unsuccessful) reforms was to move toward a union between the Reformed and Lutheran churches. Such policies likely were intended to help build a united Protestant front against re-Catholicization efforts.[16] During the early years of his reign, the elector thought this goal could be accomplished through education. Eventually, however, he determined that integrating the liturgies of both churches into a common set of rituals would promote harmony among subjects from different confessions.[17] In 1677, Karl Ludwig decreed his intent to unify the religious ceremonies of the two churches. He claimed that he "meant in no way to introduce a mixture of different contradictory points of belief, nor to order a syncretism of the same." Instead, he believed that the ordinary citizen, "who makes up the largest proportion of civil society as well as the church, . . . pays more attention to the differences of the outward church rituals and rules . . . or the spirituality associated with them than the theological

---

14. NkRKB, EOK; for the religious affiliation of the sponsors, see "Religionsverzeichnis," 1706, GLA 61/5479.

15. Benrath, "Die konfessionellen Unionsbestrebungen," 194–200; Paul Michel, "Täufer, Mennoniten und Quäker in Kriegsheim bei Worms," *Der Wormsgau* 7 (1965/66): 41–52; Mary Maples Dunn and Richard S. Dunn, eds., *The Papers of William Penn*, vol. 1, *1644–1679* (Philadelphia, 1981), 451–54.

16. The elector of Brandenburg-Prussia attempted a similar union at about the same time. Gawthrop, *Pietism*, 60–63.

17. Benrath, "Die konfessionellen Unionsbestrebungen," 200–237.

18. May 8, 1677, GLA 61/5479.

points . . . in which they are, in fact, grounded."[18] He proposed creating a unified liturgy to ease the religious tensions plaguing local villages and to promote toleration.

Karl Ludwig's religious policies, then, allowed for diversity and promoted toleration but within the traditional institutional structure of one state church. The Reformed Church was the only church supported by government taxes, and it owned the property that had always belonged to the official church in the Palatinate. For individual families, like the Wüsters, the elector's policies did not change the earlier separation between public religious identity and personal belief.

Karl Ludwig had barely started the formal process of uniting the Reformed and Lutheran churches in 1680 when he died. His son Karl (r. 1680–85) was markedly different from his father. Whereas Karl Ludwig intended to mediate theological differences by unifying religious practice, his son sought to make the official church the guardian of social and moral reform. Karl issued stricter rules about church attendance, renewed mandatory clerical visitations and inspections, and reinstituted the police code that had lapsed during his father's rule.[19]

Karl was a short-lived elector who died without a direct heir five years after assuming power; the position of elector passed to the Catholic Pfalz-Neuburg line of the family. Before his death, Karl had reached an agreement with his Catholic heir Philipp Wilhelm (r. 1685–90), to protect the dominant position of the Reformed Church in the Palatinate. The *Schwäbisch-Hallischen Rezess* permitted the former state church to maintain a semiofficial position. It guaranteed the governing status of the Reformed consistory, and it allowed Reformed pastors and teachers to retain their positions. The agreement also insured that Reformed advisors would continue to administer the property belonging to the former state church. In addition, the *Rezess* continued the policies of toleration that Karl Ludwig had established. It guaranteed that Lutheran congregations could support their pastors through private funds. To avoid discrimination against Protestant subjects, the *Rezess* decreed that public government officials would retain their positions regardless of their religious affiliation and that the addition of Catholic officials would occur in small numbers.[20]

Karl had not yet signed the *Rezess* when he died. Nevertheless, Philipp Wilhelm, upon taking power in 1685, publicly affirmed that he would honor it. To pacify his overwhelmingly Protestant subjects, the new Catholic elector reaffirmed his religious toleration several times. Throughout his five-year reign, he defended both Lutheran and Reformed congregations when Catholic Church leaders tried to take

19. Oct. 15 and 28, 1683; Feb. 11, Mar. 10, May 23, and Oct. 31, 1684, GLA 61/5479; Hans, *Kurpfälzische Religionsdeklaration*, 11–18.

20. Hans, *Kurpfälzische Religionsdeklaration*, 15–16.

away their privileges.[21] Despite his efforts to preserve his Reformed predecessor's agreement and to appease his Protestant subjects, Philipp Wilhelm's rule paved the way for religious tensions and disputes. For the first time since the Thirty Years' War, Catholics could worship publicly and own church property. The law no longer required subjects to be baptized, married, and buried in a single official church. The Catholic Church also sent missionaries from several religious orders (Jesuits, Franciscans, Carmelites, and Capuchins) into the Palatinate to win converts and educate parishioners.[22] Suddenly the Reformed Church, which had been the official church for more than forty years, began to lose its political dominance.

New competition fueled tension as clergy worked to define who belonged to their congregations. Theological differences that had been subsumed under one state church became visible in the transition to two official churches. In Palatine villages, religious diversity created new conflicts. Disputes about public ceremonies, the observance of religious holidays, and church property filled local courts. Repeated government mandates ordering subjects to live peacefully with one another and not to engage in religious quarrels signaled the difficulties of the transition.[23]

War exacerbated threats to the already tenuous position of Protestants under Catholic rule. The French invasion in 1688 increased efforts to rebuild the Catholic Church. As French troops seized Palatine villages, they forced Protestant inhabitants to follow the religious policies of Louis XIV. The invaders claimed Reformed Church buildings and property for Catholic villagers, who almost always were a minority of the inhabitants, and they required Protestants and Catholics alike to perform Catholic Mass.[24]

In the midst of the war, the elector died and his Catholic son, Johann Wilhelm (r. 1690–1716), succeeded him. The new ruler initially affirmed his father's religious policies and recognized the *Rezess,* in which the Reformed Church maintained its property and position within the Palatinate. Before long, however, Johann Wilhelm endorsed the policies of Louis XIV and encouraged Catholic Church leaders seeking political power. When he negotiated the Treaty of Ryswick ending the war in 1697, the new elector gave the property confiscated by the French to the Catholic Church. In doing so, he blatantly ignored the *Rezess,* which had guaranteed the government would not touch property belonging to the Reformed Church. By signing the treaty, Johann Wilhelm indicated his support for the Catholic Church at the expense of his Protestant subjects.[25]

---

21. Ibid. 18–22.
22. Schaab, "Die Wiederherstellung des Katholizismus," 175–80.
23. Feb. 3, July 17, Nov. 10, 1686; June 11, Aug. 8, Aug. 14, Oct. 13, 1687; June 28, 1688; GLA 61/5479; Hans, *Kurpfälzische Religionsdeklaration,* 22–24.
24. Schaab, "Die Wiederherstellung des Katholizismus," 149–51.
25. Hans, *Kurpfälzische Religionsdeklaration,* 36–110.

In 1695, during the war and Johann Wilhelm's early reign, Hans Caspar Wüster married Anna Catharina Müller, the daughter of an elder in the Reformed Church. Although he likely had been raised as a Lutheran, Wüster married in the Reformed Church at Gaiberg (Waldhilsbach had no church) because Johann Wilhelm's Catholic government still did not officially recognize the Lutheran Church. For Wüster, who had just arrived in Waldhilsbach, affiliation with the former state church was the most expedient way to secure his place within the local village social hierarchy. Given the uncertainty of the new elector's religious policy, he also may have perceived it as the best way to maintain his position within the bureaucracy. The couple baptized their first two children, Caspar (the immigrant) and Dorothea, in the Reformed Church at Bammental in 1696 and 1697, respectively.[26]

The same year as Dorothea's baptism, however, Johann Wilhelm signed the Treaty of Ryswick and the religious climate of the Palatinate changed significantly. In 1698 the elector determined that Reformed congregations should share their church buildings with both Catholic and Lutheran congregations. For Lutheran parishioners, the introduction of the simultaneous use of churches (*Simultankirchen*) meant that they could worship publicly in officially recognized congregations—a concession Catholics had gained with the *Rezess*. At the same time, the elector granted Lutheran Church leaders their own consistory, independent from the Reformed administration.[27]

The elector's new stance brought immediate changes for Hans Caspar Wüster and other Lutheran parishioners in Amt Dilsberg. The congregations, which had worshiped privately, now hired Johann Christoph Kern as the pastor of a new church in Neckargemünd. Since they had no property of their own, the Lutherans shared the town's only church building with their Reformed and Catholic neighbors. By staggering the hours of their services, all three congregations worshiped in the building that previously belonged to the Reformed Church.[28]

With the formation of a Lutheran congregation in Neckargemünd, Wüster and his wife began to baptize their children there instead of at the Reformed Church in Bammental where they had baptized Caspar and Dorothea. The couple's seven children who were baptized between February 26, 1700, and July 18, 1713, were officially identified as Lutheran. Wüster already knew Kern, the congregation's pastor, who had sponsored the baptism of his younger brother in 1682. Ironically, Johann Wilhelm's attempt to diminish the power of the

26. BRKB, EOK.

27. Schaab, "Die Wiederherstellung des Katholizismus," 150–51; Häusser, *Geschichte,* 810–13; Hans, *Kurpfälzische Religionsdeklaration,* 120–26.

28. On Sunday mornings, the Reformed parishioners held church services at 7 o'clock, the Catholics at 9 o'clock, and the Lutherans at 12 o'clock. Wüst, *Neckargemünd,* 397–98.

Reformed Church created a new kind of religious toleration for the forester. For the first time, the law permitted Wüster to receive the sacraments and show outward allegiance to his own family's confession.[29]

The law afforded Hans Caspar Wüster the opportunity to align his religious identity and his beliefs; nevertheless, the politics of his position likely encouraged him to do so as well. In 1697 and 1698, Johann Wilhelm ignored the *Rezess,* which had guaranteed government officials their jobs regardless of their religious affiliation. At the same time, the elector favored his Lutheran over his Reformed subjects; he granted them a church consistory and supported some of their clergy from government funds that had previously belonged to the Reformed Church. Consequently, Wüster, who had recently received his forester's job and still had no written contract, may have worried that continued identification with the Reformed Church could jeopardize his government position.[30] It was both politically expedient and, for the first time, legal for Wüster to change his church affiliation to match his personal belief.

Although they permitted an unprecedented alignment between affiliation and belief for individual subjects, Johann Wilhelm's religious policies created new disputes between clergy and church administrators over property and tithes. Church buildings and land traditionally belonged to the state church. All villagers supported the clergy of the official church through their tithes and taxes, regardless of their religious beliefs. By redistributing church property and changing the governing organization of the three churches, the elector instituted a major shift in the relation between the church and state.

When Johann Wilhelm's religious policies began to pose serious threats to the Reformed Church, its leaders petitioned other Protestant European governments for help. Between 1698 and 1705, politicians in the Netherlands, England, Sweden, and various Protestant German territories pressured the elector to reform his tactics. Johann Wilhelm ignored their actions until events in the War of the Spanish Succession threatened his chances for becoming the emperor. In 1705, he was finally ready to work out a compromise.[31]

29. BRKB; NkRKB; NgLKB, EOK.

30. For documents concerning Wüster's contract that had not yet been signed in 1706, see GLA 145/50. Wüst, in *Neckargemünd,* 297–98, maintains that the higher officials in the Palatinate remained Lutheran throughout the reigns of the Catholic electors. Certainly Lutherans dominated the middle level of government officials in Amt Dilsberg. In 1706, at least three of the four foresters in the Amt were Lutheran as was Kaufmann, the administrator who monopolized several of the district offices. The positions of local officials (*Anwälder* and *Schultheißen*) were more evenly distributed between Lutherans and Reformed. Of the forty-eight officials listed in Amt Dilsberg, twenty-one were Reformed, nineteen were Lutheran, and eight were Catholic. "Religionsverzeichnis," 1706.

31. Schaab, *Geschichte der Kurpfalz,* 2:156–58; Hans, *Kurpfälzische Religionsdeklaration,* 134–88.

The result was the Religious Declaration of 1705, a document that defined the relationship between the Palatine church and state for the eighteenth century. Instead of two churches sharing official status, three religious groups—Catholics, Reformed, and Lutherans—received a *written guarantee* of their rights and privileges. Public church property was divided between the Catholic and Reformed churches: the Catholic Church received two-sevenths and the Reformed Church received five-sevenths. The agreement gave the Lutherans no property except what they had accumulated as a private church. It outlined in explicit detail which church received which buildings, land, tithes, and taxes. The Religious Declaration of 1705 also restructured the government of the church. It created a single board made up of Catholic and Reformed advisors to administer the property of the two churches. The Lutheran Church had been granted its own governing body in 1698. In essence, the Religious Declaration of 1705 took away the elector's right to determine the religious affiliation of his subjects, and it established the three official churches under the umbrella of the elector's government.[32]

Theoretically, the Religious Declaration of 1705 should have ended religious disagreements and tensions in the Palatinate. It clearly defined which buildings and property belonged to which church, and it officially guaranteed the rights of each group to practice religion according to its own rituals. Instead, the division caused new rifts within villages where Reformed, Catholic, and Lutheran neighbors had lived side by side but under the auspices of one official church. The commission set up to divide church property faced ongoing disputes about such issues as which congregation owned church bells and when they should be rung, and which clergy should receive tithes from villages without a church building.[33]

Furthermore, institutional changes produced new social tensions within villages. The Religious Declaration of 1705 allowed children to choose their religious affiliation when they came of age. Since their income and political power now often depended on the size of their congregations, clergy fought hard to win the souls of children. Consequently, at a time when institutional changes brought together affiliation and belief, the construction of confessional identity became increasingly contested.

Conflicts surrounding church membership were particularly acute in the Wüsters' region of Amt Dilsberg, where religious diversity was especially prominent. In 1706, 44 percent of the total population identified themselves as Reformed, 40 percent as Lutheran, and 16 percent as Catholic.[34] Twenty years later, the percentage of Lutheran and Catholic subjects had increased to

32. A copy of the Religious Declaration of 1705 is in Nov. 21, 1705, GLA 61/5479. Schaab, *Geschichte der Kurpfalz*, 2:156–58; Schaab, "Die Wiederherstellung des Katholizismus," 151; Hans, *Kurpfälzische Religionsdeklaration*, 270–356.

33. "Religionsdeklaration," Nov. 21, 1705, GLA 61/5479.

34. "Religionsverzeichnis," 1706, GLA 61/5479.

TABLE 2 Religious Affiliation in Amt Dilsberg, 1706 and 1727

Date	Reformed		Lutheran		Catholic		Total Population
1706	2,034	44%	1,889	40%	771	16%	4,694
1727	2,268	37%	2,594	42%	1,294	21%	6,156

Sources: "Religionsverzeichnis," 1706, GLA 61/5479; "Statistical Table Heidelberg," 1727, GLA 145/364.

42 percent and 21 percent, respectively, while the number of Reformed congregants had dropped to 37 percent (see Table 2).[35] If religious identity within the region had shifted, it was no less diverse—only more so.

A similar trend is evident within individual villages. In 45 percent of the villages, membership was so mixed that no single church claimed two-thirds or more (66 percent or more) of the inhabitants. Even in those villages where either Reformed or Lutheran parishioners constituted a majority, a minority of villagers belonging to the other two churches was always present (see Table 3).

The concentration of religious diversity is even more apparent when examining the subdistricts within Amt Dilsberg. The Meckesheimer Zent, the subdistrict where the Wüsters lived, was composed almost exclusively of heterodoxic villages where no single church held more than 66 percent of the inhabitants. Waldhilsbach's population, for example, was 48 percent Reformed, 26 percent Catholic, and 26 percent Lutheran. In contrast, villages in which an overwhelming majority (81 percent or more) of inhabitants belonged to one church were located almost exclusively in the Stüber Zent, the eastern half of Amt Dilsberg. While the Reformed Church dominated the northern half of the Stüber Zent, the Lutheran nobility maintained tight control over the churches in the southern region (see Map, page 64).

Religious heterodoxy not only permeated villages, it also existed within families in Amt Dilsberg. "Mixed marriages" (*Mischehe*) formed a new social construction that emerged as a result of institutional changes.[36] Although couples from different confessions had intermarried previously, their unions had not affected where their children were baptized or educated. But after the government officially recognized the Reformed, Lutheran, and Catholic churches, couples from mixed marriages faced new interference in family decisions.

Mixed marriages consisted of unions between Protestants and Catholics as well as between Reformed and Lutheran parishioners. Hans Caspar and Anna Catharina Wüster belonged to the 35 percent of married couples in Amt

35. "Generaltabelle des Oberamts Heidelberg über die Städte, Flecken und Dörfer (Seelenzahl, Religion, Bedienstete, Viehstandt und Schatzungskapital)," 1727, GLA 145/364 (hereafter "Statistical Table Heidelberg," 1727).

36. For examples of how the government dealt with mixed marriages during the period, see "Die Taufe der Kinder aus gemischten Ehe," 1698–1749, GLA 77/4227; "Die Taufe in gemischten Ehe," 1717, GLA 77/4311; "Die Ehepakten in gemischten Ehen," 1724–1809, GLA 77/4363, 4364.

TABLE 3 Religious Diversity Within the Villages of Amt Dilsberg, 1706

Villages	Catholic		Reformed		Lutheran		Total
	N	%	N	%	N	%	N
			MECKESHEIMER ZENT				
Heterodoxic Villages							
Baiertal	20	56%	12	33%	4	11%	36
Dilsberg	64	49%	30	23%	37	28%	131
Gaiberg	11	11%	59	61%	27	28%	97
Gauangelloch	37	28%	51	38%	46	34%	134
Langenzell	(missing data)						
Lobenfeldt	50	61%	19	23%	13	16%	82
Mauer	45	36%	24	19%	56	45%	125
Mückenloch	17	17%	38	39%	43	44%	98
Schatthausen	47	34%	31	22%	62	44%	140
Spechbach	48	43%	22	20%	41	37%	111
Waldhilsbach	15	26%	28	48%	15	26%	58
Waldwimmersbach	13	16%	45	56%	22	28%	80
Wiesenbach	41	40%	40	40%	20	20%	101
Zutzenhausen	35	11%	119	36%	174	53%	328
Predominantly Lutheran (66%–80%)							
Daisbach	5	8%	13	20%	47	72%	65
Mönchzell	15	21%	3	4%	54	75%	72
Predominantly Reformed (66%–80%)							
Bammental	15	7%	173	78%	33	15%	221
Meckesheim	12	5%	180	78%	38	17%	230
Overwhelmingly Lutheran (81%+)							
Eschelbronn	7	5%	6	5%	117	90%	130

Dilsberg who crossed religious boundaries—Hans Caspar identified himself as Lutheran while Anna Catharina was affiliated with the Reformed Church. Since the majority of the population was Protestant, a larger portion of mixed marriages (21 percent) were between Lutheran and Reformed Church members. Nevertheless, an increasing number of households were headed by couples who crossed Catholic-Protestant lines as well. Catholic-Lutheran unions made up 8 percent of the married population while 6 percent of the marriages were between Catholic and Reformed spouses (see Table 4).

The creation of mixed marriages and the emergence of religious diversity brought new sources of tension for church leaders in the Palatinate. Clergy received fees for each baptism, marriage, and funeral they performed. In the case of mixed marriages, decisions about which minister should carry out such rituals often led to disputes or even physical brawls between pastors and priests

TABLE 3 *(cont'd)* Religious Diversity Within the Villages of Amt Dilsberg, 1706

Villages	Catholic		Reformed		Lutheran		Total
	N	%	*N*	%	*N*	%	*N*
STÜBER ZENT							
Heterodoxic Villages							
Asbach	9	10%	54	61%	25	29%	88
Epfenbach	32	22%	71	48%	45	30%	148
Guttenbach	38	33%	71	61%	7	6%	116
Predominantly Lutheran (66%–80%)							
Breitenbronn	19	20%	11	12%	63	68%	93
Predominantly Reformed (66%–80%)							
Neunkirchen	55	19%	212	72%	27	9%	294
Reichenbuch	14	30%	32	68%	1	2%	47
Schwarzach	14	13%	79	72%	17	15%	110
Overwhelmingly Lutheran (81%+)							
Aglasterhausen	11	6%	19	10%	151	84%	181
Bargen	30	15%	7	4%	160	81%	197
Daudenzell	1	1%	3	3%	102	96%	106
Flinsbach	21	13%	5	3%	132	84%	158
Helmstatt	9	7%	8	7%	102	86%	119
Michelbach	3	4%	11	15%	61	81%	75
Reichertshausen	2	2%	3	3%	105	95%	110
Overwhelmingly Reformed (81%+)							
Haag	1	1%	146	97%	3	2%	150
Katzenbach	6	12%	42	86%	1	2%	49
Moßbronn	0	0%	99	97%	3	3%	102
Schönbronn	7	3.5%	191	95%	3	1.5%	202
Schwanheim	0	0%	80	98%	2	2%	82
TOTALS	771		2,034		1,889		4,694

Source: Data is taken from the "Religionsverzeichnis," 1706, GLA 61/5479.

trying to protect their economic interests. In addition, religious leaders began massive efforts to win church members by controlling village schools. As a result, religious ceremonies and childhood education were particularly fraught with conflict in villages with high rates of mixed marriages.[37]

Church leaders tried to direct internal family decisions about baptism when couples belonged to two churches. In 1688, a special government conference determined that the children of mixed marriages should be baptized according to their father's faith, a decision which Johann Wilhelm confirmed in 1691. During the

37. June 19, July 7, Oct. 10, 1721; June 15, Aug. 16, Oct. 16, 1726; Jan. 2, 1727; GLA 61/5479.

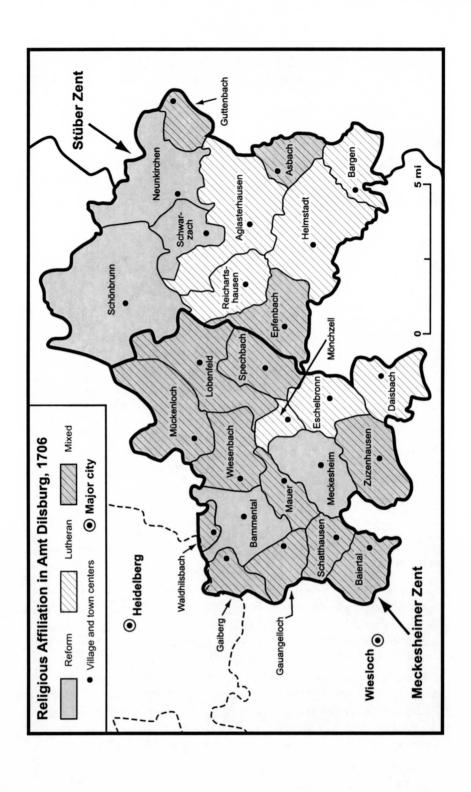

Religious Affiliation in Amt Dilsburg, 1706

Reform
Lutheran
Village and town centers
Mixed
Major city

Stüber Zent

Guttenbach
Neunkirchen
Schwarzach
Asbach
Bargen
Aglasterhausen
Helmstadt
Schönbrunn
Reicharts-hausen
Epfenbach
Mönchzell
Lobenfeld
Spechbach
Mückenloch
Eschelbronn
Daisbach
Wiesenbach
Meckesheim
Zuzenhausen
Bammental
Mauer
Schatthausen
Baiertal
Waldhilsbach
Gaiberg
Gauangelloch

Heidelberg

Wiesloch

Meckesheimer Zent

5 mi
0

TABLE 4 Marriage and Religious Affiliation in Amt Dilsberg, 1706

Households Headed by Married Couples	N	Percent	Total Percent
Single-church marriages			65%
Reformed/Reformed	322	41%	
Lutheran/Lutheran	106	13%	
Catholic/Catholic	79	10%	
Anabaptist	7	1%	
Mixed marriages			35%
Reformed/Lutheran	167	21%	
Catholic/Lutheran	65	8%	
Catholic/Reformed	46	6%	
TOTAL	792	100%	

Source: "Religionsverzeichnis," 1706, GLA 61/5479.

French invasion, however, the government ordered Catholic priests to baptize all children in areas occupied by French troops, regardless of their parents' religious affiliation. At the end of the war, the elector reconfirmed his original position that the father alone determined the religious confession of the household.[38]

Not all families followed the government's decrees. In Amt Dilsberg, ministers and priests baptized children whose mothers attended their churches as a way of increasing membership (and income). In 1702, the district administrator ordered village mayors and magistrates to prohibit clergy from baptizing children whose fathers did not belong to their churches.[39] Hans Caspar and Anna Catharina Wüster, however, followed the law in making their decisions about baptism. After a Lutheran Church was founded in Neckargemünd in 1698, Wüster became affiliated with it and Lutheran ministers baptized their children.[40]

If the baptism of the Wüster children indicates adherence to the law, baptismal sponsorship presents a more confusing image of the family's religious politics. Whereas the godparentage of Andreas Wüster's children at baptism signaled Lutheran belief in spite of their Reformed affiliation, the same was not true for Hans Caspar and Anna Catharina Wüster's children. The two children baptized during the period in which both parents were affiliated with the Reformed Church had Reformed baptismal sponsors. But when Hans Caspar began worshiping in the Lutheran Church at Neckargemünd and the couple became identified as a mixed marriage, sponsorship became complicated. Some of the children baptized between 1700 and 1713 in the Lutheran Church had

38. Hans, *Kurpfälzische Religionsdeklaration,* 189–98.
39. Jan. 10, 1702, GLA 61/5479.
40. BRKB and NgLKB, EOK.

Reformed sponsors, and some had Lutheran sponsors. Nor is there any correlation between the affiliation of godparents and the sex of the child, a signal that the couple may have chosen to have their sons raised according to their father's beliefs and their daughters according to their mother's. Reformed godparents sponsored the baptisms of Maria Barbara and Albertina, whereas Anna Barbara and Maria Margretha had Lutheran sponsors. Johannes had two Reformed sponsors, and the affiliation of Johann Ludwig's and Georg Bernhard's sponsors remain unknown. Godparentage does not chart clearly the internal religious politics of the Wüster family after its members could receive the sacraments in the church of their choice.[41]

In addition to baptism, couples of mixed religious identity faced another new decision: how to formally educate their children. In the early modern Palatinate, churches ran village schools. With the shift to a Catholic elector, the Catholic Church began intensive efforts to expand educational institutions. The Reformed leadership countered Catholic attempts by refilling lapsed teaching positions and founding new schools. Protestant Church leaders also tried to minimize the effects of the law requiring children of Catholic fathers to be baptized in the Catholic Church by encouraging parents to *educate* their sons according to the father's religion and their daughters in their mother's religion. As with baptism, church leaders tried to influence family decisions regarding education.[42]

It is difficult, at best, to determine which church dominated the Wüster children's education. Waldhilsbach, as Wistar noted in his autobiography, was too poor to have its own school.[43] Consequently, the children in the village attended school in Bammental, Gaiberg, or Neckargemünd.[44] Wistar, the oldest son of Hans Caspar and Anna Catharina Wüster, went to school in Neckargemünd, where the Reformed school shared its facilities with the Lutheran and Catholic parishioners of the town from 1699 until 1707. Although he claims not to have received much education, he clearly learned to read and write prior to his emigration. The only other evidence of his education is a reference to "old school friends" in a letter he received from Georg Friederich Hölzer after he migrated

41. The role of sponsorship in early modern Europe is difficult to ascertain. For the Wüsters, however, it remained an important indication of connections even after some of the family migrated to America. The death record for Maria Barbara Wüster Bauer Hüttner in the St. Michael's and Zion Lutheran Church records at Philadelphia dated Jan. 22, 1770, included the name of her sponsor at baptism along with her parents' names and the names of her surviving children. See Annette Burgert, *Eighteenth-Century Emigrants from German-Speaking Lands to North America*, vol. 1, *The Northern Kraichgau* (Breinigsville, Pa., 1983), 184.

42. Schaab, "Die Wiederherstellung des Katholizismus," 170–84; Hans, *Kurpfälzische Religionsdeklaration*, 198–99.

43. Wistar, "Short Report," Wistar Family Papers, HSP; documents dated 1722, GLA 229/109147.

44. *Stadt- und Landkreise*, 1:298–303, and 2:952–53; Schmidt, *Chronik*, 92–102; Wüst, *Waldhilsbach*, 332–36; *Bammental*, 419–22.

to Pennsylvania. Hölzer belonged to a prominent Reformed family and would have gone to the Reformed school in Neckargemünd.[45]

Whether Wistar went to the Reformed or Lutheran school in Neckargemünd is impossible to tell. If he had attended a Reformed school, he likely would have gone to either Bammental or Gaiberg, with the rest of the Reformed children from Waldhilsbach.[46] Therefore, he may have gone to Neckargemünd's Lutheran school while his schoolmates attended classes with the Reformed schoolmaster. Still, at least three of his sisters were confirmed in the Reformed Church between 1709 and 1717, which suggests that they were educated by that church.[47] The only other potential indicator of the Wüster children's education is a census taken in 1706, when Wistar was ten years old, indicating the religious identity of every person in every household. In this case, the five children, all specified as "still small," are listed as Reformed (even those who were baptized in the Lutheran Church).[48] The recovery of family decisions about the religious education of their children is, at best, difficult to determine for mixed marriage couples like the Wüsters.

Missionary efforts further complicated educational decisions. During Wistar's childhood, Johann Georg Kneitz, the Catholic priest at Neckargemünd from 1704 to 1727, aggressively used local schools to expand church membership and improve his personal status. Kneitz's activities in places like Bammental, Gaiberg, and Waldhilsbach led to legal battles with the people living there.[49] In 1706, he won a suit against several of the villages, forcing them to pay him a tithe to support his ministry.[50] In more than one case, he claimed vacant school buildings that belonged to the Reformed Church and installed new schools in them. He also encouraged his schoolmasters to use Reformed Church gardens that were not in use.[51] In Bammental, the Reformed pastor complained that

45. Feb. 23, 1742, Hölzer to Wistar, Wistar Family Papers, HSP. Neckargemünd's Reformed school dated from the end of the Thirty Years' War. With the introduction of the simultaneous use of churches, however, the government forced the Reformed Church to share its school. As a result, all three congregations sponsored schools in the same building. Wüst, *Neckargemünd*, 430–34.

46. See Schmidt, *Chronik*, 92; Wüst, *Waldhilsbach*, 332–35.

47. Confirmation records for the remaining children are not extant. See the records for Dorothea (conf. 1709), Anna Barbara (conf. 1713), and Albertina (conf. 1717) in the Bammental Reformed Church, BRKB, EOK.

48. "Religionsverzeichnis," 1706, GLA 61/5479.

49. Wüst, *Neckargemünd*, 403–4.

50. Jan. 25, 1706, GLA 61/5465.

51. May 4, July 7, Oct. 14, 1719; Feb. 14, 1721; GLA 61/5479. In a case in Gaiberg, Kneitz demanded that his schoolmaster there be able to use the old schoolhouse and part of the church garden plot. In defending his claim, Kneitz argued that the entire village, both Reformed and Catholics, had built the school. Reformed villagers argued that there had been no Catholic inhabitants in the village before 1716. In fact, 11 percent of the village population was Catholic in 1706. The number increased to 21 percent during Kneitz's ministry. July 14, 31, Aug. 2, 1719; Feb. 26, Mar. 23, June 18, Sept. 26, 1721; July 24,

Kneitz and his schoolteacher had confiscated more than forty songbooks and catechisms from his Reformed parishioners. "Since the people, because of their poverty, cannot buy any others," the pastor requested help from the government. He maintained that Kneitz had no right to deter villagers from using the state-approved songbooks and catechisms.[52]

Kneitz's conflicts with Protestant clergy and villagers in his jurisdiction reveal the complex tensions that arose as each church tried to secure its position in the new competitive environment. Between clergy and within villages, the disputes frequently centered on who controlled income, usufruct rights, and property. But Kneitz's proselytizing also interfered with internal family politics as well. The families of mixed marriages, like the Wüsters, were particularly prone to competition as clergy fought over the right to baptize and educate their children.

Kneitz clearly sought to increase the size of his parish and its property by converting children to Catholicism. While his overall efforts apparently did not succeed, he did win new converts (see Table 5). Within the Wüster family, Dorothea, the oldest daughter, who had been baptized and confirmed in the Reformed Church in Bammental, joined the Catholic Church prior to her marriage, which Kneiz performed in 1720.[53] Another daughter, Albertina, married at the Catholic Church in Langenbrücken in 1722.[54] Johann Ludwig, the youngest of the Wüster sons to survive to adulthood and the only son to remain in Europe, also converted to Catholicism.[55] Evidently Kneitz's efforts succeeded, even in families where both parents were Protestant.

It is impossible to know for certain how Wistar's family dealt with the internal family politics surrounding religious identity and education. They did, however, manage to negotiate religious diversity, as church records and Wistar's letters suggest. His parents remained in a mixed marriage until their deaths. Hans Caspar Wüster's burial was recorded in the Neckargemünd Lutheran Church records; his wife Anna Catharina was buried in the cemetery of the Reformed Church at Gaiberg.[56] Nevertheless, Wistar continued to communicate with his mother and siblings in letters filled with religious language and sentiment.

1723; June 3, 1726; GLA 61/5479; "Religionsverzeichnis," 1706, GLA 61/5479; "Statistical Table Heidelberg," 1727, GLA 145/364.

52. Feb. 14, 1721, GLA 61/5479. By June 6, 1726, town officials could report that there were no religious complaints among any of the inhabitants of Bammental; June 6, 1726, GLA 61/5479.

53. Married Aug. 11, 1720, NgKKB. She was confirmed in 1709, BRKB, EOK.

54. International Genealogical Index, Genealogical Society of the Church of the Latter-Day Saints. Marriage in Aug. 1722; four children were baptized in the Catholic Church at Langenbrücken. She was confirmed in 1717 in the Reformed Church, BRKB, EOK.

55. See Chapter 2. Johann Ludwig converted before Feb. 28, 1729, GLA 77/1732.

56. Jan. 15, 1726, NgLKB, EOK; May 24, 1743, BRKB, EOK; Georg Friedrich Hölzer, Neckargemünd, to Caspar Wistar, Philadlephia, May 17 and May 27, 1743, Wistar Family Papers, HSP.

TABLE 5 Catholic Missionary Activity in Bammental, Gaiberg, Waldhilsbach, and Wiesenbach, 1706–1727

Village	Catholic		Reformed		Lutheran		Total
	N	%	N	%	N	%	
Bammental							
1706	15	7%	174	78%	33	15%	222
1727	24	7%	275	78%	55	15%	354
Gaiberg							
1706	11	11%	60	59%	27	27%	101
1727	21	21%	46	47%	30	31%	97
Waldhilsbach							
1706	15	26%	29	50%	14	24%	58
1727	24	26%	45	49%	23	25%	92
Wiesenbach							
1706	42	38%	41	37%	27	25%	110
1727	50	32%	60	38%	47	30%	157

Sources: "Religionsverzeichnis," 1706, GLA 61/5479; "Statistical Table Heidelberg," 1727, GLA 145/364.

Wistar's complex and fluid Palatine religious circumstances influenced his decisions and behaviors in the British colonies in two ways. First, having grown up in an area with a state church tradition, Wistar clearly grasped the importance of having the same confessional allegiance as those in positions of power for one's social and economic security. Even though Pennsylvania had no official church, Wistar recognized that Quakers held dominant political and social positions, and he understood the advantages that could accrue if he joined their ranks. Becoming a member of the Society of Friends was a logical step for the son of a Lutheran forester who married in a Reformed Church at a time when it was most expedient to do so. Second, the religious diversity within villages and families that Palatine religious policies created helped to prepare Wistar for the pluralism of Pennsylvania. He seemed to move with ease among a wide variety of colonists: he did business with Anglo-American Quakers and Anglicans; sold land to German-speaking members of the Lutheran and Reformed churches; and retrieved legacies and loaned money to those who belonged to a variety of religious "sects" as well as "church" Germans. Wistar's Palatine religious background posed no obstacles to pursuing his goals in Pennsylvania; instead it provided a road map for navigating the colony's diversity.

Until the Lord of all Lords inspired me to travel to Pennsylvania, which I also made up my mind to do and did against all of my friends' and father's and mother's wishes as also against my master's will, and [they] tried to keep me from taking my intended trip but they could not. So I, with God, began my journey in May 1717, which God knows was very difficult and hard for me to do—to at once renounce and also take my leave from my dear parents and brothers and sisters and all [my] other friends [to go to] a strange land as this new land Pennsylvania was, because at that time it was not so well known as now, so that it was thought one would never more be heard from again, much less seen again. This made it difficult in both respects. I did eventually take my leave, however, with sadness and heavy hearts and crying and tears.

And the first part of the trip began on Pentecost Monday [when I went] from [Wald]Hilsbach to Gaiberg to one of my good friends, Jörg Müller, who had in his safe-keeping my little bit of money that I had saved from time to time, which was between 40 and 50 Gulden, which once again did not occur without crying. Having collected my money, I set out to travel to Heidelberg from where the ship that was to take us to Rotterdam should leave the next morning. But as I arrived, I heard that the ship could not leave for another eight days which brought even more sadness for me, because the leave that I had taken yesterday from my parents and brothers and sisters and other good friends had been so hard for me and had brought me so much sadness. So [I] thought I would visit my father's two sisters, who lived in the west over the Rhine, one of whom was my cousin David Deschler's mother, rather than take my leave from home once again.

As soon as I had left my things with the ship captain and finalized where I wanted to meet him, I made my way out of Heidelberg with a heavy heart. When I was about half an hour out of the city, I got the idea that I should turn around one more time and look at the city once more, [because] I would perhaps never see it again. So I turned around to look at the city. There I saw from afar someone running and waving with his hat. I stood there waiting until he came. Who should it be but my father's servant who said to me that my mother could not find peace until she had seen me once more and she would be here shortly. We came together, embraced each other around the neck, and cried with one another. [We] could not speak with one another until some time had gone by and the crying had stopped. She told me that I should go back home with her after all, but I said that if I went with her my heart was so taken with the new land that I could not stay. And because it was so, I pleaded with her sincerely to let me go now in God's name. My mother could not convince me to go home with her. I told her I wanted to go visit Father's two sisters and after that I wanted to also visit her sisters who lived in Amt Simmern and then perhaps things would change.

That is what I did. [I] visited the friends and in Bacharrach I waited on the ship until it came and after that [we went] to Rotterdam, from Rotterdam to London. There we paid our ship freight, for which Abraham Rim loaned me three pistolines.

—CASPAR WISTAR, "A Short Report"

CHAPTER 4

Leaving Home
THE DECISION TO EMIGRATE

The most memorable part of Wistar's journey to Pennsylvania, as recorded by him twenty-five years later, was the difficulty of leaving home. In contrast to many other immigrants, he recorded nothing about his transatlantic voyage.[1] Instead, Wistar told of the heart-wrenching emotions that accompanied saying good-bye to his family and friends.

Wistar himself suggests two reasons for his emotional departure: first, he was leaving against the wishes of his parents and friends and, second, Pennsylvania was not as well known in 1717 as it was in the 1740s when he wrote down his memories. Each of these suggestions raises more questions. Why did he decide to leave home? Certainly migration was nothing new for people living in Wistar's Palatinate. Artisans, pilgrims, vagrants, and students all moved routinely from place to place throughout Europe. Families migrated to new places, too. Although several hundreds of thousands of people moved into the German southwest territories in the seventeenth and eighteenth centuries, more than 800,000 people left the region in the same period—the overwhelming majority of them traveling to eastern Europe.[2] Why did Wistar choose to go west instead of east? What did he know about Pennsylvania? And why did he choose Pennsylvania over Carolina—the other British colony whose proprietors were actively soliciting German-speaking settlers? The specific answers to these questions remain obscure. Wistar attributed his choice to migrate to divine providence. Nevertheless, by studying the information about the colonies that may have been available to him and exploring his circumstances on the eve of his departure, we catch glimpses of the context for his inspiration.

1. "Diary of Samuel Guldin, Relating to His Journey to Pennsylvania, June to September, 1710," *Journal of the Presbyterian Historical Society* 14 (1930): 28–41, 64–73; R. W. Kelsey, ed. and trans., "An Early Description of Pennsylvania: Letter of Christopher Sower. Written in 1724, Describing the Conditions in Philadelphia and Vicinity, and the Sea Voyage from Europe," *PMHB* 45 (1921): 243–54; and Gottlieb Mittelberger, *Gottlieb Mittelberger's Journey to Pennsylvania in the Year 1710 and Return to Germany in the Year 1754,* trans. and ed. Oscar Handlin and John Clive (Cambridge: Harvard University Press, 1960).

2. Hans Fenske, "Internal Migration: Germany in the Eighteenth Century," *Central European History* 13 (1980): 332–47. See Fertig, *Lokales Leben,* 65–69, for a good summary of the literature on early modern European migration.

Wistar's decision came early in the eighteenth century, before the peak periods of migration to Pennsylvania.[3] But by 1717 people from the Rhine Valley had
been moving to British America for more than thirty years. The colonial proprietors and their agents circulated promotional pamphlets and recruited settlers
throughout continental Europe. Although it is impossible to know whether or
not Wistar himself read this literature, the channels through which it and other
news about the colonies circulated linked people who lived close to him. His
exposure to information about America may have influenced his decision to
leave home and likely shaped his expectations about life in the British colonies.
The timing of his "inspiration" to migrate also suggests that his family's struggle
to secure a place within the local social and economic hierarchies may have
encouraged him to seek a living elsewhere.

By the time Wistar determined to cross the Atlantic, information about the
British colonies was spreading throughout Europe in both written and spo-
ken form. He and other emigrants attributed their decisions to leave home to
divine inspiration but they also acknowledged the influence of books and pamphlets. When asked in 1709 who had told him about the colonies, one emigrant
responded that "God had given him the idea" to go to the British colonies. That
same year, another man stated that he first heard about America from "English
agents at Frankfurt and writings brought by them." Johannes Willig "had a book
about the Island," as continental Europeans erroneously referred to all British
colonies. Another emigrant had bought a book at Frankfurt for 3 *Batzen* in
which "there was writing about the Island."[4]

For those who either did not own the books or could not read, their friends
and neighbors passed on information. One 1709 emigrant from the Rhine River
Valley heard "of books about the Island" through people "from Darmstadt who
are going." Another heard about books in neighboring villages that the schoolmaster had brought. A third reportedly heard about the colonies through people
from the Palatinate. And Philipps Petri noted, "people everywhere are talking
about [them]."[5]

The "books" emigrants referred to were pamphlets advertising the new British colonies. In 1681, William Penn published *Some Account of the Province of*

3. Wokeck, *Trade in Strangers*, 37–58.

4. The responses are from interviews that government officials conducted with emigrants from
Nassau-Weilburg. Copies of the original documents are in the Library of Congress, Preussisches Staats-
archiv Wiesbaden, Bestand VI 1, Nassau-Weilburg, Gen. XIV c., Nr. 17. German transcriptions of the
interviews are in Julius Goebel, ed., "Neue Dokumente zur Geschichte der Massenauswanderung im
Jahre 1709," *Deutsch-amerikanische Geschichtsblätter* 13 (1913): 181–201. Excerpts from the interviews are
translated in Henry Z. Jones, *The Palatine Families of New York, 1710*, vol. 1 (University City, Calif.,
1985), iv–v. Quotes are from Jones's translations.

5. Jones, *Palatine Families*, 1:v.

Pennsylvania to recruit settlers. The booklet described Pennsylvania's landscape and natural resources. Penn also outlined its constitution, his policies for granting settlers land, the kinds of people best suited for migration, and preparations required for the long transatlantic journey.[6] Shortly after its initial publication, Benjamin Furly, an English Quaker living in the Netherlands and Penn's agent, translated the pamphlet into Dutch and German for distribution throughout Europe.[7]

Penn's pamphlet was the first in a series of publications printed during the next four decades aimed at potential German-speaking colonists.[8] Among the German-language literature most widely disseminated, the works of three authors were linked to migrations from Wistar's home region. Francis Daniel Pastorius, after traveling to Pennsylvania and founding Germantown in 1683, wrote a series of pamphlets and letters that were published in Europe.[9] Daniel Falkner, who arrived in Pennsylvania with a group of Pietists in 1694, returned to the Continent shortly before 1700 as an emissary from the American Pietists "to make known the true state and spiritual condition of the Germans who had emigrated to Pennsylvania" and to solicit aid and recruits.[10] In 1702 he published

6. *Some Account* is reprinted in Albert Cook Myers, ed. *Narratives in Early Pennsylvania, West New Jersey and Delaware, 1630–1707* (New York: Barnes and Noble, 1912), 202–15.

7. Rosalind J. Beiler, "Bridging the Gap: Cultural Mediators and the Structure of Transatlantic Communication," in *Atlantic Communications: The Media in American and German History from the Seventeenth to the Twentieth Century,* eds. Norbert Finzsch and Ursula Lehmkuhl (Oxford: Berg, 2004), 45–64; Myers, *Narratives,* 199–201; Richard S. Dunn, "Penny Wise and Pound Foolish: Penn as a Businessman," in *The World of William Penn,* eds. Richard S. Dunn and Mary Maples Dunn (Philadelphia: University of Pennsylvania Press, 1986), 43; Gary Nash, *Quakers and Politics: Pennsylvania, 1681–1726* (Princeton: Princeton University Press, 1968; rev. ed. Boston: Northeastern University Press, 1993), 11–15; Sally Schwartz, *"A Mixed Multitude": The Struggle for Toleration in Colonial Pennsylvania* (New York: New York University Press, 1987), 23–24; William Hull, *William Penn and the Dutch Quaker Migration to Pennsylvania* (Swarthmore, Pa.: Swarthmore College, 1935), 236.

8. For a summary of Pennsylvania's promotional literature, see Julius Sachse, "Pennsylvania: The German Influence in Its Settlement and Development," *Pennsylvania German Society Proceedings and Addresses* 14 (1905): 8–12. Facsimiles of the title pages for promotional literature are reprinted in an appendix in Julius Sachse, "Title Pages of Books and Pamphlets That Influenced German Emigration to Pennsylvania," *Pennsylvania German Society Proceedings and Addresses* 7 (1897): 201–56. For a recent scholarly treatment of this literature, see Mark Häberlein, "Nachrichten aus der Neuen Welt: Die Erweiterung des deutschen Nordamerikabildes im 18. Jarhundert," in *Nord und Süd in Amerika gemeinsamkeiten Gegensätze, europäischer Hintergrund,* Wolfgang Reinhard, Peter Waldmann, and Peter Eisenmann, eds. (Freiburg: Rombach, 1992), 1125–41.

9. The best known of these was Francis Daniel Pastorius, *Umständige Geographische Beschreibung Der zu allerletzt erfundenen Provintz Pensylvaniae, In denen End-Gräntzen Americae In der West-Welt gelegen Durch Franciscum Danielem Pastorium, J. U. Lic. und Friedens-Richtern daselbsten. Worbey angehencket sind einige notable Begebenheiten, und Bericht-Schreiben an dessen Herrn Vatern Melchiorem Adamum Pastorium, Und andere gute Freunde,* published in 1700 and reprinted in translation in Myers, *Narratives,* 360–448. Pastorius's *Umständige Beschreibung* was usually bound together with a German translation of Gabriel Thomas's *Historical and Geographical Account of Pensilvania and of West-New-Jersey* (London, 1698) and Daniel Falkner's *Curieuse Nachricht.* Myers, *Narratives,* 359.

10. Julius Sachse, ed. and trans., *Falkner's Curieuse Nachricht von Pensylvania: The Book That Stimulated the Great German Emigration to Pennsylvania* (Philadelphia: Pennsylvania German Society, 1905), 37.

Curieuse Nachricht von Pensylvania . . ., which contained the answers to more than one hundred questions about the colony.[11] Josua Kochertal, a Lutheran pastor from the Neckar Valley, published a pamphlet about the colony of Carolina in 1706, titled *Außführlich- und umständlicher Bericht von der berühmten Landschaft Carolina.*[12] Each of the authors participated in overlapping and intersecting communication networks that spanned the Rhine River and included Amt Dilsberg; each was connected to people who were migrating from villages close to Waldhilsbach. Whether or not he actually read any of these pamphlets, Wistar likely was familiar with the information they contained.

Pastorius was a member of the Frankfurt Company, a group of investors in Pennsylvania land. The company's original members were closely connected to Philip Jacob Spener (1635–1705), an early Lutheran Pietist leader.[13] In the 1670s, Spener and his friend Johann Jakob Schütz began weekly meetings to read and discuss devotional literature and to promote personal piety.[14] Both men corresponded extensively with people throughout Europe who were interested in reforming the Protestant Church and society through religious practice

11. Sachse, *Falkner's Curieuse Nachricht*, 23–28.

12. Walter A. Knittle, *Early Eighteenth-Century Palatine Emigration: A British Government Redemptioner Project to Manufacture Naval Stores* (Philadelphia: Dorrance, 1938; repr. Baltimore: Genealogical Publishing, 1970), 14–19; Jones, *Palatine Families*, 1:471–72; introduction to facsimile of Josua Kochertal, *Außführlich- und umständlicher Bericht von der berühmten Landschafft Carolina In dem Engelländischen America gelegen* (Frankfurt, 1709).

13. Sachse, *Falkner's Curieuse Nachricht*, 22–25; F. Ernst Stoeffler, *The Rise of Evangelical Pietism* (Leiden: E. J. Brill, 1971), 229. The literature on Spener and German Pietism is vast. For a brief overview and a good synthesis, see the multivolume series Martin Brecht, Klaus Deppermann, Ulrich Gäbler, and Hartmut Lehmann, eds., *Geschichte des Pietismus* (Göttingen: Vandenhoeck und Ruprecht, 1993–2004), esp. vols. 1 and 2.

14. Elizabeth Fisher, "'Prophesies and Revelations': German Cabbalists in Early Pennsylvania," *PMHB* 109 (1985): 302–16; Andreas Deppermann, *Johann Jakob Schütz und die Anfänge des Pietismus* (Tübingen: Mohr Siebeck, 2002), 81–206, 322–27; Richard S. Dunn and Mary Maples Dunn, eds. *The Papers of William Penn*, vol. 1, *1644–1700* (Philadelphia: University of Pennsylvania Press, 1981), 447–56.

15. Their correspondents came from a variety of religious perspectives and cultural backgrounds. Spener sought to reform the Lutheran Church from within, but he exchanged letters with religious seekers who held views significantly different from his own. Martin Brecht, "Philipp Jakob Spener, sein Programm und dessen Auswirkungen," in *Geschichte des Pietismus*, vol. 1, *Das Pietismus vom siebzehnten bis zum frühen achtzehnten Jahrhundert*, ed. Martin Brecht (Göttingen: Vandenhoeck und Ruprecht, 1993), 278–89; Johannes Wallmann, ed., *Briefe aus der Frankfurter Zeit, 1666–1686*, vols. 1–4 (Tübingen: Mohr and Siebeck, 1992–2005). Schütz corresponded with German Reformed and Lutheran Pietists; intellectuals who explored the mystical elements of the Cabbala; and separatists like Anna Maria von Schurmann, Johanna Eleonora von Merlau, and Johann Wilhelm Petersen, who became separatists by the early eighteenth century. Depperman, *Johann Jakob Schütz*, 222–336; Fisher, "Prophesies and Revelations," 299–333.

16. Dunn and Dunn, eds. *Penn Papers*, 1:215–19, 448–51, 459–63; Marjorie Nicolson, ed., *Conway Letters: The Correspondence of Anne, Viscountess Conway, Henry More, and Their Friends, 1642–1684* (New

and devotion.[15] In 1677, Penn and Furly visited the Frankfurt Pietists on a missionary journey to Europe and began corresponding with Schütz.[16] After Penn received the charter for his colony in 1681, Furly, acting as Penn's agent, began funneling promotional literature through these same communication channels. He sent private letters to the Pietists in Frankfurt, encouraging them to migrate to Pennsylvania. As a result of his efforts, the Frankfurt Company purchased 15,000 acres in the colony.[17]

In late spring 1683, Pastorius, acting as an agent of the Frankfurt Company, set out for Pennsylvania. On his way, he stopped at Kriegsheim, where he visited with Furly's friends among the Quakers and Mennonites there, and in Krefeld, where he met another group of investors who had purchased Pennsylvania land. After his arrival in the colony when it became clear the other investors were not joining him there, Pastorius worked with the immigrants from Krefeld and later arrivals from Kriegsheim to establish Germantown.[18]

The colonists Pastorius joined were linked to another set of contacts near Wistar's home: Mennonites who belonged to a network of congregations that reached from Amsterdam in the north, to Danzig in the east, and Switzerland in the south. In 1710, some Swiss Mennonites, who had settled temporarily in the Palatinate, migrated to Pennsylvania. Within a few years they sent Martin Kindig back to Europe to recruit additional emigrants. Palatine ministers reported to Dutch religious leaders in 1717 that 300 Mennonites were traveling to Rotterdam en route to the British colonies.[19] Many of the emigrants came from villages in Amt Dilsberg that included Mennonite congregations (see Map 5).[20] Wistar's arrival on the same ship with members of this group and

---

Haven: Yale University Press, 1930), 309–436; D. Elton Trueblood, *Robert Barclay* (New York: Harper and Row, 1968), 64–67, 74–75, 84–92; Depperman, *Johann Jakob Schütz*, 322–27.

17. Samuel Pennypacker, *Historical and Biographical Sketches* (Philadelphia: Robert A. Tripple, 1883), 13–14.

18. Beiler, "Bridging the Gap," 54–56; Hull, *William Penn*, 290–92, 336–37; Depperman, *Johann Jakob Schütz*, 327–35; Harold S. Bender, "The Founding of the Mennonite Church in America at Germantown, 1683–1708," *Mennonite Quarterly Review* 7 (1933): 238–46. For a brief biography of Pastorius, see Craig Horle and Marianne Wokeck et al., eds., *Lawmaking and Legislators in Pennsylvania: A Biographical Dictionary*, vol. 1, *1682–1709* (Philadelphia: University of Pennsylvania Press, 1991), 586–90.

19. Rosalind J. Beiler, "Distributing Aid to Believers in Need: The Religious Foundations of Transatlantic Migration," *PA Hist* 64 Supplemental Issue (1997) 73–87; Richard K. MacMaster, *Land, Piety and Peoplehood: The Establishment of Mennonite Communities in America, 1683–1790* (Scottdale, Pa.: Herald Press, 1985), 33–59.

20. "Religionsverzeichnis," 1706, GLA 61/5479; "Register," 1716, GLA 145/292; Harold Bender, ed., "Palatinate Mennonite Census Lists, 1664–1774, I," *Mennonite Quarterly Review* 14 (1940): 14–15. The villages that included Mennonites were: Zuzenhausen, Bammenthal, Meckesheim, Eschelbronn, Mauer, Langenzell, Helmstadt, Angelloch, Hof Hohenhardt, Daisbach, Schatthausen, Kloster Lobenfeld, Ochsenbach, Bayerthal, Biederbach, and Bruchhausen. Bender, "Palatine Mennonite Census," 20–23.

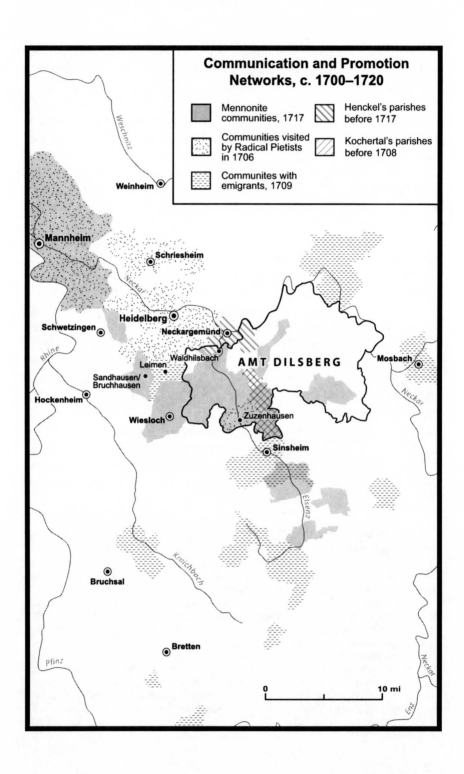

Communication and Promotion Networks, c. 1700–1720

- Mennonite communities, 1717
- Communities visited by Radical Pietists in 1706
- Communites with emigrants, 1709
- Henckel's parishes before 1717
- Kochertal's parishes before 1708

Weschnitz

Weinheim

Mannheim

Schriesheim

Neckar

Heidelberg

Schwetzingen

Neckargemünd

Rhine

Leimen

Waldhilsbach

AMT DILSBERG

Mosbach

Sandhausen/ Bruchhausen

Neckar

Hockenheim

Wiesloch

Zuzenhausen

Sinsheim

Bruchsal

Elsenz

Kraichbach

Bretten

Pfinz

Neckar

Enz

0   10 mi

his later business relationships with many of the immigrants suggest their role as important sources of information prior to his decision to leave home.

Another potential source of information for Wistar was a group of people linked indirectly to Daniel Falkner. Falkner had migrated to Pennsylvania in 1694 with Johannes Kelpius, a Lutheran Pietist who believed the establishment of God's kingdom on earth was imminent.[21] Falkner, Kelpius, and others in their group communicated with August Hermann Francke, a correspondent of Spener's, who had recently established an orphanage and educational founda-tions at Halle (which would become the center of German Pietism in the eigh-teenth century).[22] In 1699, he and Heinrich Bernard Köster returned to Europe to collect money for a new church, recruit immigrants, and solicit a pastor for the Lutherans in Pennsylvania.[23] While there, Falkner visited Francke.[24] Among the topics they discussed was the potential for establishing an American Pietist colony. Francke drafted a list of questions about conditions in Pennsylvania to which Falkner responded. His replies first circulated in manuscript form, but in 1702, the Frankfurt Company published them as *Curieuse Nachricht von Pensyl-vania.*[25] Falkner's Pietist American colony never materialized. Nevertheless, his pamphlet describing conditions in Pennsylvania was disseminated through his and Francke's correspondence networks.

Radical Pietists with connections to these communication networks arrived in Wistar's home region in 1706 when an itinerant preacher visited Heidel-berg.[26] That same year, a member of the Reformed Church consistory reported that "for some time the so-called Pietists have been getting the upper hand here in the city [Heidelberg] as well as in various places in the country, especially in Schriesheim." He noted that "they meet from time to time in their homes and

21. Fisher, "Prophesies and Revelations," 299–333; Journal of Johannes Kelpius, 1695–1708, AM .0880, HSP; an English translation of Kelpius's journal is in Julius Sachse, *Pennsylvania: The German Influence in Its Settlement and Development: A Narrative and Critical History,* pt. 27, *The Diarium of Magister Johannes Kelpius* (Lancaster: Pennsylvania-German Society, 1917).

22. Falkner, Lübeck, to August Hermann Francke, Halle, Aug. 26, 1691, Francke Nachlass 32/11:3 [10902]; Falkner, Lüneburg, to August Hermann Francke, Feb. 8, 1692, Francke Nachlass 32/11:4 [10903]; Falkner, Hamburg, to August Hermann Francke, Halle, Jan. 27, 1693, Francke Nachlass 32/11:5 [10904], Staatsbibliothek zu Berlin—Preussischer Kulturbesitz, Berlin.

23. Julius Sachse, *The German Pietists of Provincial Pennsylvania, 1694–1708* (Philadelphia, 1895; repr. New York, AMS Press, 1970), 93–99; Jacob Bruno Wigers, London, to Henry July Elers, Halle, May 3, 1699, Hauptarchiv B71a, S. 69–74, Archiv der Franckesche Stiftung, Halle, Germany (hereafter AFSt).

24. For a brief summary of the extensive literature on Francke, see Martin Brecht, "August Her-mann Francke und der Hallische Pietismus," in *Geschichte,* 1:439–539.

25. Sachse, *Falkner's Curieuse Nachricht,* 22–38; 45–245. One copy of Falkner's original manuscript is in Hauptarchiv D85: S. 469–597, AFSt.

26. Durnbaugh, *European Origins,* 32–56; Heinz Renkewitz, *Hochmann von Hochenau, 1670–1721: Quellen Studien zur Geschichte des Pietismus,* vol. 5, *Arbeiten zur Geschichte des Pietismus* (Wittenberg: Luther-Verlag, 1969), 1–41; 217–36.

hold conventicles."[27] Government officials eventually arrested the itinerant and his followers and sentenced them to hard labor. But Pietists already had become established in Amt Dilsberg. One government official claimed, "It is not to be doubted that the fanatics, who have infiltrated from time to time, have set foot in almost all of the territory."[28] The itinerant preacher whose visit created such a flurry had undergone a conversion experience in Halle under Francke's influence.[29] His followers from Amt Dilsberg participated in their communication networks and would have been familiar with Falkner's *Curieuse Nachricht*.[30]

Furthermore, Kocherthal, another pamphlet author with connections to Wistar's home area, was a Lutheran minister at Eschelbron, Münchzell, and Daisbach, all within four to eight miles of Waldhilsbach. Unhappy with the conditions of the Palatine Lutheran Church, he had traveled to London in 1704 to assess the opportunities for emigration. After returning and publishing his pamphlet, he led a group of forty-one people to England in 1708, where they eventually received support from Queen Anne for their transportation to New York. The following year, thousands of emigrants, hoping to find a better life in America, sailed down the Rhine to Rotterdam, London, and the British colonies.[31]

Many of the 1709 and 1710 emigrants came from towns close to Wistar's home. Nearly a dozen families left from villages close to Sinsheim in the Kraichgau.[32] Johann Nicolaus Hornig, Johann Georg Kast, Georg Herchheimer, and their families left from Leimen and Sandhausen, two villages within two miles of the hunting lodge at Bruchhausen where Wistar served as a hunter's apprentice. Several of Wistar's shipmates in 1717 had friends or acquaintances who had followed Kochertal's group to New York.[33]

27. Quote is from GLA 77/4330 as translated in Durnbaugh, *European Origins*, 40.

28. Translation from Durnbaugh, *European Origins*, 41–42.

29. Max Goebel, *Geschichte des christlichen Lebens in der rheinisch-westphälischen evangelischen Kirche*, vol. 2, *Das siebenzehnte Jahrhundert* (Coblenz, in Commission bei Karl Bädeker, 1862), 811–13; Durnbaugh, *European Origins*, 36.

30. Sachse, *Falkner's Curieuse Nachricht*, 22–30; Durnbaugh, *European Origins*, 38–79, 281–320.

31. Knittle, *Palatine Emigration*, 14–19, 32–46; Otterness, *Becoming German*, 25–51; Kochertal, *Ausführlich- und umständlicher Bericht*, intro. Documents from German archives concerning the 1708–10 migrations are reprinted in Julius Goebel, ed., "Briefe Deutscher Auswanderer aus dem Jahr 1709," *Deutsch-Amerikanische Geschichtsblätter* 12 (1912): 124–89.

32. The Castners of Elsenz, the Kasselmanns of Adelshofen, the Meyers of Steinsfurt and Rohrbach, the Mussiers from Steinsfurt, the Rauschers of Dühren, the Straubs of Sinsheim, Wägelis of Bonfeld, and the Wanners of Sinsheim all arrived in New York in 1710. Jones, *Palatine Families*, 1:119–22, 432–37; 2:630–31, 682–83, 751–52, 1007–9, 1069–70, 1200. For later migrations from the same region, see Fogleman, *Hopeful Journeys*, 36–65.

33. Jones, *Palatine Families*, 1:388–90, 402–3, 437–38. Although they emigrated before Wistar's apprenticeship, some of their friends and relatives, who remained behind, migrated in later years. Jost Schwab, the father-in-law of Abraham Rhiem, the only "friend" Wistar had on the ship, had sponsored

Even closer to home, Anthony Henckel, the Lutheran minister at Neckargemünd (the church Wistar's father belonged to and where his younger siblings
were baptized), determined to leave the Palatinate for Pennsylvania. He had
preceded Kochertal as the pastor at Eschelbronn, Münchzell, and Daisbach and
his parish included those congregations again in 1717. Henckel had spent years
squabbling with Catholic officials over the use of church buildings and property. When he petitioned the consistory for permission to emigrate, he claimed
he could not support his family of seven children on the meager income his
poor parishes supplied.[34] Oral traditions record that Henckel migrated to New
Hanover, Pennsylvania, with some of his parishioners.[35]

Wistar did not acknowledge any connection to Henckel, nor is there evidence to suggest he established connections with the minister after he was in
the colony. Wistar claimed that the only friend who accompanied him to Pennsylvania was Abraham Rhiem. But local and regional officials remarked upon
Henckel's departure; the event also would have been well publicized among the
members of his congregations.[36] It was no accident that Wistar decided to leave
home at the same time colonial promotional literature was luring so many of his
neighbors and acquaintances away from the area.

Each of the promotional tracts circulating through these communication networks that crisscrossed Wistar's home region provided appealing images of
Britain's American colonies.[37] Regardless of colonial realities that did not always
match promoters' promises, the pictures they painted resonated with potential
Palatine immigrants like Wistar.

---

the baptism of Herchheimer's son in 1700. For the genealogy of Abraham (Eberhard) Rhiem and Johann
Jost Schwab, see Elmer Denniston, *Genealogy of the Stukey, Ream, Grove, Clem and Denniston Families*
(Harrisburg, Pa.: pub. by author, 1939), 245–50; and Emily S. Morse and Winifred M. McLachlan, *The
Swope Family Book of Remembrance: A History of the Origins of the First Schwab, Schwob, Swope Families
in Early Lancaster County, Pennsylvania, and Some of Their Descendants*, vol. 2, *Jost Schwab* (Provo, Utah:
J. Theron Smith, 1972), 1289–96.

34. Henckel's conflicts with Catholic officials occurred while he was the pastor at Breitenborn and
Daudenzell. In 1714 he became the pastor at Neckargemünd and the Meckesheimer Cent, where his
ministry coincided with that of Johann Georg Kneitz, the Catholic priest at Neckargemünd from 1704
to 1727. The records from his ministry there are in the NgLKB, EOK.

35. For a history of his life and the reproduction of many documents concerning his ministry in
the Palatinate, see articles by Burt Brown Barker in *Henckel Family Records* 3 (1928): 90–116; 4 (1929):
118–30; 6 (1931): 212–30; 8 (1932): 314–40. See also Ann Hinckle Gable, *The Pastoral Years of Rev. Anthony
Henckel, 1692–1717* (Camden, Maine: Penobscot Press, 1991). Henckel served a congregation at New
Hanover that Falkner reportedly had led prior to his arrival.

36. July 1, 1717, GLA 229/71466, 11. A facsimile of the original is reproduced in Gable, *Pastoral Years*,
116–21.

37. For a good summary of the debates on push and pull factors in migration from the German
Southwest to America and the influence of promotional literature, see Fertig, *Locales Leben*, 96–135.

Umständige Geogra-
phische
Beschreibung
Der zu Allerletzt erfundenen
Provintz
PENSYLVA-
NIÆ,
In denen End-Gräntzen
AMERICÆ
In der West-Welt gelegen/
Durch
FRANCISCUM DANIELEM
PASTORIUM,
J. V. Lic. und Friedens-Richtern
daselbsten.
Worbey angehencket sind eini-
ge notable Begebenheiten / und
Bericht-Schreiben an dessen Herrn
Vattern
MELCHIOREM ADAMUM PASTO-
RIUM,
Und andere gute Freunde.

Franckfurth und Leipzig/
Zufinden bey Andreas Otto. 1700.

FIG. 6 Title page, Pastorius's *Umständige geographische Beschreibung*, 1700.
Courtesy of the Library Company of Philadelphia.

First, and not surprisingly, the pamphlets promised inexpensive and abundant land. Pastorius declared that in Pennsylvania, both the wealthy and the poor could obtain property. Those with capital could purchase land at a reasonable rate while those without money could rent it for a penny per acre. Even immigrants who signed indentures to pay for their trip could receive fifty acres for an annual rent of a half penny per acre upon the completion of their contracts.[38] Kochertal's descriptions of land in Carolina were even more compelling. That colony's proprietors reportedly guaranteed each head of household fifty acres of land as a gift. If a householder required more land, he could obtain as much as one hundred acres. Householders received their land rent-free for the first three years, and thereafter they needed to pay only a ground rent of an "*Englischen Stuber*," which, according to Kochertal, was only one-third of the value of a "*Kreutzer.*"[39]

In addition to highlighting the inexpensive cost of land in the British colonies, promoters pointed to its fertility and abundance. Falkner claimed that Pennsylvania's land was excellent and that the colonists' yields of grain were comparable to those in the Palatinate or Magdeburg or Halberstadt. The colony's rich soil, however, meant that crops grew twice as fast and made a second harvest possible.[40] Kochertal promised that South Carolina was "one of the most fertile regions which can be found" and was preferable in many places to Germany or England.[41] Furthermore, the vast array of crops and produce in the American "islands" seemed to grow with less human energy than in Europe. In Pennsylvania, Falkner declared, peaches and cherries were plentiful and "grew like weeds."[42] Kochertal attested that Carolina's colonists raised grains, rice, and tobacco very profitably and that wild grapes could be harvested for wine. In addition, other nut and fruit trees simply grew wild, without being planted from seed.[43] Such glowing images of natural abundance would have been particularly appealing for people from Wistar's home region, where memories of recent wars were only too vivid. A combination of plundering enemy armies; supplying food for friendly troops; and devastating, harsh winters led to food shortages and crop failures by the first decade of the eighteenth century.

A second incentive prominent in the promotional literature was the nonintrusive government and tax structures of the British colonies. Pastorius emphasized that in Pennsylvania, "each year certain persons are elected from the whole

38. Myers, *Narratives*, 374.
39. Kochertal, *Außführlich- und umständlicher Bericht*, 10.
40. Sachse, *Falkner's Curieuse Nachricht*, 102–3.
41. Kochertal, *Außführlich- und umständlicher Bericht*, 12.
42. Sachse, *Falkner's Curieuse Nachricht*, 104–5.
43. Kochertal, *Außführlich- und umständlicher Bericht*, 12–13.

people" to the colonial Assembly. These legislators "make the necessary laws and ordinances for that year according to the condition of the time and the people, and thereby prevent encroaching vices."[44] Pastorius also maintained that colonists elected officials by secret ballot, so that "none may know who has voted for, or against, him." He believed this prevented bribery and encouraged virtuous behavior, since "if anyone has conducted himself improperly this year, a better man may be chosen next time."[45] If he read the promoter's pamphlet, Wistar, who had witnessed his father's political struggle with Ziegler, would not have missed the implications of Pastorius's comment.

Pastorius also stressed the colonists' role in determining taxes. He claimed that "neither the king himself nor his envoys, bailiffs, nor governors may lay any kind of burden or tax upon the subjects, unless those subjects themselves have first voluntarily resolved and consented to give a specified amount." Furthermore, he claimed, "no tax may remain in force for longer than a single year."[46] In comparison to the Palatinate, where subjects paid various taxes and tithes to the elector, local governments, landlords, and the church, Pennsylvania's taxation policies must have seemed a fantasy.

In describing Carolina, Kochertal also emphasized low taxes. He promised that instead of giving local government officials tithes for supporting the clergy, the colonists themselves collected tithes to distribute to their ministers. Almost incredulously, Kochertal added, "the entire annual contribution due to the authorities comes only from the groundrent." The settlers were "otherwise completely freed from all obligations, compulsory labor, serfdom, and all other burdens, whatever they may be named, and the authorities are prepared to give security that it will always remain so in the future."[47] For Palatine villagers who still performed compulsory labor and were struggling against an expanding state and growing tax obligations, Carolina sounded like paradise.[48]

A third incentive that colonial promoters used to attract potential settlers was religious toleration. Pastorius declared that in Pennsylvania, "no one sect may raise itself above the others, each shall enjoy freedom of conscience, and no one shall be forced to be present at any public services for the worship of God, and no one shall be disturbed in his belief or religion."[49] Falkner, in surveying religious toleration in all of the British colonies, averred that in Pennsylvania,

44. Myers, *Narratives*, 436.
45. Ibid., 377.
46. Ibid., 437.
47. Kochertal, *Ausführlich- und umständlicher Bericht*, 11.
48. See Chapter 2, above. For discussions of the tensions between villagers and the state in the Kraichgau, see Fogleman, *Hopeful Journeys*, 36–65.
49. Myers, *Narratives*, 377.

"all sects except the Jews and such as absolutely deny Christianity, are not only countenanced, but they are granted the free exercise of their religion and are undisturbed and protected by the public authorities."[50] He compared this to Maryland, Virginia, and New England, which he claimed all allowed the "sects" and Jews to worship in private but not in public. In describing Carolina, Kochertal declared that the Lutherans and Reformed as well as the Mennonites would enjoy religious toleration and freedom of conscience.[51]

Religious toleration was a critical incentive between 1680 and 1730, the earliest period of German-speaking migration to the colonies, when government officials were harassing, imprisoning, and banishing Mennonites, Quakers, and Pietists. Pastorius and Falkner were both closely tied to the Pietist conventicles at Frankfurt and Halle at a time when their status was tenuous.[52] They appealed directly to emigrants interested in religious toleration. Kochertal responded to tactics that had already proven profitable in Pennsylvania at precisely the time when officials were negotiating another forced exile of Swiss Mennonites.[53]

Freedom from an intrusive official church, however, may have enticed Lutheran, Reformed, and Catholic congregants to emigrate as well. Squabbles and conflicts between local clergy and parishioners intruded constantly into the lives of Palatine villagers. Kochertal himself was caught in the midst of these disputes.[54] The promise that no one would force them to attend any particular church or interfere with family decisions about baptism, marriage, and burial rites would have appealed to villagers even when they did not suffer from overt religious persecution.[55]

Wistar claimed that God inspired his decision to go to Pennsylvania, yet the timing of his inspiration suggests earthly concerns as well. When he determined to leave home in 1717, the young man's future looked uncertain. He was working as a hunter's apprentice for Georg Michael Förster, the chief hunter at Bruchhausen. Just the year before, the new elector, Karl Philipp, had instituted a series

50. Sachse, *Falkner's Curieuse Nachricht*, 201.

51. Kochertal, *Außführlich- und umständlicher Bericht*, 9–10.

52. Samuel W. Pennypacker, "The Settlement of Germantown, Pennsylvania and the Causes Which Led to It," *Historical and Biographical Sketches* (Philadelphia, Robert A. Tripple, 1883), 17; Sachse, *Falkner's Curieuse Nachricht*, 31–43.

53. Beiler, "Distributing Aid," 79–81.

54. Heinz Schuchmann, "Der 1708 nach Amerika ausgewanderte Pfarrer Josua Kocherthal hieß ursprünglich Josua Harrsch," *Pfälzische Familien u. Wappenkunde: Biographie, Genealogie, Heraldik*, Supplement: *Mitteilungen zur Wanderungsgeschichte der Pfälzer* 6 (Nov. 1967): 121–28. See especially the comment that Kochertal suffered the same difficulties as his predecessor, Anthony Jakob Henckel, p. 127. Schuchmann's article is translated by Frederick S. Weiser in "Notes on the Origins of Joshua Kocherthal," *Concordia Historical Institute Quarterly* 41 (1968): 147–53.

55. See Chapter 3, above.

of government reforms that resulted in frozen salaries for the forestry department. Almost immediately, the hunters at Bruchhausen began to request assistance; on January 13, 1717, they petitioned for their salaries from the last half of 1716. The hunters argued that they needed their salaries for survival because they received no supplement of "crops, wine, or household goods, but have only a small allowance and money for clothing." Whenever they wanted food or drink, they needed cash. During the wolf hunts that were then in progress, the hunters had borrowed nearly 100 *Gulden* from Chief Hunter Förster.[56]

The hunters' petition brought no relief, however; in spite of repeated complaints, the salary freeze continued until 1719. In the meantime, Chief Master of the Hunt Karl von Venningen reorganized the department, cutting excess positions and consolidating costs. The plan he outlined reduced the department from 115 positions to 87.[57] From Wistar's perspective, his future prospects as a hunter or forester looked grim.

At the same time, Wistar's father was embroiled in his ongoing battle with Andreas Ziegler for social status and control of resources in Waldhilsbach. For a period of time in 1716 and 1717, it looked as if Wistar's father might lose his forestry position, one that Wistar, as the oldest son, might inherit, along with the little bit of social status it brought him.[58] Life in the village among neighbors who consistently tried to constrain the forester held little promise for his son.

Religious factors also may have played a role in the timing of Wistar's decision to leave home. When he came to power in 1716, Karl Philipp increased the government's support for the Catholic Church and its efforts to expand. At the same time, a group of nobles from the Kraichgau who had converted to Catholicism became the elector's advisors at the highest levels of government. Karl Philipp's early actions appeared to support his predecessor's encouragement of spreading the Catholic faith. The government did not persecute Protestants; nevertheless, local religious conflicts increased dramatically and the prospects for Lutheran and Reformed government officials looked less hopeful. Religious changes may also have threatened to jeopardize Wistar's future economic success.[59]

56. Jan. 13, 1717, GLA 77/1738.

57. 1716–19, GLA 77/1738.

58. See Chapter 2, above.

59. Schaab, *Geschichte der Kurpfalz*, 2:158–60, 171–73. Regardless of the reality for Protestants in the Palatinate, political leaders from other Protestant European states viewed the Catholic electors' policies with the utmost suspicion. For example, the emigrants who arrived in London in 1709 and 1710 were labeled "Protestant Palatines," fleeing religious persecution at the hands of the Catholics even though most of them left home for economic reasons; Otterness, *Becoming German*, 37–56. By the 1720s, Karl Philipp's religious policies were making news in the British American colonies. The *American Weekly Mercury* reported on letters written by the king of Prussia and the States General to the elector on behalf of his Protestant subjects. *American Weekly Mercury*, Jan. 26, 1720; Feb. 16, 1720; Apr. 28, 1720; May 12, 1720; June 30, 1720; July 7, 1720.

Thus Wistar's inspiration to emigrate to Pennsylvania came at a critical time when there seemed to be little hope for improving or even maintaining his position in the Palatinate. He was twenty-one when he made his decision, the age when he should have been setting up his own household. His chances for doing so seemed especially grim in 1716 and 1717. Wistar may not have known as much about Pennsylvania as later emigrants, but what information he did have held out the promise of opportunity. At least one emigrant from Wistar's region, Martin Kindig, brought back positive reports of Penn's colony—reports that convinced 300 of his fellow Mennonites to leave home. The pastor of the church Wistar's father attended believed he stood a better chance of earning a living for his large family in Pennsylvania. If he was willing to risk the move, why not Wistar?

In determining to leave home, Wistar took a gamble that the promise of the "new world" was better than his chance for securing a forester's position in the old one, a position that could easily disappear with the stroke of an administrator's pen. It was the knowledge that he was taking a chance on the unknown while risking the disapproval of family and friends that created the emotional trauma in saying good-bye.

PART II

Wistar's American World

I arrived healthy in Philadelphia the 16th of September 1717, through the help of God. And because the same year many ships had arrived in Philadelphia, the Germans, in the end, were viewed poorly which did not serve me so well. Because there was no more than 9 pence in my savings and [I] was also in debt 3 pistolines and [I] had no other friends except for the one I owed 3 pistolines and [I] could not ask him for more for fear he might say pay me first what you owe me, as we came to unload [our things] I took my little sack and went with the large group to an inn and as the others were being given something to eat and drink, I had to first go for a walk because I did not have the means [to pay for food]. So I took my 9 pence and bought me a loaf of bread for 5 pence; then my misery was that I had only 4 pence and did not have enough to buy another [loaf of] bread.

After this I walked around to see the city and met a man who made cider, who I helped. He gave me apples—as many as my pockets could hold. Then I was rich in apples and my bread; that lasted for 2 or 3 days. I came to a soap maker who gave me very hard work and I was more weak and faint from the ship so that the same work seemed to me to be incredibly difficult for I worked hard and it was still too little. The soap maker's wife was somewhat impatient and I could not understand her. [I] thought all the time that I did not work enough for her since she was so unhappy. I stayed with the soap maker named John Bearde 16 months and a half in soap-making and [I] carted ashes together with a wheelbarrow until I learned the craft of button-making.

—CASPAR WISTAR, "A Short Report"

CHAPTER 5

Establishing Professional and Family Connections
NEW BEGINNINGS IN PENNSYLVANIA

Wistar's most vivid memories of his arrival in Philadelphia were his supposed poverty and the difficulty of being German in a British colonial city.[1] His training as a Palatine hunter was meaningless in Philadelphia, and he had no friends or patrons in high places to loan him money. Even when he managed to find work, language difficulties threatened Wistar's progress.

Wistar's "Short Report" comes to an abrupt end after his arrival in Philadelphia. We do not know how he interpreted his early struggle to find security, although the beginning of the story he tells has an uncanny resemblance to Benjamin Franklin's later autobiography. Wistar's near-penniless arrival, his walk around the city, his purchase of bread, and the image of the young immigrant pushing a wheelbarrow through the streets foreshadow Franklin's interpretation of a self-made American man.[2] Indeed, contemporaries recognized Wistar's meteoric rise from rags to riches, and his descendants perpetuated an image of his early poverty.[3]

A careful reading of historical evidence, however, suggests that Wistar's experience was more complex. He may have arrived in British America without significant savings or language skills, but he was not as destitute as he believed or as he viewed himself from his later position of prosperity. Wistar brought a wealth of knowledge and experience with him from the Palatinate that shaped his response to Pennsylvania's circumstances in very specific ways. Like his father and grandfather before him, the young man set out to build professional and social connections through religious affiliation, political patronage, and family networks. In doing so, he adapted strategies he learned in Europe to British America's very different circumstances.

1. For a description of the attitudes toward German-speaking immigrants in 1717, see Schwartz, *"Mixed Multitude,"* 85–88. Wistar claims to have saved between 40 and 50 *Gulden* before leaving for Pennsylvania. Although he portrays himself as impoverished, he did not arrive as an indentured servant, as did many other young single male immigrants.

2. J. A. Leo Lemay and P. M. Zall, eds., *Benjamin Franklin's Autobiography: An Authoritative Text, Backgrounds, Criticism* (New York: W. W. Norton, 1986), 19–21.

3. Gov. James Hamilton to Thomas Penn, Sept. 24, 1750, PPOC, 5:55, HSP; Sauer, obituary for Caspar Wistar, *Pennsylvania Berichte,* Apr. 1, 1752, HSP.

When he stepped onto the dock on September 16, 1717, Wistar encountered a world that contrasted sharply with the one he had left behind. Philadelphia in 1717 was a young, rapidly growing city. William Penn, the colony's proprietor, had founded Pennsylvania only thirty-five years earlier in 1682. A steady stream of settlers from Britain and its other colonies made the city one of the busiest seaports in British North America.[4] By the mid-1720s, Christopher Sauer, a fellow German-speaking immigrant, reported that "the city has already 2000 houses." Although it "was a wilderness forty years ago, . . . now there live there at least eight hundred important merchants and shopkeepers." He deemed the city "handsomely built" with "straight streets . . . laid out at right angles."[5] Sauer may have exaggerated the number of merchants and shopkeepers in Philadelphia, but other visitors also commented on its accelerated growth, brick houses, and wide streets laid out in a grid pattern. An English visitor to the city in 1726 attested that it was "built square in [the] Form of a Chess-Board" and contained "several Streets near two Mile[s] long" that were "built after the English Manner."[6]

The broad straight avenues of Penn's planned town looked strikingly different from the narrow, winding streets and alleys of Heidelberg, the medieval European city Wistar had turned to look at one last time as he left home. Like Heidelberg, where the elector's court was located, Philadelphia was the seat of Pennsylvania's provincial government. The colony's governor, council, and assembly met regularly there. Both places had roughly the same number of inhabitants: Heidelberg's population was around 6,100 and Philadelphia's was 4,200.[7] And

4. Arthur Jensen, *The Maritime Commerce of Colonial Philadelphia* (Madison, Wis.: State Historical Society of Wisconsin for the Department of History, University of Wisconsin, 1963), 1–6; Edwin Bronner, *William Penn's "Holy Experiment": The Founding of Pennsylvania, 1681–1701* (Philadelphia, 1962; repr. Westport, Conn.: Greenwood Press, 1978), 31–33; Susan E. Klepp, "Demography in Early Philadelphia, 1690–1860," *Proceedings of the American Philosophical Society* 133 (June 1989): 85–111; P. M. G. Harris, "The Demographic Development of Colonial Philadelphia in Some Comparative Perspective," *Proceedings of the American Philosophical Society* 133 (June 1989): 262–304.

5. Christopher Sauer to friends in Germany, Aug. 1, 1725, translated in Donald Durnbaugh, ed., *The Brethren in Colonial America: A Source Book on the Transplantation and Development of the Church of the Brethren in the Eighteenth Century* (Elgin, Ill.: Brethren Press), 34. See also Christopher Sauer to friends in Germany, Dec. 1, 1724, in Kelsey, "Early Description of Pennsylvania," 252.

6. Richard Castleman, *The Voyage, Shipwreck, and Miraculous Escape of Richard Castleman, Gentlemen, with a Description of Pensylvania and the City Philadelphia (1726)* in *The Voyages and Adventures of Captain Robert Boyle, in Several Parts of the World by W. R. Chetwood* (London, 1728), 363. See also John George Käsebier to Count Casimir, Nov. 7, 1724, Durnbaugh, *Brethren in Colonial America*, 30, and [Jacob Duche], *Caspipina's Letters, Containing Observations on a Variety of Subjects, Literary, Moral, and Religious* (Bath, 1777), 7–10.

7. For the population of Heidelberg in 1714, see Karl Kollnig, *Wandlungen im Bevölkerungsbild des pfälzischen Oberrheingebietes* (Heidelberg: Carl Winters Universitätsbuchhandlung, 1952), 36. In 1717, Philadelphia's population was 4,224. By 1726 it had reached 6,100; Klepp, "Demography," 103–4. See also Nash, *Urban Crucible*, 407; Gary Nash and Billy G. Smith, "The Population of Eighteenth-Century Philadelphia," *PMHB* 99 (1975): 366.

FIG. 7 The South East Prospect of the City of Philadelphia, c. 1720. Courtesy of the Library Company of Philadelphia.

FIG. 8 Heidelberg, view from the north, c. 1683. Courtesy of the Kurpfälzisches Museum, Heidelberg.

both cities were located on rivers—Heidelberg on the Neckar River and Philadelphia at the confluence of the Delaware and Schuylkill rivers. There, however, the similarities ended.

In spite of its orderly and planned development, Philadelphia lacked the "refinements" and institutions of the older European city. Pennsbury, the proprietor's country estate located some distance up the Delaware River, could not compare to the elector's castle and gardens overlooking Heidelberg.[8] Nor did colonial government officials participate in anything close to the court culture of the Palatinate.[9] In 1717, Philadelphia had no university, no cathedral, no hospital, no guilds. The skyline boasted no spires or steeples, and the city had few public buildings. Many of its religious groups met in private homes or warehouses.[10] Philadelphia remained a small, rural town in comparison to the government seat of the Palatinate.

No doubt Wistar noticed the striking visual differences between the two cities when he stepped onto one of the many wharves jutting out into the Delaware River. We do not know on which ship he arrived or to whom the vessel belonged. We know only that he was one of the 363 travelers aboard the ships for which Captains Richmond, Towor, and Eyers presented passenger lists to the provincial council on September 19, 1717.[11] In subsequent years, German immigrants would proceed first to the courthouse, where the government required them to take an oath of allegiance to the king of England.[12]

In the year Wistar arrived, this requirement was not yet in place. In fact, the governor informed his council on September 17 that "Great numbers of fforeigners from Germany, Strangers to our Language and Constitutions" had arrived and had "dispersed themselves immediately after Landing, without producing any Certificates." Council members determined, therefore, that ship captains should appear before them to give them an account "of the number and

8. Samuel M. Janney, *The Life of William Penn; with Selections from his Correspondence and Autobiography* (Philadelphia: Lippincott, Grambo, 1852), 427–36; Richard Dunn and Mary Maples Dunn, eds., *The Papers of William Penn*, vol. 3, *1685–1700* (Philadelphia: University of Pennsylvania Press, 1986), 608–9.

9. *Stadt- und Landkreise*, 2:20–22; Richard Benz, *Heidelberg: Schicksal und Geist* (Konstanz: J. Torbecke, 1961), 242–76; Friedrich Walter, *Geschichte des Theaters und der Musik am kurpfälzischen Hoffe* (Leipzig: Verlag von Breitkopf und Härtel, 1898), 25–84.

10. Martin Snyder, *City of Independence* (New York: Praeger, 1975), 29–31; Edwin B. Bronner, "Village into Town, 1701–1746," in *Philadelphia: A 300-Year History*, ed. Russell Weigley (New York: W. W. Norton, 1982), 33–35; Robert Shoemaker, "Christ Church, St. Peter's, and St. Paul's," *Transactions of the American Philosophical Society*, n.s., 43 (1953): 11; George B. Tatum, *Penn's Great Town: 250 Years of Philadelphia Architecture Illustrated in Prints and Drawings* (Philadelphia: University of Pennsylvania Press, 1961), 27–28.

11. *MPC*, 3:29.

12. Wokeck, *Trade in Strangers*, 137–41.

Characters of their Passengers." The council required the immigrants to take an oath of allegiance before the city recorder within one month.[13]

Wistar may have disembarked at the public wharf on Dock Street, built in the cove where Philadelphia's first ships cast anchor.[14] Or perhaps he arrived at William Fishbourne's wharf on the eastern end of Walnut Street, where John Stedman, a ship captain who transported German-speaking immigrants to the colony in the 1730s, docked his ships and had a store.[15] Either route sent Wistar into Philadelphia through its waterfront, the center of the city's commercial activity. At the wharves, ships of all sizes arrived and departed daily. In 1698, Gabriel Thomas claimed that Philadelphians participated in "Commerce both by Sea and Land, viz. to New-York, New-England, Virginia, Mary-Land, Carolina, Jamaica, Barbadoes, . . . Maderas, . . . and Old-England; besides several other places."[16] From the wharves, large oceangoing vessels carried flour, bread, lumber, meat, and corn to the West Indies and tobacco and fur to England. They brought wine and salt from Madeira and Lisbon and people and manufactured goods from Great Britain and Ireland. Smaller vessels came and went from coastal ports carrying commodities for transshipment to overseas destinations. By the time Wistar arrived, roughly 116 vessels a year sailed from Philadelphia.[17] The bustling hub of activity along the waterfront clearly indicated the city's budding role as a colonial entrepôt.[18]

To support the city's maritime trade, merchants' stores, warehouses, and homes sprouted beside the wharves and along Water and Front streets. When Penn first planned his city, he sold only a few lots on "the bank," the strip of land between Front Street and the Delaware. By 1717, however, the bank was lined with stores and warehouses.[19] Sprinkled among the wharves were many of the city's taverns and "public houses." After they disembarked, Wistar and his shipmates sought food and lodging at an inn. They may have gone to the Blue Anchor Tavern at the Dock, which dated back to the earliest days of the city,

13. *MPC*, 3:28–29.

14. Gary B. Nash, "City Planning and Political Tension in the Seventeenth Century: The Case of Philadelphia," *Proceedings of the American Philosophical Society* 112 (1968): 60–64; Michael McMahan, "'Public Service' Versus 'Mans Properties': Dock Creek and the Origins of Urban Technology in Eighteenth-Century Philadelphia," in *Early American Technology: Making and Doing Things from the Colonial Era to 1850*, ed. Judith A. McGaw (Chapel Hill: University of North Carolina Press, 1994), 114–17.

15. *Pennsylvania Gazette*, Dec. 5, 1734, Feb. 3, 1737, and Mar. 1, 1739; Wokeck, *Trade in Strangers*, 69–75, 93–95.

16. Thomas, *Historical and Geographical Account*, 24–25.

17. Jensen, *Maritime Commerce*, 5.

18. Ibid., 1–10; Carl and Jessica Bridenbaugh, *Rebels and Gentlemen: Philadelphia in the Age of Franklin* (New York: Oxford University Press, 1962), 5–7; McCusker and Menard, *Economy*, 189–208; Frederick B. Tolles, *Meeting House and Counting House* (Chapel Hill: University of North Carolina Press, 1948; repr. New York: W. W. Norton, 1963), 85–88.

19. Nash, "City Planning," 69–72.

or perhaps, like Franklin several years later, they went to the Crooked Billet on Water Street.[20] In addition to purchasing food and lodging, merchants transacted business, politicians met and campaigned, and ordinary people heard the latest news in Philadelphia's taverns and inns. Until 1710, the Common Council of Philadelphia and the justices of the peace, like the court at Waldhilsbach, also met in taverns.[21]

Unable to afford a tavern meal with his fellow passengers, Wistar set off to explore the city. Most likely he started up Front Street, lined with the homes of Pennsylvania's most prominent merchants. Here were the stores and houses of men like Jonathan Dickinson, William Fishbourne, Samuel Carpenter, and Charles Read.[22] One of the brick houses he walked past belonged to Anthony Morris, a wealthy brewer and merchant. Typical of the city's early Quaker merchants, Morris began his career as an artisan. He migrated from England to New Jersey, settled in Philadelphia in 1685, and soon joined the city's growing ranks of merchants.[23] By 1717, he owned a tavern and ran a brewery. Morris, like other Philadelphia merchants whose houses lined Front Street, was also active in city and provincial politics; he served as a city councilman, alderman, mayor, justice of the peace, legislator, and provincial councilor.[24] Morris's rise from artisan to prominent merchant and politician represented the opportunity Philadelphia provided for its earliest immigrants.

Continuing past Morris's house and Chestnut Street, Wistar likely turned west onto High Street, the center of the city's public life. Here, in the middle of the street, was the site where the "great town bell, erected upon a mast" had once stood.[25] From under the bell, provincial and royal proclamations had been announced. Here too was the "cage," built in 1682 to house the city's offenders. By the time Wistar arrived, the city had converted the "cage" into a watchtower

20. Robert Earle Graham, "The Taverns of Colonial Philadelphia," *Transactions of the American Philosophical Society*, n.s., 43 (1953): 318; Lemay and Zall, *Benjamin Franklin's Autobiography*, 21; John Watson, *Annals of Philadelphia and Pennsylvania in the Olden Time* (Philadelphia, 1857), 1:464.

21. Peter Thompson, *Rum Punch and Revolution: Taverngoing and Public Life in Eighteenth-Century Philadelphia* (Philadelphia: University of Pennsylvania Press, 1999), 111–44; Ellis P. Oberholtzer, *Philadelphia: A History of the City and Its People* (Philadelphia: S. J. Clarke Publishing, 1912), 103; Bronner, "Village into Town," 57.

22. Craig Horle, Joseph Foster, and Jeffrey Scheib et al., eds., *Lawmaking and Legislators in Pennsylvania: A Biographical Dictionary*, vol. 2, *1710–1756* (Philadelphia, 1997), 266, 311, 366–71, 881–82; Doerflinger, *Vigorous Spirit*, 39–42.

23. Moon, *Morris Family*, 1:45–47, 79–80.

24. Horle et al., *Lawmaking and Legislators*, 1:554–58; Moon, *Morris Family*, 65–66. During his tenure as a legislator, committees often met at Morris's house. Across the street was William Monnington's house, another Philadelphia Quaker merchant who became Wistar's business partner. Horle et al., *Lawmaking and Legislators*, 2:701. For a discussion of Philadelphia's social structure and the place of Quaker merchants at the turn of the century, see Nash, *Quakers and Politics*, 285–87, 319–28.

25. Watson, *Annals*, 1:350.

FIG. 9 Old Courthouse and Second Friends Meeting. Courtesy of the Library Company of Philadelphia.

and replaced it with a prison, which was already so decrepit that its inhabitants often escaped. Public punishments were meted out at a whipping post and pillory, which stood beside the watchtower and in front of the prison.[26]

By 1717, the bell had been moved to a tower on top of the city's courthouse, which perched high upon arched pillars just beyond the prison and west of the intersection of High with Second Street. In contrast to Heidelberg, where bells were rung from the cathedral's towers, the placement of Philadelphia's bell tower signified a secular state—one without an official, state-sponsored religion. Built in 1707, the courthouse was the center of political life. Here the Common Council of Philadelphia, the city's governing body, met after 1710. Here Philadelphia County's justices of the peace climbed the double set of steps to hold court four times a year, instead of at a tavern. And here departing mayors feasted with the city's gentlemen.[27]

The courthouse was more than the city's political center; it also housed the provincial government. Until the 1740s, Pennsylvania's assembly met either in the courthouse or in private homes.[28] From the second-floor balcony government

26. Ibid., 1:350, 356–59; Snyder, *City of Independence*, 27–28. Oberholtzer, *Philadelphia*, 104.
27. Judith Diamondstone, "Philadelphia's Municipal Corporation, 1701–1776," *PMHB* 90 (1966): 183–201; Nash, *Urban Crucible*, 30–32.
28. Bronner, "Village into Town," 51–53.

officials read royal decrees and colonial governors made their inaugural speeches. On May 31, 1717, just a few months before Wistar arrived, the commission of Sir William Keith, the new governor, was "published and proclaimed in due form, at the Court house in Philadelphia, The Mayor & Corporation, & Gentlemen & Inhabitants of the sd. City attending."[29] Philadelphia's freeholders lined the steps leading to the balcony to vote for provincial legislators. Election inspectors assembled on one staircase insured that only qualified voters climbed to the top, cast their vote, and then exited by the other staircase. During contentious elections, like those of the 1720s or the 1740s, voting dissolved into riots as competing factions attempted to control the courthouse steps.[30]

Across from the courthouse on the corner of High and Second streets Wistar passed the Society of Friends Meetinghouse.[31] Quakers dominated the city's early political and economic life; they held the important official positions and monopolized much of the city's trade. Nevertheless, the province had no official, tax-supported church. Penn's tolerant religious policies required parishioners in each congregation to fund their own minister's salary, church buildings, and schools. In the first several decades of settlement, Quakers and Anglicans, the other major religious group in the colony, struggled to achieve dominance. Political and religious leaders disagreed over doctrinal and institutional issues.[32] But sectarian power struggles in Philadelphia never included state property as they had in the Palatinate. And the voluntary nature of churches meant that clergy recruited parishioners less zealously than Wistar had experienced at home.

Penn's religious policies resulted in an unusual degree of religious diversity for the British colonies. Promoters and visitors frequently remarked on the variety of religious groups in Pennsylvania. Pastorius declared in 1684 that his household included "those who hold to the Roman, to the Lutheran, to the Calvinistic, to the Anabaptist, and to the Anglican church and only one Quaker."[33] An English visitor asserted in 1726, "All Religions are tolerated here, which is one Means to increase the Riches of the Place." He made specific references to the Anglican, Quaker, and Swedish Lutheran meetinghouses.[34] The Anglicans had completed Christ Church on Second Street, just north of High Street in

29. *MPC*, 3:13.

30. Horle et al., *Lawmaking and Legislators*, 2:20–23; William Parsons, "The Bloody Election of 1742," *PA Hist* 36 (1969): 293–300.

31. Edwin B. Bronner, "Quaker Landmarks in Early Philadelphia," *Transactions of the American Philosophical Society*, n.s., 43, pt. 1 (1953): 210–12; Tatum, *Penn's Great Town*, 24–25.

32. Schwartz, *"Mixed Multitude,"* 36–80; Deborah Mathias Gough, *Christ Church, Philadelphia: The Nation's Church in a Changing City* (Philadelphia: University of Pennsylvania Press, 1995), 5–22; Nash, *Quakers and Politics*, 127–224.

33. Myers, *Narratives*, 396.

34. Castleman, "Voyage," 364. For additional discussions on religious diversity, see Schwartz, *"Mixed Multitude,"* 63–65.

High Street & Market Shambles.

FIG. 10 High Street and Market Shambles, 1830. Courtesy of the Library Company of
Philadelphia.

1696 and the Presbyterians had a church that they shared with the Baptists just
up the street from the Friends Meetinghouse.[35]

Nevertheless, for German-speaking immigrants like Wistar the city had
few options for worshiping in one's native language. During the first several
decades of settlement, many of the immigrants were Quakers, Mennonites, or
radical Pietists of one sort or another. The Lutheran and Reformed churches in
the German states showed little interest in supporting fledgling Pennsylvania
congregations.[36] Thus Philadelphia's German parishioners from those confessions suffered a chronic shortage of clergy. They either joined one of the many
sects or attended services led by Anglican, Presbyterian, or Swedish Lutheran
ministers.[37] Indeed, Anthony Henckel, the pastor of the church Wistar's father
attended in Neckargemünd, founded one of the earliest German Lutheran

35. Shoemaker, "Christ Church," 187–90; Gough, *Christ Church*, 10–11; Alexander Mackie, "The
Presbyterian Churches of Old Philadelphia," *Transactions of the American Philosophical Society*, n.s., 43,
pt. 1 (1953): 217–18.

36. Klaus Deppermann, "Pennsylvanien als Asyl des frühen deutschen Pietismus," *Pietismus und
Neuzeit* 10 (1982): 190–212; Fisher, "Prophesies and Revelations," 299–333; Fogleman, *Hopeful Journeys*,
3.

37. Schwartz, *"Mixed Multitude,"* 72–74.

congregations in Pennsylvania at New Hanover, thirty-some miles from Philadelphia, after his arrival in 1717.[38]

Directly in front of the Friends Meetinghouse and the Presbyterian church and in the middle of the street, Wistar encountered another prominent feature of High Street's public life: the market. The Delaware wharves may have been the city's center for overseas trade but the market was its link to outlying regions. From Philadelphia's founding, Penn planned to use High Street as the city's retail center. He convinced Robert Turner, one of the colony's wealthiest settlers, to take a lot close to High Street for that reason.[39] In the earliest days of settlement, market was held on Wednesdays and Saturdays in a grassy area at the intersection of Front and High streets. Later, farmers, traders, and Indians from the surrounding countryside and New Jersey brought their produce, livestock, and furs to the "shambles," movable stalls, which were set up between Front and Second streets. By 1717, the new market with permanent brick stalls extended beyond the courthouse between Second and Third streets.[40]

Market days brought lavish displays of the abundant natural resources in Pennsylvania—especially during harvest, the time of year Wistar arrived. Visitors to the colony inevitably raved about the lushness of the vegetation and the plentiful wildlife. One Englishman declared that "the Woods afford fine Pigeons, Pheasants, Quails, Partridges, Woodcocks, Snipes, wild Turkies, and various other Birds." He also praised the extensive variety of fish and oysters found in the colony's rivers and bays and promised that "when any of these are brought to Market, you may buy 'em very reasonably."[41]

To German-speaking immigrants from the war-torn Palatinate, Pennsylvania's richness was almost overwhelming. Johann Georg Käsebier wrote glowingly that it was "a precious land with the finest wheat, as well as unusual corn, fine broomcorn, maize, and white beets of such quality as I never saw in Germany." He especially was impressed by the apples, harvested "in great quantities from trees which grow up wild without being grafted." They were "so delicate to look at that I have not seen the like in Germany." Even more astonishing were the spoiled apples, which were so numerous "that a wagon loaded with them could not be budged by four horses. Many trees are full of apples which are frozen because there is a shortage of workers."[42] The bountiful produce presented

38. Glatfelter, *Pastors and People,* 19–22.
39. Nash, "City Planning," 63–64.
40. Oberholtzer, *Philadelphia,* 73–74; Watson, *Annals,* 1:359, 362–64; "Notes and Documents," *PMHB* 23 (1899): 408–9; Bronner, "Village into Town," 62.
41. Castleman, "Voyage," 359–60.
42. Johann Georg Käsebier to Count Casimir, Nov. 7, 1724, as translated and reprinted in Durnbaugh, *Brethren in Colonial America,* 30.

to bustling crowds at the market booths stood in stark contrast to the Palatinate, where neighbors brawled over fruit on village-owned trees.

To reap the benefits of the market's thronging customers, artisans, shop-keepers, and retail merchants built their shops and houses on either side of High Street facing the market. Market days offered the best opportunity to sell and trade hardware, dry goods, other imported merchandise, and services to fellow colonists who came to the city to sell their produce and purchase supplies. As he walked up the street, Wistar passed the properties of artisans like John Rutter, smith; Jonathan Cockshaw, weaver; and Edward Warner, carpenter.[43] In 1717, Philadelphia offered seemingly unlimited opportunity for craftsmen and labor-ers. Early letters from German-speaking immigrants outlined in great detail the different wages artisans would earn at their trades and what kinds of laborers were most needed.[44]

In spite of Philadelphia's bustling growth and the opportunity it presented for economic prosperity, the conditions Wistar encountered when he arrived placed him at the bottom of colonial society. In contrast to the Palatinate, Pennsylvania had no forestry department; neither Penn nor his descendants commanded a corps of hunters. Although Philadelphia was a busy port city, Pennsylvania was still largely unsettled "wilderness" rather than villages and forests—forests, that is, in the organized, administered, Palatine sense of the word.[45] The difference between the two worlds dictated that Wistar could not practice the profession for which he had trained in Europe. Instead, he was reduced to collecting ashes with a wheelbarrow for a soap maker named John Bearde, a job well below the social status of a hunter and forester.[46]

Although his station as a wage laborer during his first year in Philadelphia made a lasting impression, Wistar did not remain in his humble position for long. He recognized that in Pennsylvania, as in the Palatinate, economic secu-rity depended, in part, on commanding specialized skills. Even though he was already an adult and had completed one apprenticeship, he became an appren-tice to a brass button maker in January 1719. Wistar did not identify his master, but stories of his training have become family tradition. According to one tale, Wistar's master "met with a severe accident which confined him to his bed" shortly after the apprenticeship began. The accident "had such a discouraging effect upon the enterprising German, that the Button-maker allowed him to

43. Philadelphia County Deeds, F-3:486–91, microfilm copy, HSP. For a contemporary description of the artisan's houses along High Street, see the column by "Busy Body," *American Weekly Mercury*, June 19, 1729.

44. Durnbaugh, *Brethren in Colonial America*, 30–41.

45. See Chapter 1, above.

46. Wistar, "Short Report," Wistar Family Papers, HSP.

bring his work to the chamber and there instructed him in the art." Wistar supposedly worked so hard to learn his new trade, that "when it was necessary to desist, he would be unable to open his fingers and was obliged to reverse his clenched hand to allow the hammer to slip through."[47]

Whether Wistar's success as a brass button maker resulted from his diligence or perhaps from the elimination of his master's competition due to his accident remains unclear.[48] The immigrant did, however, establish a successful business. He remarked to one correspondent in 1733, "I am, according to my primary occupation, a button maker and brazier (*mesing gieser*)."[49] At his death in 1752, Wistar's button-making tools, supplies, and apprentices were worth 676 Pennsylvania pounds (£400 sterling).[50] For Wistar, promotion from a wage laborer to an artisan signaled the first step in securing his livelihood in Philadelphia.

Wistar's apprenticeship also immersed him in Anglo-American culture and the English language. Like some of the immigrants who signed indentures with him in later years, Wistar may have learned English as part of his formal contract.[51] More likely, he picked up the language during his daily contact with English speakers, for his written English displays the same rudimentary phonetic spelling as his written German.[52] Little evidence remains for determining when he acquired language skills. On July 10, 1721, Wistar signed his name in German script as "Caspar Wüster."[53] By December 18, 1722, he had changed his signature to "Caspar Wistar" and signed in English letters.[54] Throughout the

47. Brown, "Interesting Records," Salem County Historical Society, Salem, N.J.

48. A search of Philadelphia wills and administrations revealed no deaths for button makers between 1717 and 1726. But there is a will probated for Ann Bird, widow of Andrew Bird, brazier, in 1722. Andrew Bird had already died when she wrote her will on Sept. 12, 1720. Philadelphia County Wills, bk. D, 207, microfilm copy, HSP. Other possibilities for Wistar's master are: Thomas Paglan and Austin Paris (both brass founders in Philadelphia in 1717), and John Hyatt (Philadelphia brass founder from 1723 to 1735); James Biser Whisker, *Pennsylvania Workers in Brass, Copper and Tin, 1681–1900* (Lewiston, N.Y.: Edwin Mellen Press, 1993), 116, 149.

49. Caspar Wistar to Johann Martin Franck, Nov. 10, 1733, Wistar Family Papers, HSP.

50. Inventory of the Goods and Chattels of Caspar Wistar, Apr. 4, 1752, Wistar Family Papers, HSP, 16; Philadelphia County Wills, bk. I, 493, microfilm copy, HSP. Exchange rate is based on John J. McCusker, *Money and Exchange in Europe and America, 1600–1775* (Chapel Hill: University of North Carolina Press, 1978), 185.

51. Wistar's contract with John Peter Lambert, May 2, 1746, "Account of Servants Bound and Assigned Before James Hamilton, Mayor of Philadelphia," *PMHB* 31 (1907): 358–59. See also the contract between Philip Hime and John Gebherd, Nov. 14, 1745 "Account of Servants," *PMHB* 31 (1907): 92.

52. See, e.g., a receipt in Wistar's handwriting dated March 10, 1749, in which he paid John Potts £3 "for one years ground Rent for one lod of grent in thirt stritt." In October 1751, five months before his death, Wistar's heavy accent was still apparent; he paid another £3 "ground rent for one lad thirt strett." Receipt Book of Caspar Wistar, 1747–84, Am .941, HSP.

53. Philadelphia County Wills, bk. D, 199, microfilm copy, HSP.

54. Deed from William Lawrence, Phila., to Joshua Lawrence, Phila., Cadwalader Papers, Thomas Cadwalader Section, Penn Agent, Deeds, box 33, Dec. 18, 1722, HSP; affidavit, Caspar Wistar, Nov. 9,

remainder of his life, Wistar always used his English signature, even when the documents he signed were written in German.[55] Language acquisition was yet another hurdle he crossed in his initial adjustment to his new environment.

Scant evidence survives for Wistar's activities during his first decade in Pennsylvania. Nevertheless, the glimpses that remain show him striving to secure his position in the colony. Wistar quickly recognized the prominent position of Quakers in the province.[56] Just as his father and grandfather used their confessional identity to secure their government positions and enhance their social standing, so Wistar realized the benefits of religious membership for establishing his reputation in Pennsylvania. As early as 1721 he indicated his Quaker sympathies by signing a declaration of allegiance to the king of England rather than swearing an oath. The declaration was a legal tool designed to permit Quakers, who had scruples against taking oaths, to promise loyalty to Great Britain. By 1726, Wistar had become a member of the Philadelphia Monthly Meeting of Friends and thereby gained entrance into the dominant network of merchants and political leaders in the province.[57]

Within a very short time after his arrival, Wistar began to purchase property. In Pennsylvania, as in Waldhilsbach, land ownership was a critical indicator of economic and social status. In 1721 Wistar purchased a prime city lot on High Street between Third and Fourth streets. Precisely how he raised £210 "American Money" (£153 sterling) at a time when specie was scarce and only four years after he had arrived with no resources remains a mystery.[58] Perhaps he turned

1731, in possession of Mrs. Robert T. Price, Centreville, Md., copy on file at the Library Company of Philadelphia, Philadelphia.

55. See, e.g., his signature on a copy of a statement regarding an agreement between Jörg Jäcobus and Claus Riedenhaus, Nov. 9, 1731, photocopy of original, Library Company of Philadelphia. Wistar's accounts for the United Glass Company were kept in German, but he always used his English signature when signing them; Caspar Wistar Account Book, 1743–69, bk. G, Wistar Family Papers, HSP. It is impossible to tell how Wistar signed his name when writing to family and friends as extant letters are fragments without signatures from his copy book. Wistar Family Papers, HSP.

56. Tolles, *Meeting House*, 113–19; Gary Nash, "The Early Merchants of Philadelphia: The Formation and Disintegration of a Founding Elite," in *World of William Penn*, ed. Dunn and Dunn, 337–51.

57. A photograph of Wistar's declaration of allegiance is on file at the Germantown Historical Society. On January 28, 1726, he applied to the Philadelphia Monthly Meeting for a certificate to the Abington Monthly Meeting for "his clearness with respect to marriage." William W. Hinshaw, *Encyclopedia of American Quaker Genealogy*, vol. 2, *Records and Minutes of Four of the Oldest Monthly Meetings which ever Belonged to the Philadelphia Yearly Meeting of Friends* (Ann Arbor, Mich., 1938; repr. Baltimore: Genealogical Publishing, 1994), 690.

58. Philadelphia County Deeds, F-3:422–24, microfilm copy, HSP. For conversion rates, see McCusker, *Money and Exchange*, 184. Wistar's capital may have come from goods that he smuggled with his personal belongings when he crossed the Atlantic—a practice that was not unusual among early German-speaking immigrants. Rosalind J. Beiler, "Smuggling Goods or Moving Households?

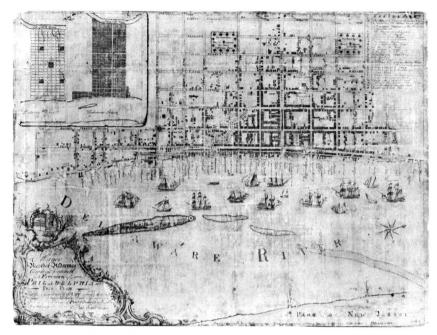

FIG. 11 Wistar's Philadelphia, 1762. Courtesy of the Library Company of Philadelphia.

once again to his friend Abraham Rhiem for a loan.[59] More likely, however, he borrowed money or took out a mortgage from one of Philadelphia's wealthy Quakers, whose patronage he sought. One month after buying the property, Wistar witnessed the will of Anthony Morris Sr., a "weighty" Friend who had connections to the German community in Germantown and who was Wistar's neighbor. He may have borrowed money from Morris or from Quakers in Germantown with whom he eventually became business partners.[60]

The Legal Status of German-Speaking Immigrants in the First British Empire," in *Menschen zwischen zwei Welten: Auswanderung, Ansiedlung, Akkulturation,* eds. Walter G. Rödel and Helmut Schmahl (Trier: WVT Wissenschaftlicher Verlag Trier, 2002), 9–23.

59. For Rhiem's activities, see James Steele's Letterbook, 1715–32, HSP, 27; *Pennsylvania Archives,* 2nd ser., *Minutes of the Board of Property of the Province of Pennsylvania,* vol. 19 (Harrisburg, 1876–93), 725 (hereafter *Minutes*); Denniston, *Genealogy,* 245–64; Morse and McLachlan, *Swope Family Book,* 2:1294–96.

60. Philadelphia County Wills, bk. D, 199, microfilm copy, HSP; John Jordan, ed., *Colonial and Revolutionary Families of Pennsylvania,* vol. 1 (New York: Lewis Publishing, 1911; repr. Baltimore: Genealogical Publishing, 1978), 258; Horle et al., *Lawmaking and Legislators,* 1:554–59; Margaret H. Collins and Ellinor C. Aird, *Ancestors of the Distaff Side of the First Five Generations of the Collins Family in America,* vol. 3 of *The Collins Family* (Ardmore, Pa., 1980), 87–92; Moon, *Morris Family,* 1:32–123; Pennypacker, "Settlement of Germantown," 57, 84, 102, 124, 128–30, 290; and Hull, *William Penn,* 244, 248, 318, 320, 332.

Wistar's 1721 purchase seems odd in light of the poor economic conditions in the colony. Yet it also represents the opportunity Philadelphia offered artisans of the "middling sort." During the depression of 1720 and 1721, unemployment drove many laborers out of the city in search of work. As a result, property prices began to fall. A combination of paper currency issued in 1723 and wages that kept pace with the cost of living curtailed the depression and helped to stabilize the economy. By 1724 trade flourished once again. For artisans who had modest savings or access to credit, available lots for affordable prices made Philadelphia a city with more opportunities than either Boston or New York.[61]

Wistar clearly was in a position to benefit from the city's opportunities. Memories of his father's constant struggle to get ahead likely fueled his desire for more land. Not content with one city property, he purchased the adjoining lot with two buildings for an additional 130 Pennsylvania pounds (£91 sterling) on October 26, 1724.[62] Wistar's new property was ideal for a brass button maker's apprentice setting up shop. It was at the corner of High and Third streets, just a short distance from the end of the market stalls. Like his artisan neighbors, he could sell his buttons to the crowds who arrived twice a week to buy and sell produce.[63]

Wistar may have shared aspirations for wealth with his Anglo-American neighbors, but he remained an alien in a British colony. His status as a foreigner posed barriers to participating in civic life that fellow property owners did not face. According to British law, foreigners could not pass their land on to their children unless they became naturalized subjects. Nor could they participate in overseas trade without first seeking naturalization. Although provincial governments tried to guarantee such rights for their settlers, Parliament, the crown, and the English courts frequently blocked their attempts.[64]

Indeed, Penn had worked to secure the property of German-speaking immigrants. In 1683 he promised foreign landowners that their heirs could inherit their property in spite of their legal status. He also convinced the assembly to enact legislation naturalizing all non-British inhabitants (mostly Dutch and Swedish) who were living in the province when he received his charter from the king. In spite of Penn's best efforts, however, the status of his foreign settlers remained ambiguous. Attempting to clarify the issue, the Pennsylvania assembly passed two laws in 1700. One law specified naturalization procedures and privileges while the other protected *all* property owners and their heirs—regardless

61. Nash, *Urban Crucible*, 119–23.
62. Philadelphia County Deeds, F-3:486–88, microfilm copy, HSP.
63. Ibid., 488–91.
64. Beiler, "Smuggling Goods," 11–14.

of their status as British subjects or aliens. The crown, however, rejected both laws because they granted Penn powers beyond those explicitly stated in his charter from Charles II.[65]

German-speaking immigrants in Germantown and Philadelphia responded with great concern when the crown refused to approve the laws. In 1704, eighty-two of the foreigners petitioned the colony's provincial council and assembly for naturalization. They did so because following "the repeal of the late laws . . . for encouragement of the peopling and settling of this colony, some doubts and questions" had arisen about whether they were "capable to hold what they purchased."[66] When the act finally passed in 1709, it signaled both the Germans' intent to secure their property and their awareness of the act's jurisdiction. The law guaranteed that the petitioners could hold property as if they "were free and natural-born subjects and people of this *province*."[67] The Pennsylvania assembly recognized that its power was limited to the colony's borders. Nevertheless, the queen did not confirm the act until 1714, ten years after the immigrants first submitted their petition.[68]

News of the legal difficulties that Pennsylvania Germans faced in leaving legacies of land spread back to Europe. Several months after Wistar arrived, the colony's commissioners of property warned some of his shipmates that the government could not guarantee their rights to pass on land to their heirs unless they were naturalized. The newcomers replied that they already knew about the colony's laws and that they would petition to become subjects.[69]

Wistar, like his fellow immigrants, clearly understood the potential danger of losing his investment in real estate. Although most of his shipmates did not become British subjects until much later, he submitted a naturalization petition to the legislature in December 1723.[70] After several lengthy discussions and amendments, Assemblymen Anthony Morris (Jr.) and Samuel Levis presented Wistar's bill to Governor William Keith.[71] The governor and provincial council approved the act the following spring, granting Wistar, fellow German John Cratho, and French immigrant Nicholas Gateau the right to "have and enjoy

---

65. Schwartz, *"Mixed Multitude,"* 26–29.

66. *Statutes at Large of Pennsylvania*, 2:298.

67. *Statutes at Large of Pennsylvania*, 2:300, emphasis added; Schwartz, *"Mixed Multitude,"* 26–29; *MPC*, 2:241, 248, 480, 488, 494; Horle et al., *Lawmaking and Legislators*, 1:499, 586–90; *Votes and Proceedings of the House of Representatives of the Province of Pennsylvania* (Philadelphia, 1752), vol. 1, pt. 2, 26, 47.

68. *Statutes at Large of Pennsylvania*, 2:298.

69. *Minutes*, 19:679. For a history of the 1717 immigrants, see MacMaster, *Land, Piety and Peoplehood*, 81–85.

70. *Votes*, 2:1561; *MPC*, 3:234–35.

71. *MPC*, 3:234; *Votes*, 2:1570, 1572, 1579–80, 1583–84.

all lands and tenements ... as if they had been born natural subjects of this province."[72]

The success of Wistar's naturalization act indicates that he had established his reputation among the "better sort" of Pennsylvanians. Simultaneous to its discussions of his bill, the assembly debated another naturalization petition from "a great number" of German-speaking settlers.[73] The majority of the petitioners had settled in the Tulpehocken region in 1723 at the special invitation of Governor Keith. The governor's efforts to win supporters for his policies among the "lower sorts" of colonists had offended political leaders loyal to the proprietary family. They believed Keith was using the Germans in his quest for political power.[74] Isaac Norris, a provincial councilor, declared that "the late popular Schemes have Alarm'd Every body, who have anything like Estates in the province." He believed that the petitioners were "mostly unknown to the Assembly or the better sort of the Inhabitants."[75]

The legislators, who previously had been on friendly terms with Keith, echoed Norris's sentiment. Local officials, they determined, should inquire into the petitioners' "Characters, Belief and Behavior" before issuing certificates qualifying them for naturalization.[76] In contrast, the assembly required no character references for Wistar; he already had proven his reputation. Only two days after its resolution on the Tulpehocken Germans' petition, the assembly approved his bill.[77]

Wistar's naturalization signaled the start of a new stage in his diverse American career. By 1724 Wistar most likely had completed his apprenticeship as a button

72. *MPC*, 3:235; *Statutes at Large of Pennsylvania*, 3:424–26. For the naturalization of Wistar's fellow shipmates in 1730, see *Statutes at Large of Pennsylvania*, 4:147–50.

73. *Votes*, 2:1568–69; *MPC*, 3:241. Isaac Norris claimed the petition for naturalization was from "near 4 hundrd forreigns at once." Isaac Norris Sr. to S. Clements, Apr. 30, 1725, Isaac Norris Sr. Letterbook, 1716–30, 422, Norris Papers, HSP. This is likely an exaggeration unless the petition included more than the families living in the Tulpehocken Valley.

74. For details on Keith's role in Pennsylvania politics during the 1720s and his alliances with the "common sorts," see Nash, *Quakers and Politics*, 330–35; Alan Tully, *William Penn's Legacy: Politics and Social Structure in Provincial Pennsylvania, 1726–1755* (Baltimore: Johns Hopkins University Press, 1977), 15–19; Schwartz, *"Mixed Multitude,"* 96–99; Thomas Wendel, "The Keith-Lloyd Alliance: Factional and Coalition Politics in Colonial Pennsylvania," *PMHB* 92 (1968): 289–305; Horle et al., *Lawmaking and Legislators*, 2:561–89.

75. Isaac Norris Sr. to S. Clements, Apr. 30, 1725, Isaac Norris Sr. Letterbook, 1716–30, 422, Norris Papers, HSP.

76. *Votes*, 2:1569.

77. *Votes*, 2:1570, 1572, 1579–80, 1583–84, 1588. During the next session, Keith used Wistar's act in an effort to convince the assembly to drop the required investigation into the Tulpehocken Germans' reputations. He pointed out that the assembly had not thought it necessary in former cases. *Votes*, 2:1678–80.

maker and had set up his own business. He had lived in the colony long enough to be familiar with the career paths of Philadelphia's "better sort." Like many of them, Wistar expanded his profession as an artisan to include investment and trade. His naturalization act also granted Wistar the right to trade as if he were a natural-born subject of Great Britain.[78] The following year, Wistar purchased a share in the Abbington Iron Furnace in Newcastle County. He recognized from his forestry training the potential for investments in industries that converted natural resources into marketable commodities. One of Wistar's partners, Thomas Rutter, was a Germantown resident with Quaker background; Rutter's brother John (another partner) was Wistar's neighbor. Several partners, including William Fishborne, William Monnington, and Evan Owen, were members of the assembly.[79]

Wistar's business partnership with prominent Philadelphia merchants and his success in receiving the patronage of Quaker politicians suggest that he understood well who controlled the colony's economy and dominated provincial politics.[80] Like his grandfather and father, who sought patrons in the elector's government bureaucracy to elevate their social position, Wistar pursued connections to wealthy, established Quaker merchants and government officials to secure his reputation.

Having established himself as a Quaker investor and merchant, Wistar turned his efforts toward starting a family. Early in 1726 he applied to the Philadelphia Monthly Meeting for permission to marry, as was customary for Quakers in good standing. One of the men appointed to verify his status as an upstanding Friend was Evan Owen, Wistar's partner in the Abbington Iron Furnace and a former legislator.[81] In May his request was approved and he married Catharine Jansen.[82] Catharine's parents were well-established Quakers in Germantown

---

78. *Statutes at Large of Pennsylvania*, 3:424–26.

79. J. Thomas Scharf, *History of Delaware, 1609–1888* (Philadelphia: L. J. Richards, 1888) vol. 2, 951; Newcastle County Deeds, H-1:222–26, microfilm copy, HSP. The partners were Samuel James, Reese Jones, Samuel Nutt, Evan Owen, William Branson, Thomas Rutter, John Rutter, Caspar Wistar, John Leacock, William Fishbourn, Edward Bradley, and William Monnington. For their social and political status, see Tully, *William Penn's Legacy*, 74–75; Tolles, *Meeting House*, 98–100, 109–43; and Horle et al., *Lawmaking and Legislators*, 2:366–73, 700–4, 789–92.

80. Tolles, *Meeting House*, 113–19; Nash, "Early Merchants of Philadelphia," 337–51; and Nash, *Quakers and Politics*.

81. Horle et al., *Lawmaking and Legislators*, 2:789–92.

82. On January 28, 1726 [28th 11th month] he applied to the Philadelphia Monthly Meeting for a certificate to the Abington Monthly Meeting (of which Catharine was a member) for "his clearness with respect to marriage." On February 25, 1726, he received permission from the Abington Monthly Meeting to marry Catharine; Hinshaw, *Encyclopedia*, 2:690. According to a transcription of the marriage certificate at the HSP, the couple was married on May 25, 1726 [25th 3rd month]. A transcription of the Abington Monthly Meeting Minutes at the Genealogical Society of Pennsylvania, however,

and had lived in the colony for more than twenty-five years. As a young girl, Catharine had attended Pastorius's school.[83] By the time of Wistar's marriage, her father was a substantial landowner and justice of the peace for Philadelphia County.[84]

In marrying Catharine Jansen, Wistar chose a wife whose background was similar to his own family's class of officials in Amt Dilsberg. A justice of the peace was the closest position in Pennsylvania's local government structure to Waldhilsbach's village magistrate. Just as his father had married the daughter of a government official and Reformed elder in an attempt to secure his position in Waldhilsbach, so Wistar chose the daughter of a Quaker justice of the peace as his wife. An alliance with the Jansen family anchored his place in Pennsylvania society and signaled his acceptance among the German Quaker community.

By 1726, Wistar had overcome his supposed poverty and his status as a foreigner to establish his place in Pennsylvania. He recognized that Pennsylvania's government bureaucracy did not offer the same opportunities the forestry administration had provided his grandfather. He needed to acquire new professional skills and a new language. And to secure his property, Wistar needed to become a British subject. Wistar trained as an artisan and entered the career path of prominent Philadelphia merchants. Relying on his European experience to inform his decisions, he changed his religious affiliation and sought patronage among those who held political power in the colony to help build his reputation. Like his father, Wistar married the daughter of a local magistrate who belonged to the dominant religious group. Within a decade of his arrival, he had used his knowledge and European experience to overcome the difficulties of arriving without significant financial resources or connections.

records the marriage as occurring on April 25, 1726 [25th 2nd month] after declaring their intentions before two meetings. Family Bible records list the event as occurring on May 25, 1726 [25th 3rd month]. Wistar family records, Salem County Historical Society, Salem, N.J.

83. Although Pastorius died shortly after Wistar's arrival, he had been closely connected to Dirck and Margaret Jansen, Wistar's in-laws. In 1782, Catharine Jansen Wistar, in a legal document testifying to her father's signature on a land deed, noted that she had attended Pastorius's school. (I'm grateful to Jim Duffin for pointing out this connection.) Wistar's and Jansen's marriage certificate lists Hannah, Pastorius's daughter, as one of the witnesses. A copy of the certificate is in Marriage Certificates, HSP.

84. Samuel W. Pennypacker, *Settlement of Germantown* (New York, 1899; repr. 1970), 158–59; Mark F. Lloyd, "The Johnson (Jansen) Family and Their Houses in Eighteenth-Century Germantown," *Germantown Crier* 33, no. 2 (1981): 36–43; Sandra M. Lloyd, Historic Structures Report, Wyck House, Dec. 1986, 37–52. Jansen served as a justice of the peace for Philadelphia County, 1726, 1727, 1733, 1735/6, 1737, 1738. *MPC*, 3:257, 282, 491, 531; *Minutes*, 19:724. For some of Jansen's land records, see Patent Bk. A-6:164; A-7:471, 472; Commission Bk. A-3:263, 265, RG-17, Records of the Land Office, PSA.

This was for some years past a very good country, and like all other new colonies, little inhabited; in consequence those who came here from time to time could purchase for a small sum of money large tracts of land, and because the wild land called for much labor, although the inhabitants were few, we were glad when ships arrived here bringing Germans, for these were at once redeemed, and by their labor earned so much that they too soon were able to purchase land. . . . For several years it has happened that not only many thousand Germans, but also Englishmen and Irishmen, have settled here, and have filled up the land everywhere, so that he who now wishes to obtain land must seek it far in the wilderness, and pay dear for it besides.

—CASPAR WISTAR, letter to potential immigrants, November 8, 1732

CHAPTER 6

Securing a Legacy
WISTAR'S PENNSYLVANIA LAND SPECULATION

In the years following his marriage, Wistar turned his attention toward acquiring the wealth he needed to support his growing family. Between 1727 and 1741, Wistar's wife, Catharine, gave birth to six children, five of whom lived to adulthood (see Appendix 3). In addition, his father died in 1726, making him, as the oldest son, the patriarch of his European family. Wistar worked to insure the well-being of his widowed mother, four married sisters, and two young, unmarried brothers from across the Atlantic. Motivated by his responsibilities as the head of households on two continents, he set out to improve his economic status. Mimicking the role of Palatine foresters, Wistar shrewdly acted as the man in the middle. In Pennsylvania, however, that middle position was between German-speaking immigrants and their Anglo-American neighbors and government. He used his land speculation, transatlantic trading activities, and glass-making enterprise to become a leader among the colonial American German community and to earn a fortune.

Wistar's most profitable attempts to obtain a legacy for his children were in real estate. Pennsylvania had, at least in theory, plenty of the one resource the Palatinate lacked: land and land-based resources waiting to be turned into marketable commodities. Whereas villagers in Wistar's home region competed with their neighbors, the government, and the church for land, Pennsylvania's limited government struggled against squatters to maintain control of the "unimproved" territory it claimed. Instead of fighting with his neighbors to purchase property, as his father had done, Wistar, through his land speculation, helped to clear titles for both the government and fellow colonists. He also inadvertently shaped Pennsylvania's ethnic landscape when he sold his large tracts of land in parcels to fellow German-speaking immigrants.

Late in 1728, Pennsylvania's commissioners of property "at length agreed," that Wistar, after "having often applyed" to them for land, should receive a warrant for 2,000 acres "to be taken up back in the Province."[1] Between then and his death in 1752, Wistar purchased more than 22,000 acres of Pennsylvania land that he subdivided and sold at a tremendous profit. Wistar's own description,

1. *Minutes*, 19:758.

of his investments are no longer extant except in his last will and testament; the only written evidence that remains are the hundreds of pages recording his transactions in public records. Nevertheless, his actions tell a story that frequently has been overlooked. Wistar's real estate investments not only provided his family with substantial legacies, they also enabled him to become a patron within the immigrant community.

Two particular sets of circumstances aided Wistar's real estate pursuits: the chaotic nature of Pennsylvania's proprietary affairs in the 1720s and the simultaneous arrival of German-speaking immigrants. Wistar astutely recognized both the governing family's needs and those of his fellow immigrants. His Palatine background had taught him that government service should provide opportunities for upward mobility. But the Palatinate's unwieldy bureaucracy had threatened to squeeze him out. Pennsylvania's proprietors lacked a significant governing apparatus; they struggled to maintain control of the colony. Acting as an entrepreneur rather than a government official, Wistar set out to furnish solutions that would enhance his personal gain.

Timing was one of the crucial factors in Wistar's success as a land speculator. The young man entered Pennsylvania at a moment when the ownership of the colony was disputed. In 1718, one year after Wistar's arrival, William Penn died. In his will, Penn left most of his American holdings to three sons from his second marriage, John, Thomas, and Richard. Penn's children by his first marriage contested the will, and a lengthy legal battle ensued for control of the colony. While the suit wound its way through the British court system, the trustees assigned to oversee Penn's affairs in America refrained from selling land because they were uncertain who held appropriate authority for granting clear titles.[2]

A mortgage Penn had contracted on Pennsylvania before his death further complicated the colony's legal status. Even after the British courts established the legality of the will in 1727 and granted Pennsylvania to John, Thomas, and Richard Penn, it took another two and a half years to clear the mortgage. By the time Pennsylvania's proprietary status was completely clarified, fourteen years of confusion and inactivity had paralyzed the colony's land office.[3]

A boundary dispute between Pennsylvania and Maryland created additional confusion. An official border between the two colonies had never been drawn; consequently, the Penns and Baltimores argued over whether their charters placed it ten miles north of Philadelphia or twenty miles south of the city. In

---

2. Tully, *William Penn's Legacy*, 3–5.

3. Dunn, "Penny Wise," 48–52; Richard S. Dunn and Mary Maples Dunn, eds., *The Papers of William Penn*, vol. 4, *1708–1718* (Philadelphia: University of Pennsylvania Press, 1987), 399–508; William R. Shepherd, *History of Proprietary Government in Pennsylvania* (New York: Columbia University Press, 1896), 183–204; Bronner, *William Penn's "Holy Experiment,"* 75–77.

the seventeenth century, both families agreed on the line south of the city. But the Baltimores raised the issue again after Penn's death. Throughout the 1720s, the agents of both families refused to negotiate their positions while uncertainty and conflict prevailed in the disputed region.[4]

The final constraint that hindered the commissioners of property was that one of the Penns needed to negotiate with neighboring Native Americans for more land. During his lifetime, William Penn had insisted on purchasing Indian rights to Pennsylvania territory before selling it to European immigrants. Furthermore, as the proprietor of the colony, he retained his right as sole negotiator for Native American land. Between 1681 and 1718, the Delaware Indians had sold Penn the region between the Delaware and Susquehanna rivers and Duck Creek and the Lehigh Mountains. By the late 1720s, however, colonists had bought most Pennsylvania acreage already cleared of Delaware claims. Before the commissioners of property could guarantee new buyers full rights to their real estate, the proprietors had to purchase additional Delaware territory.[5]

Meanwhile, growing numbers of German and Scots-Irish immigrants arrived in the colony. Between 1717 and 1726, a handful of ships with German-speaking settlers docked at Philadelphia.[6] Many of the immigrants were connected to Germantown colonists, who had come at Penn's personal invitation, or to the religious channels through which Pastorius's promotional literature circulated. The earliest newcomers invested in land at Conestoga before Penn's death, and those who followed settled close to their friends and fellow congregants.[7] Another group of "Palatines" migrated from New York a few years later. The British crown had sent them to New York as part of a government scheme to produce naval stores after they had been lured to London in 1709 and 1710 by Kochertal's pamphlet. The government plan failed, however, and conflicts between the immigrants and provincial leaders arose. While on a visit to Albany, Pennsylvania's Governor Keith invited the settlers to move to his colony. Beginning in 1723, the first of the New York "Palatines" settled along the Tulpehocken Creek on land that belonged to the Delaware Indians.[8]

4. Tully, *William Penn's Legacy*, 6–7; Mabel P. Wolff, *The Colonial Agency of Pennsylvania, 1712–1757* (Lancaster, Pa., 1933), 16–17, 59–71; James Lemon, *The Best Poor Man's Country: A Geographical Study of Early Southeastern Pennsylvania* (Baltimore: Johns Hopkins University Press, 1972), 58–59.

5. Francis Jennings, "Brother Miquon: Good Lord!" in *World of William Penn*, ed. Dunn and Dunn, 195–214; Donna Munger, *Pennsylvania Land Records: A History and Guide for Research* (Wilmington, Del.: Scholarly Resources, 1992), 6–10.

6. Wokeck, *Trade in Strangers*, 37–58; Fogleman, *Hopeful Journeys*, 4–6; Schwartz, *"Mixed Multitude,"* 80–103.

7. Beiler, "Distributing Aid," 77–83; MacMaster, *Land, Piety, and Peoplehood*, 50–60; 79–81; Lemon, *Best Poor Man's Country*, 43–49.

8. Otterness, *Becoming German*, 7–77, 137–60; Paul A. W. Wallace, *Conrad Weiser, 1696–1760: Friend of Colonist and Mohawk* (Philadelphia, 1945; repr. Baltimore: For Wennawoods Publishing by Gateway Press, 1996).

The German-speaking immigrants (as well as a growing number of Scots-Irish colonists) wanted to buy land, but throughout the 1720s, the commissioners of property refused to issue patents because they could not guarantee cleared titles.[9] James Logan, one of the trustees listed in Penn's will and the family's Pennsylvania agent, noted constantly the problems these circumstances created. In 1726, he warned Hannah Penn, "Your lands to the Northw[ar]d are overrun by a number of those unruly Palatines . . . invited hither in 1722 by Sr. William [Keith] . . . and the southern parts are in the same manner possessed by as disorderly persons who have lately floc'd in . . . from Ireland."[10] Because the commissioners refused to grant patents, immigrants simply squatted on tracts that appeared uninhabited and claimed they would pay for them when Penn's estate was resolved. By 1726 Logan believed close to 100,000 acres were "possessed by persons, who resolutely sitt down and improve, without any manner of Right or Pretense to it."[11] He soon learned, moreover, that another large contingent of German-speaking immigrants planned to move to Pennsylvania the following year.[12]

In fact, Logan's worst fears came true. Instead of the three ships of Germans they expected, six ships with more than 1,200 foreigners arrived.[13] In addition, eight or nine ships from northern Ireland landed at New Castle. The "Palatine" and Scots-Irish newcomers all predicted that many of their compatriots planned to make the journey the following year. "Both these sorts sitt frequently down on any spott of vacant Land they can find without asking questions," lamented Logan. He believed that few of those who improved the land had the means to purchase it.[14]

In response to the wave of new arrivals, Logan, the other provincial councilors, and the governor tried to halt immigration. They solicited aid from British ministers and parliamentarians.[15] Early in 1728, they even convinced the Pennsylvania assembly to send a memorial to the Board of Trade, calling for an act

9. Schwartz, "Mixed Multitude," 81–87; Tully, William Penn's Legacy, 53–57; Lemon, Best Poor Man's Country, 42–70; Wokeck, Trade in Strangers, 167–219.
10. James Logan to Hannah Penn, Feb. 9, 1726, PPOC, 1:181, 313, HSP.
11. James Logan to Hannah Penn, Mar. 11, 1726, PPOC, 1:185, HSP. See also James Logan to James Steel, Nov. 18, 1729, PPOC, 2:101, HSP; James Steel to John, Thomas, and Richard Penn, Aug. 8, 1731, James Steel's Letterbook, 1730–41, 25–26, Logan Papers, HSP.
12. James Logan to John Penn, Sept. 23, 1727, James Logan Letterbook, 4:145, Logan Papers, HSP.
13. James Logan to John Penn, Sept. 23, 1727 and Oct. 22, 1727, James Logan Letterbook, 4:145–46, Logan Papers, HSP.
14. James Logan to the Penns, Nov. 15, 1727, James Logan Letterbook, 4:153–54; 160, Logan Papers, HSP.
15. James Logan to John Penn, Dec. 12, 1726, PPOC, 1:233, 255, HSP; James Logan to John Penn, July 10, 1727, PPOC, 1:283, HSP; James Logan to John Penn, Sept. 23, 1727, James Logan Letterbook, 4:145, Logan Papers, HSP (the same letter is also in PPOC, 1:287); Patrick Gordon to John Penn, Oct. 25, 1727, PPOC, 1:297–99, HSP; James Logan to John Penn, Dec. 6, 1727, PPOC, 1:311, HSP.

of Parliament to limit the flow of German-speaking settlers.[16] But to no avail; neither Parliament nor the Board of Trade agreed to stem the tide.

Facing growing numbers of squatters and a pressing need to raise money for the Penn family, the commissioners of property "at length agreed" to sell land to Wistar. Although questions remained about the legality of the sale, Wistar "passed his Bills of Exchange, payable to the Propr[ietar]y Trustees in London," for £133 sterling for 1,200 acres and promised to pay an additional £128 "money of Pennsilvania (in Gold)" for the remaining 800 acres.[17] The commissioners probably agreed to Wistar's purchase in part because of the high price he was willing to pay. He offered the Penns £16 Pennsylvania currency per hundred acres at a time when the going rate was £10 per hundred.[18] Acknowledging the pressure to bring order to the colony and raise money for the proprietors, Logan promised John Penn that "We [the trustees] are deeply affected with the unhappy situation of your affairs & would gladly lend a helping hand to heal their Disorders. But the whole of them, as well in Governmt as Property, at this time yeilds a very melancholy prospect." He sent Penn Wistar's bills and an additional £268 in gold and furs to apply toward the mortgage but added, "This is all I can doe this fall and is even more than I expected."[19]

Wistar's 1729 purchase confirms his success at establishing credit networks in the Anglo-American merchant community. His bills of exchange were drawn on Benjamin Horne, a Quaker and an independent coal factor in London with close connections to Wistar's Abbington furnace business partners. Barely a decade after his arrival in the colony, Wistar had garnered the reputation and credibility necessary to supply the proprietors with much-needed income. Furthermore, he did so at a time when bills of exchange were scarce in Pennsylvania.[20]

Before long, Wistar proved a lucrative client to the Penns. Not only was he willing to pay the going rate of 50 percent on his bills of exchange, he paid cash

16. Patrick Gordon to John Penn, Dec. 8, 1727, PPOC, 1:309, HSP; James Logan to John Penn, June 28, 1728, PPOC, 2:17, HSP; Patrick Gordon to the Penns, June 28, 1728, PPOC, 2:19, HSP; Patrick Gordon to the Duke of Newcastle, Dec. 8, 1727, Additional Miscellaneous, 1:25, Penn Manuscripts, HSP; *Votes*, 3:1874–78.

17. *Minutes*, 19:758; Copied Surveys, Survey Book (hereafter Survey Bk.) D-88:206, RG-17, Records of the Land Office, PSA. On April 18, 1729, Wistar submitted £32:15:2 Pennsylvania currency and the remaining balance of £95:4:10 on June 10, 1729; Pennsylvania Journals (hereafter PA Journals), 1:67, 69, Penn Papers, HSP.

18. Tully, *William Penn's Legacy*, 5.

19. James Logan to John Penn, Oct. 8, 1728, James Logan Letterbook, 3:275, Logan Papers, HSP.

20. Horne's brother Edward was a Pennsylvania legislator and a close associate of Wistar's business partners. Michael W. Flinn, *The History of the British Coal Industry*, vol. 2, *1700–1830: The Industrial Revolution* (Oxford: Clarendon Press, 1984), 276–77; Norman Penney, *My Ancestors* (Bishopsgate, England, 1920), 77–78; Horle et al., *Lawmaking and Legislators*, 2:510–13; James Logan to John, Thomas, and Richard Penn, July 29, 1728, James Logan Letterbook, 4:182–87, Logan Papers, HSP.

for additional land.[21] In November 1729, Wistar submitted £77 Pennsylvania currency for 483 acres to be added to the tracts already surveyed to him.[22] Over the next three years, he was one of the few sources of income Pennsylvania provided for the debt-ridden proprietors. When he bought additional real estate in early 1732, the Penns complained to James Steel, their receiver general, that Wistar's money and another small sum were the only funds he had sent them.[23] By the time Thomas Penn arrived in the colony in the summer of 1732, the proprietors knew they could depend on Wistar's credit and cash.[24]

Wistar also assumed the risks involved in collecting money from German-speaking colonists. In 1727, Logan proposed to the proprietors that they might grant the squatters' land to third parties who could pay cash for large tracts and extend credit to those lacking funds to purchase land outright. The only other option was for the Penns to rent directly to the settlers. Rents, however, had proven impossible to collect in the Lower Counties, where the boundary dispute with Lord Baltimore threatened colonists' titles. Logan predicted that German-speaking squatters would use a similar rationale for refusing to pay rents until the Penns had resolved their legal problems.[25] Norris, another one of the trustees, was pessimistic about obtaining money from the German "free Booters or those voluntary or unlicensed settlers on your lands." He believed that the "large number, the insolence of some, & the povertie of most" would make the situation difficult to handle. He suggested that it would "require some person or Persons of great care & discretion to be the active agents in agreeing with those settlers."[26]

Wistar performed precisely the task Logan and Norris proposed. Between 1729 and his death in 1752, he received patents for more than 22,000 acres of land in Philadelphia, Bucks, and Lancaster counties.[27] He resold the large majority

21. PA Journals, 1:71, Penn Papers, HSP. Wistar paid £133 6s 8d at 50 percent according to Logan's letter to John Penn, Oct. 8, 1728, James Logan Letterbook, 3:275, Logan Papers, HSP. According to McCusker, *Money and Exchange*, 184, the average exchange rate for the winter of 1728/29 was 150 Pennsylvania pounds per £100 sterling. Thus Wistar was paying the current London exchange rate of 50 percent.

22. Nov. 15, 1729, PA Journals, 1:71, Penn Papers, HSP.

23. James Logan to John Penn, Oct. 8, 1728, James Logan Letterbook, 3:275, Logan Papers, HSP; Apr. 29, 1731, John, Thomas, and Richard Penn to James Steel, Thomas Penn Letter Books, 1:27, Penn Papers, HSP; June 7, 1731, Correspondence of James Logan, vol. 1, 1729–31, 116, Logan Papers, HSP; Aug. 3, 1731, PA Journals, 1:77, Penn Papers, HSP; Thomas Penn to James Steel, [Jan. 1732], Thomas Penn Letterbooks, 1:44, Penn Papers, HSP.

24. Munger, *Pennsylvania Land*, 66–67.

25. James Logan to the Penns, Nov. 25, 1727, James Logan Letterbook, 4:160, Logan Papers, HSP.

26. Isaac Norris to John Penn, Apr. 30, 1729, Isaac Norris Letterbook, 1716–30, 522–25, Norris Papers, HSP.

27. Patent Books (hereafter Patent Bk.), A-6:106, 162; A-7:2, 257, 486; A-8:351, 354, 387; A-9:164; A-10:247, 249, RG-17, Records of the Land Office, PSA.

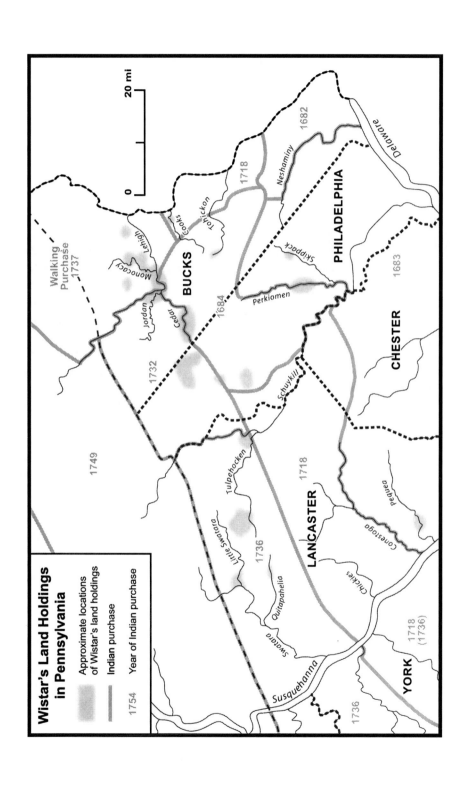

Wistar's Land Holdings
in Pennsylvania

Approximate locations
of Wistar's land holdings

Indian purchase

1754   Year of Indian purchase

Walking
Purchase
1737

1749

1732

1684

1682

1718

1683

BUCKS

PHILADELPHIA

CHESTER

LANCASTER

YORK

1718

1718
(1736)

1736

1736

20 mi

0

Lehigh

Monocacy

Cooks

Tohickon

Neshaminy

Delaware

Jordan

Cedar

Perkiomen

Skippack

Schuylkill

Tulpehocken

Little Swatara

Quitapahelia

Swatara

Susquehanna

Conestoga

Pequea

Chickies

of his property to German-speaking immigrants and their descendants. All of those who bought Wistar's Philadelphia County land had German names.[28] A similar overwhelming majority of the people purchasing his real estate in the areas that became Berks, Bucks, Lancaster, Montgomery, and Northampton counties were German immigrants or their children.[29] In buying land from the proprietors and reselling it to fellow immigrants, Wistar assumed financial risks for the Penns. He paid the proprietors cash and extended credit through mortgages and bonds to the immigrants purchasing his acreage.[30]

In addition, Wistar provided the funds necessary for the proprietors to purchase Native American land. In several instances he paid for property before the Penns had bought it from the Indians. His first investment in "unimproved" Pennsylvania property was surveyed in six tracts. Among these were two parcels in Maxatawny and Macungy, located in territory that still belonged to the Delaware Indians.[31] During Steel's visit to London in 1729 and 1730, the proprietors agreed to grant Wistar an additional 2,271 acres, more than one-third of which was surveyed on Delaware land.[32] Wistar solved, at least in part, the debt-ridden Penns' problem of how to raise revenue so that they could earn a profit from their Pennsylvania claims. He was willing to ignore Indian claims and risk receiving clear titles to his new property as long as he could purchase it early. In turn, his money furnished the Penns with the capital they desperately needed to negotiate for Indian lands on which squatters were already settling.[33]

Driven by the potential profits from his real estate investments, Wistar eagerly participated in at least one of the Penns' less successful and more controversial revenue raising strategies—the Lottery Scheme of 1735. Facing debtors' prison

28. The only exception was a deed between Wistar and Nicholas Skull (Philadelphia County Deeds, H-11:126) for a tract of land in the Forks of the Delaware which was in Bucks County but recorded in the Philadelphia County deed book. Philadelphia County Deeds, F-5:176, 290, 291; F-6:142, 463; F-8:157; G-1:54, 122, 147, 209; G-1:54–55; G-4:265; G-6:522; G-7:720; G-9:256; H-3:232; H-5:32, 38; H-10:302; H-12:142; H-15:496; I-2:403; I-7:337; I-10:330; I-15:398, 402; I-16:160. All county deed citations are taken from microfilm copies at the HSP or PSA.

29. See the deeds for those counties indexed under Wistar as grantor.

30. Lancaster County Deeds, B:160–62, 452–53; A:85, 88; C:122–24, 275–78; Philadelphia County Wills, bk. I, 493, microfilm copy, HSP.

31. Patent Bk. A-6:106; Philadelphia County Deeds, F-5:176–78, 290–92; F-6:463–65, 469. At least two of these tracts were in what later became Berks and Lehigh counties. The "Commonwealth of Pennsylvania, Genealogical Map of the Counties," printed by the Historical and Museum Commission, shows that this land was purchased from the Indians on October 11, 1736. According to Francis Jennings, however, this "purchase" was a release signed by the Iroquois to any right they had to the land. In fact, the land belonged to the Delaware Indians. Francis Jennings, *The Ambiguous Iroquois Empire: The Covenant Chain Confederation of Indian Tribes with English Colonies from Its Beginnings to the Lancaster Treaty of 1744* (New York: W. W. Norton, 1984), 322–24.

32. Francis Jennings, "The Scandalous Indian Policy of William Penn's Sons: Deeds and Documents of the Walking Purchase," *PA Hist* 37 (1970): 22.

33. Jennings, "Scandalous Indian Policy," 21–24.

in England, John Penn fled to Philadelphia in 1734. He brought along a detailed design for a land lottery in which "adventurers" could purchase a forty-shilling ticket to win tracts in unsettled territory. The original scheme included 100,000 acres and was to provide the Penns with £15,000 in revenues. The winning ticket holders were to receive parcels calculated at a rate of £15.10 per hundred acres. They could locate their tracts anywhere in the province except on "Manor land, already surveyed or agreed for with the Proprietors or their Agents, or that have been actually settled and improved" before the date of the drawing.[34]

Unfortunately for the Penns, the scheme did not prove popular. In fact, Thomas Penn discovered that Pennsylvania had a statute against lotteries.[35] In October 1736, one of the lottery's managers observed to John Penn that the "Drawing [of] itt is totally supprese'd and the money paid for the Tickets (by the intended adventurers) is now to be returned [to] them except they accept of lands on the terms in the proposals." He thought some purchasers might agree to take land but others would request refunds.[36]

Wistar was one of the purchasers willing to accept land on the terms of the original scheme. Between 1735 and 1752 he bought nearly 6,000 acres through lottery tickets.[37] The Penns, however, still needed desperately to buy additional Indian territory, and for that they needed more funds. To help remedy their financial woes, Thomas Penn held a "small and secret lottery" in which he sold tracts belonging to the Delaware Indians in the area between the Lehigh and the Delaware rivers (known as the Forks of the Delaware). The purchasers were "confined to eight close proprietary associates" who each received 500-acre tracts.[38] Penn then used dubious copies of documents to convince the Delawares

34. "Proposal for Lottery Scheme," Aug. 16, 1735, Patent Bk. A-7:224–26, 239–40.

35. "Case about a Lottery of Lands in America, with Mr. Scry Eyres Opinion," Documents Removed from Boxes, carton 8, box 28–#8, 13, RG-17, Records of the Land Office, PSA; Thomas Penn to John Penn, Sept. 10, 1736, Penn Mss., Correspondence of the Penn Family, vol. 18, p. 26, Penn Papers, HSP; Jennings, "Scandalous Indian Policy," 26–36; Munger, *Pennsylvania Land,* 71–73; Asa E. Martin, "Lotteries in Pennsylvania Prior to 1833," *PMHB* 47 (1923): 309–13.

36. Clement Plumsted to John Penn, Oct. 4, 1736, PPOC, 3:25, HSP.

37. Survey Bk. D-88:255 lists individual tracts totaling 5,100 "surveyed to Caspar Wistar on the Lottery Scheme." Survey Bk. D-88:156 includes a note from Richard Peters dated 12 Nov. 1744: "Reicd of Caspar Wistar twenty seven Lottery Tickets wch wth four hundred recd by James Steele amount to 1854 for wch he has had already surveyed 5099 as & 100 ps & I have this day given him a Warrant for the remaining 410 as wch compleats his Lottery Land & is in full of all accounts." Nevertheless, Wistar received at least an additional 487 acres warranted to him on the lottery scheme after 1744. Patent Bk. A-16:137–38, 419–22.

38. Jennings, "Scandalous Indian Policy," 35; Jennings, *Ambiguous Iroquois Empire,* 334–35, 390–95. Jennings carefully documents his research; nevertheless, his claim that the Penns held a small, secret lottery differs significantly from Munger's argument that Pennsylvanians used lottery tickets to purchase land throughout the colony (Munger, *Pennsylvania Land,* 73). No doubt the Penns did keep their lottery land transactions in the Forks of the Delaware secret since they had not yet cleared the territory of Indian claims. But notes for "lottery land" in the registers of warrants and surveys suggest that the

that the founder William Penn had already bought the land but that the boundaries had never been established. According to his documents, the bounds of the sale were supposed to have been measured by the distance a man could walk in a day and a half. By the time the Delawares agreed to set the boundaries, Penn had already hired men who cleared a pathway and conducted a trial walk. When the official walk took place on September 19 and 20, 1737, it encompassed much more territory than the Delawares intended. The boundaries included lands south of the Lehigh River and in the Forks of the Delaware, where lottery ticket purchasers had already selected and paid for large tracts.[39]

Not surprisingly, Wistar was also one of the proprietors' "close associates" who participated in the secret lottery. Clearly he had become an insider among Pennsylvania's elite.[40] On October 14 and 15, 1736, a full year before the infamous Walking Purchase, three 500-acre plots were surveyed for him on the Lehigh River and Monacasy Creek in the Forks of the Delaware. The wording of Wistar's patent for the property, received in 1742, indicated that it was lottery land laid out before it was cleared of Indian claims.[41] Wistar also managed to obtain additional tracts within the Walking Purchase. He bought more than 1,000 acres located on Cooks Creek and Indian Coplay's Creek.[42] Clearly Wistar was more concerned with the profits his investments would bring than with the ethics of the proprietors' actions or the Native Americans he was displacing.

One set of land transactions in particular demonstrates the complex ways Wistar's speculation resolved the problems of immigration, Indian claims, legal titles, and funding for the Penns. In the mid-1720s, the German-speaking immigrants who had settled in the Tulpehocken Valley petitioned Governor Keith. They requested that "upon paying the usual prices for lands at such distance from Philadelphia, we may have sufficient rights and titles made to us for such lands as we shall have occasion to buy." Furthermore, they wanted their purchases to "be freed from the demands of the Indians of that part of the country

---

Penns continued to sell acreage through lottery tickets to others outside of any secret drawing. Wistar's documents, including Richard Peters's comment in note 37, suggest both interpretations may be valid. The "small and secret lottery" Jennings posits was likely held for the land within the Walking Purchase whereas other land already cleared of Indian claims was sold openly through lottery tickets.

39. Jennings, "Scandalous Indian Policy," 19–39; Jennings, *Ambiguous Iroquois Empire,* 325–46; Anthony F. C. Wallace, *King of the Delawares: Teedyuscung, 1700–1763* (Syracuse: Syracuse University Press, 1990; orig. pub. 1949), 13–30.

40. Wistar won the patronage of the proprietary family during a period of relatively peaceful relations between the colony's leading Quakers and proprietors. When political alliances shifted at the end of the 1730s, Wistar's position also moved. Tully, *William Penn's Legacy,* 17–20.

41. Patent Bk. A-10:405–7; Jennings, "Scandalous Indian Policy," 35–36. The patent states that the "tracts were, by agreement some time since made, surveyed to Caspar Wistar." Jennings argues that this language indicates participation in the secret lottery.

42. Patent Bk. A-8:387–88; A-10:402–5; Survey Bk. D-88:223, 252–54; D-88:226–28, 239–40.

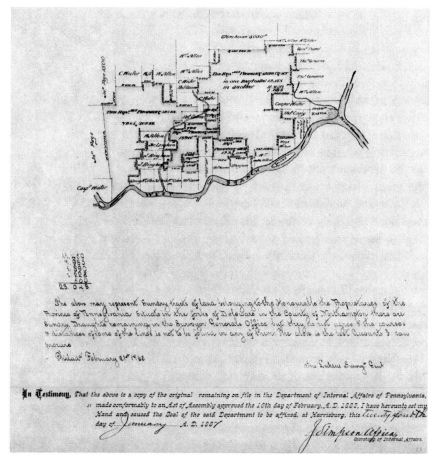

FIG. 12 Proprietaries land in the Forks of the Delaware, 1763. RG-17: Bureau of Land Records, Map Collection no. 3336. Courtesy of the Pennsylvania Museum and Historical Commission, Pennsylvania State Archives.

who pretend a right thereto."[43] At the time, William Penn's estate was tied up in court. Logan suggested that, until the Penns' mortgage was paid off, the commissioners of property could not "comprehend how ye Titles from us can be good and to take Money w[i]thout giving Titles would be unjust and therefore is not to be expected from us."[44] Nor did the family have the funds to clear the land of Indian claims.[45]

43. *MPC*, 3:241; PPOC, 1:137, HSP. The petition is reprinted in Earl W. Ibach, *The Hub of the Tulpe-hocken* (Earl W. Ibach, 1976), 11.

44. James Logan to John Penn, Sept. 11, 1728, James Logan Letterbook, 4:196–97, Logan Papers, HSP.

45. Francis Jennings, "Incident at Tulpehocken," *PA History* 35 (1968): 335–39.

Family politics further complicated Tulpehocken circumstances. Shortly after the "Palatines" moved to the region, William Penn's daughter Letitia and her husband William Aubrey prepared to sell 10,000 acres she had received from the founder as a legacy. The property was surveyed in the Tulpehocken Valley in Letitia Aubrey's name without regard to the Delaware Indians who owned it. In 1727, an additional 10,000 acres was surveyed in adjacent tracts for Gulielma Fell, Penn's granddaughter, as part of her inheritance. Logan, who recognized the value of the land and wanted to obtain some of the profits for himself, began negotiating privately with the resident Germans. He agreed to sell one parcel for the exorbitant price of £40 Pennsylvania currency per hundred acres. He also tried unsuccessfully to purchase the land privately from Sasoonan, one of the Delawares who owned it. When the Penns discovered his scheme, however, they acted decisively to thwart his efforts. The Aubreys sold their land to an English buyer and ordered a new survey directly, circumventing Logan, who usually approved warrants for surveys. The Fells granted Thomas Penn power of attorney to sell their Pennsylvania property on their behalf.[46]

Soon after Thomas Penn's arrival in the colony, Wistar bought the Fells' tract. Penn first negotiated with the Tulpehocken Delaware Indians for their land and then began the necessary steps to complete the sale. In January 1735, all of the parties who held an interest in the land granted Wistar the full 10,000 acres. The Fells, William Penn (the founder's grandson), Thomas Penn, as well as the two remaining trustees of the founder's estate, Logan and Samuel Preston, all participated in the transaction. The agreement cleared the proprietary title to the land, a fact the Penns recognized the following day when they issued a patent to Wistar confirming his sole ownership of Fells' Manor.[47] Within a week, Wistar contracted with Thomas Penn to buy the property. He agreed to pay Penn £1818 sterling with interest in six installments.[48]

Through his purchase, Wistar helped the Penns clear their land of Indian claims, satisfy William Penn's legacy, and net a higher profit than the other land they were selling—all while keeping Logan from encroaching on their profits. His acquisition of Fells' Manor also aided the Tulpehocken Germans in receiving clear titles to their lands. Although it took years and a high price to

46. Jennings, "Incident at Tulpehocken," 343–54; John Taylor's Survey, Nov. 2, 1727, Survey Bk. B-23:83; Tripartite Indenture, Jan. 3, 1733, Documents Removed from Boxes, carton 8, box 27–#8, 19, RG-17, Records of the Land Office; Survey Bk. B-18:1–2, PSA.

47. Philadelphia County Deeds, F-7:195–203; Patent Bk. A-7:486; the original document is in MS-5, Penn Deeds, P-19, PSA.

48. Lease and release, Jan. 26 and Jan. 27, 1736, Library of the Museum of Wheaton Village, Millville, N.J.; Lancaster County Deeds, A:6–9. See also warrant for survey and return, Dec. 10, 1734, Survey Bk. D-75:290, 300; undated survey, Survey Bk. B-22:198, PSA.

accomplish their goals, they secured the sole ownership of their farms through Wistar's deeds of conveyance.[49]

Wistar came out a winner too. Fells' Manor provided him with tidy returns on his investment. The German immigrants had been living in the Tulpehocken Valley for more than a decade when Wistar invested in the land. They had sufficient funds to pay for their "improvements." Wistar negotiated sales and probably already had received payments from the immigrants long before he actually paid Thomas Penn.[50] The profits he made on his Tulpehocken transactions were extraordinary. Including interest, he paid Penn £22 per hundred acres and nearly doubled his investment when he received on average £40 per hundred acres from his fellow immigrants (the same exorbitant price Logan had failed to receive).[51] His returns on Fells' Manor were modest compared to other investments. In one 1729 purchase of 2,000 acres, Wistar netted nearly 200 percent from the 698 acres he sold. The remaining plantation with its cattle he later willed to one of his daughters.[52] In another instance, he paid £12 Pennsylvania currency per hundred acres and resold it at a rate of £50 per hundred.[53]

In addition to furnishing tremendous wealth, Wistar's land speculation allowed him to become a patron within the Pennsylvania German community. He used his capital, connections to proprietary agents, and ethnic identity to mediate between the immigrants and the provincial government and to fashion a position of power.[54]

Frequent and steady land purchases throughout the 1730s and 1740s required Wistar to pay regular visits to the commissioners of property and other government officials. In his first three years of speculating, Wistar requested three warrants for surveys, had eleven tracts surveyed on his behalf, received two patents,

49. Berks County Deeds, A-1:5–9, 11–13, 107–9, 256–58, 312–14, 321–23, 349; A-2:42–45, 392–94; A-5:71–72, 103–6; Berks County Deeds, 8:101–3; 15:410–11, 489–90; 16:14–16; 18:93; 69:223; Lancaster County Deeds, C:178–80, 318; D:154; E:6, 187; H:2, 171–72, 388–89.

50. See, e.g., Berks County Deeds, A-1:11–13. In 1743, Wistar conveyed to Catharine Rith land that her husband had paid for during his lifetime.

51. Indenture, Nov. 10, 1737, Philadelphia County Deeds, G-4:40–48; deeds dating from Dec. 2, 1738 to Dec. 10, 1745, Berks County Deeds, A-1:5–9, 11–13, 107–9, 256–58, 312–14, 321–23, 349; A-2:42–45, 392–94; A-5:71–72, 103–6; Berks County Deeds, 8:101–3; 15:410–11, 489–90; 16:14–16; 18:93; 69:223; Lancaster County Deeds, C:178–80, 318; D:154; E:6, 187; H:2, 171–72, 388–89.

52. Philadelphia County Deeds, F-5:176–78, 290–92; F-6:463–65, 469; G-7:120–22; Philadelphia County Wills, bk. I, 493, microfilm copy, HSP.

53. Patent Bk. A-6:162; Philadelphia County Deeds, F-6:142–43; G-1:122–23, 147–49, 209–11; G-4:265–67; G-9:256–58; Berks County Deeds, A-1:31–34; A-2:326–28.

54. Wistar fits the pattern of early arrivals from the Kraichgau and Palatinate who acted as "brokers" for later German-speaking immigrants. Roeber, *Palatines,* 3.

and sold seven parcels of real estate.[55] Each transaction required negotiations with men in the land office. His initial pace of purchases was moderate when compared to that of the next decade. Between 1733 and 1743, Wistar and his wife signed more than thirty-five deeds conveying land to German-speaking buyers. County and provincial officials frequently acted as witnesses to their sales.[56] In addition, Wistar received ten patents for "unimproved" land and purchased at least five parcels of land that were already "improved" and patented.[57]

In the process, Wistar became well acquainted with proprietary appointees and sought to use these relationships for his own benefit. As early as 1730, the Penns referred to him as a "friend" of James Steel, their receiver general. They agreed to sell him land on Steel's recommendation.[58] After Thomas Penn arrived in the colony, Wistar negotiated directly with the proprietors to purchase property. During the same year he invested in Fells' Manor, for example, he bought a prime Philadelphia city lot from the three Penn brothers.[59] By the late 1730s he had agreed privately with Benjamin Eastburn, Pennsylvania's surveyor general, "to be jointly concern'd in taking up Lands to the amount of a certain Sum of Money, Caspar to advance 2/3ds & Benj. the other." Since Eastburn was the surveyor, he "was to be at the trouble of taking up the choicest tracts he could find and the Benefit was to be equally divided."[60] Wistar became so well known in Pennsylvania's land office that government officials filed his documents separately, a practice they observed with other prominent speculators.[61] Like his father, who had sought the favor of local government officials, Wistar used his connections to those in power to improve his economic status.

Wistar also fashioned his role as a mediator through his frequent land-speculating trips into Philadelphia's surrounding countryside. In November 1733, he explained to one correspondent that, although he was primarily a brazier and brass button maker, he was "often away from home one or two or three weeks

55. Patent Bk. A-6:106, 162; Survey Bk. D-88, 142, 155, 157, 206–8, 224–25, 231–32, 248, 250, 259, 261–64, 265, 272, 274–78; Philadelphia County Deeds, F-5:176–78; F-5:290–92; F-6:142–43, 463–65, 469; G-7:720–22; Berks County Deeds, A-2:46–48.

56. Philadelphia County Deeds, F-8:157; G-1:54–55, 122–23, 147–49, 209–11; G-4:265–67; G-9:256–58; H-5:32–34; H-19:302–4; Berks County Deeds, A-1:5–9, 31–34, 107–9, 321–23, 349; A-2:42–44, 326–28, 392–94; A-5:103–6; 8:101–3; 15:410–11; 16:14–16; 18:93; 69:223; Lancaster County Deeds, A:19–30; C:13, 318; D:154; E:6, 187; H:2, 388–89.

57. Patent Bk. A-3:351–53; A-7:2–5, 257–59, 486; A-8:354–56; A-9:164–66; A-10:247–51, 402–7; Philadelphia County Deeds, F-7:195–203; F-8:261; G-4:40–48; G-5:442–44; G-6:522–25; G-12:25–29; Lancaster County Deeds, A:4–9.

58. Survey Bk. D-88:207–8, PSA; John, Thomas, and Richard Penn to James Steel, Thomas Penn Letter Books, 1 (1729–42), 27, Penn Papers, HSP.

59. Patent Bk. A-7:257–59, PSA.

60. Richard Peters to Thomas Penn, Oct. 17, 1742, Richard Peters Letterbook, 1741–43, 36b, Peters Papers, HSP.

61. Munger, Pennsylvania Land, 66–67.

at a time."[62] Many of his land transactions were in areas where immigrants had already cleared the land and built houses. The Tulpehocken Germans, for example, had settled on Fells' Manor well over a decade before Wistar bought the land from Penn. Immigrants also lived in Macungy by the time he invested in real estate there.[63] In the process of buying and selling land, Wistar had ample opportunity to meet fellow immigrants.

Wistar's familiarity with the German-speaking community was not confined to those living in Pennsylvania. He did not formally advertise the properties he sold, but he did send information about Pennsylvania to prospective European settlers. After one ship of immigrants arrived in 1731 under particularly gruesome conditions, Wistar wrote a letter that was subsequently published throughout Europe. He felt "compelled, out of sympathy for the poor people, who are yet in the Fatherland" to give them an accurate account of "what it means to remove to this new land."[64] Wistar noted that in the past Pennsylvania was a little-inhabited colony where immigrants could purchase large parcels of property for small sums of money. Now, however, a growing number of immigrants were filling up the land and as a result new settlers needed to go farther into the "wilderness" to find affordable property. In general, Wistar painted a rather negative picture of American conditions for prospective immigrants.

Although he discouraged further German migration out of genuine sympathy for fellow immigrants, Wistar also encouraged a more selective decision-making process that would serve his interests better over time. He advised those Europeans who were willing to face the harsh conditions of the voyage to insure they could pay for the journey and have enough money left over to purchase supplies. "Let no one depend on his friends [who] may be here, for these have all they can do to get through themselves," he warned.[65] As a land speculator, Wistar wanted to sell his acreage for a profit. Lowering people's expectations prior to immigration increased his chances of finding buyers willing to pay a higher price for his land in the "wilderness." The straightforwardness and honest tone of Wistar's letter spread his reputation as a trustworthy patron among members of the immigrant community even before they arrived in Pennsylvania.

62. Wistar to Johann Martin Franck, Nov. 10, 1733, Wistar Family Papers, HSP.
63. W. W. H. Davis, *The History of Bucks County, Pennsylvania from the Discovery of the Delaware to the Present Time* (1905), chap. 32—accessed Dec. 12, 2003, at ftp://ftp.rootsweb.com/pub/usgenweb/pa/bucks/history/local/davis/davis30.txt.
64. Wistar to potential immigrants, Nov. 8, 1732, in *Perkiomen Region, Past and Present* 2 (Nov. 15, 1899):119–20. Wistar's letter was written on the "4th of the Winter month, 1732" and was first printed in a Leipzig newspaper on May 22, 1733. It was printed in Switzerland in 1734. A partial draft of the letter is in the Wistar Family Papers, HSP. See also *Pennsylvania German Society Proceedings and Address* 8 (1897): 141–44.
65. Ibid.

Given his connections to colonial authorities and his growing reputation among Germans, it is not surprising that Wistar began to mediate between Pennsylvania's immigrants and government officials. At the most basic level, he vouched for the reputations of fellow Germans or paid the proprietors money on their behalf. In 1728, for example, he submitted payment for John Herr, one of the German founders of the Mennonite settlement in Lancaster County.[66] The following year he recommended Thomas Hean as "an honest man that will pay" for his land if the commissioners of property agreed to have it surveyed.[67] Wistar's remittances for other people increased after Thomas Penn arrived in the colony in 1732. Whether he was acting as a collector for the Penns or extending credit to those whose debts he paid is not always clear. In one case Wistar most likely acted as courier when he submitted money for his father-in-law, who assumed a debt for a German settler.[68] In other instances, he simply made payments to the Penns "for" a debtor or paid cash to their accounts.[69]

Wistar's role as intermediary also worked in the other direction. At times, he represented the proprietors and their interests to German-speaking immigrants. In 1734, Wistar escorted Baron Philip Georg Friederich von Reck from Philadelphia to Trenton on Governor Gordon's orders. Von Reck had led a group of German-speaking refugees to Georgia and was returning to Europe. He used the opportunity to travel through the colonies and raise funds for the new settlement in Georgia. After visiting the governor and Thomas Penn, "a large group of upright people from Germantown" accompanied him on his way toward New Jersey. Von Reck and Wistar journeyed alone from Bristol, however. As they traveled, Wistar described the opportunities Pennsylvania provided for potential immigrants. He claimed that "the land is very fertile . . . and grain grows well."[70] Most likely the patronage he had won among Pennsylvania's officials and his ethnic identity made Wistar the choice escort.

Wistar's mediation between government officials and immigrants frequently concerned land issues. In 1736, Steel wrote to John Penn that he "repeatedly Spoke to Caspar Wistar & N[icholas] Scull about [the] Perkasie Lands." The Penns had been contemplating selling the property to a group of Schwenkfelder immigrants who had arrived a few years earlier. Steel reported that "they both say that it might be sold in parcells, as well thy own as that belonging

66. Account of John Herr, Apr. 6, 1728; PA Journals, 1:61, Penn Papers, HSP.

67. *Minutes*, 19:761.

68. Account of Martin Funk, Mar. 13, 1735, PA Journals, 1:188, Penn Papers, HSP.

69. Account of Derrick Jansen, Aug. 22, 1733, PA Journals, 1:100; Account of Henry Reiser, July 5, 1735, PA Journals, 1:158; Account of Henry Reizer, Aug. 12, 1735, PA Journals, 1:162; Account of Henry Carpenter, Jan. 3, 1736, PA Journals, 1:180, Penn Papers, HSP.

70. George Jones, ed., *Detailed Reports on the Salzburger Emigrants Who Settled in America . . . Edited by Samuel Urlsperger*, vol. 1 *1733–1734* (Athens, Ga: University of Georgia Press, 1968), 121–22.

to thy Brother Richard, at the prices mentioned in thy Letter."[71] By the mid-1730s Wistar was familiar enough with Pennsylvania's undeveloped land and the immigrant market that the Penn's agents sought his advice.

Other members of the Anglo-American elite understood Wistar's role as land speculator and mediator, too. In 1738, Virginian William Byrd II wrote to John Bartram, a Pennsylvania naturalist, "I expect every day the arrival of a little ship with Switzers and Germans to settle upon part of my Land at Roanoke." They had purchased one block of his land, but "there are 72,000 [acres] remaining, to which your friend, Caspar Wistar, is very welcome, if He or any of his Countrymen are so inclined."[72] Bartram had shown Byrd's description of his land to "several as I came home & in town [to] my friend Casper Wister to whom many of ye Palatines resorts both for advice and assistance."[73] Bartram and Byrd, like the Pennsylvania proprietors, understood Wistar's leadership position among the immigrant community.

By the late 1730s, the Penns relied on Wistar's ethnic identity and loyalty in dealing with German settlers living in the region disputed by the Maryland and Pennsylvania proprietors. Throughout the decade a series of violent and at times deadly conflicts erupted west of the Susquehanna River. The tension frequently revolved around Thomas Cressap, who claimed to represent Maryland's government. A group of fifty or sixty German immigrants living in the region became caught in the middle of the power struggle. They had sworn their allegiance to the Pennsylvania proprietors when they arrived in Philadelphia. In the meantime, Cressap convinced them that their land was in Maryland and surveyed it, apparently without official authority. After they received no legal documents from Maryland for their land and in the face of growing harassment and violence, the Germans resumed their allegiance to the Penns in 1736.[74]

Pennsylvania officials finally arrested Cressap in September 1736 on murder charges. His capture did not immediately quell hostilities, however. Charles Higgenbothom, another Marylander, continued "Cressap's War" by terrorizing

71. James Steel to John Penn, Sept. 14, 1736, PPOC, 3:9, HSP. For a fascinating account of German immigrants shopping for Pennsylvania land, see "Diary of Christopher Wiegner," Joseph Downs Collection, Henry Francis DuPont Winterthur Museum Library, Winterthur, Del., 143–50.

72. William Byrd II to John Bartram, Nov. 30, 1738, in Edmund Berkeley and Dorothy S. Berkeley, eds., *The Correspondence of John Bartram, 1734–1777* (Gainesville: University of Florida Press, 1992), 101.

73. John Bartram to William Byrd, [Nov. 1738], in Berkeley and Berkeley, *John Bartram*, 98–99.

74. Lawrence Wroth, "The Story of Thomas Cresap, A Maryland Pioneer," *Maryland Historical Magazine* 9 (1914): 1–37; Paul Doutrich, "Cresap's War: Expansion and Conflict in the Susquehanna Valley," *PA Hist* 53 (1986): 89–104; Charles Dutrizac, "Local Identity and Authority in a Disputed Hinterland: The Pennsylvania-Maryland Border in the 1730s," *PMHB* 115 (1991): 35–61; Thomas Slaughter, "Crowds in Eighteenth-Century America: Reflections and New Directions," *PMHB* 115 (1991): 13–18; Willis Shirk, "Wright's Ferry: A Glimpse into the Susquehanna Backcountry," *PMHB* 120 (1996): 67–69.

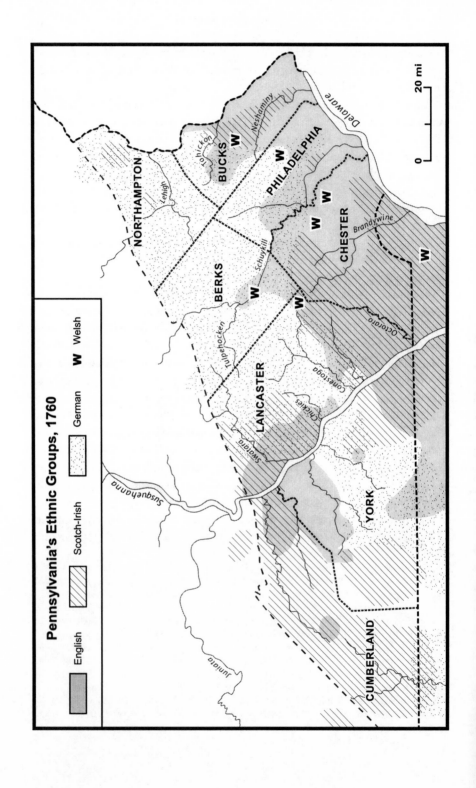

Pennsylvania's Ethnic Groups, 1760

English
Scotch-Irish
German
W Welsh

20 mi

NORTHAMPTON

BUCKS

PHILADELPHIA

CHESTER

BERKS

LANCASTER

YORK

CUMBERLAND

Delaware

Neshaminy

Tohickon

Lehigh

Schuylkill

Brandywine

Octoraro

Tulpehocken

Conestoga

Chickies

Swatara

Susquehanna

Juniata

W

settlers in the region and arresting them for not paying their taxes. He participated in a scheme to reclaim their "plantations" and sell them to Pennsylvania investors willing to move west of the Susquehanna under the auspices of the Maryland government. In December, Higgenbothom surprised a group of families who were burying a child and carried six men to jail in Annapolis. Four of the six were German-speaking immigrants.[75]

Glimpses of Wistar's role as mediator emerge in early 1737, at the height of the conflict. During their incarceration, Maryland officials had tried to turn the prisoners against the Penns by claiming that, during their attempts to arrest him, the Pennsylvanians had burned Cressap's house without warning him to get out. Wistar defended the proprietors' interests and government officials' actions and tried to convince his fellow immigrants to remain loyal to the Penns. Thomas Penn reported that "Caspar set several right" about what had happened "and twas of some use."[76] Wistar apparently also escorted some of the prisoners home from Annapolis. On February 28, Steel reimbursed him for travel expenses and cash he had advanced to the prisoners while on their journey.[77]

Wistar's defense of the Penns, however, was also in his own interests. His land holdings along the Swatara and Tulpehocken creeks were just east of the Susquehanna River. Wistar probably concurred with Samuel Blunston, a Lancaster County justice of the peace, who warned the Penns to think about their actions carefully. Blunston begged the proprietors to consider the "Effect it might have on the Inhabitants of this Side [east] of the River" if they did not defend their claims on the west side. He feared Lancaster's residents would use such a failure as "a pretence to question the proprietors Claim to the Lands" on the Lancaster side.[78] Such possibilities also made Wistar vulnerable. He had already contracted to purchase 10,000 acres in the Tulpehocken Valley.

75. Samuel Hazard, ed., *PA Archives*, ser. 1, *Selected and Arranged from Original Documents in the Office of the Secretary of the Commonwealth* (hereafter *Original Documents*), vol. 1, *1664–1747* (Philadelphia: Joseph Severns, 1852), 316–20, 492–94, 504–6, 508–9, 513–16, 522–28, 536–38; "Petition of 63 persons natives of Germany inhabiting near the River Susquehannah," Dec. 1736, Society Miscellaneous Collection, Petitions, box 4b, f. 4, HSP; James Steel's Letterbook, 1730–41, 127, Logan Papers, HSP; Thomas Penn, 1730–67, box 2 (unbound MSS), Penn Papers; *MPC*, 4:149–54; James Steel to Thomas Noxon, Jan. 28, 1737, James Steel's Letterbook, 1730–41, 129–30, Logan Papers, HSP.

76. Thomas Penn to [Samuel Blunston?], Jan. 20, 1736/7, Thomas Penn, 1730–67, box 2 (unbound MSS), file #38, Penn Papers, HSP. Thomas Penn wrote to James Steel, "I think it might be well for some German to write to those now in Annapolis Gaol to advise them to be as easy as possible under their present confinement, because it may not be so necessary to have them as immediately bailed; they should not want, yet tis necessary they should be very frugal." Wistar may have written to the imprisoned Germans on Penn's behalf. Thomas Penn to James Steel, Feb. 10, 1736/7, Thomas Penn, 1730–67, box 2 (unbound MSS), Penn Papers, HSP.

77. Account of James Steel with Caspar Wistar, Feb. 28, 1736/7, Penn-Baily Collection, HSP.

78. Samuel Blunston to Gov. Gordon, [Dec. 1736], *Original Documents*, 1:316–20.

Although Wistar argued for loyalty to the proprietors in 1737, over the next several years his own position began to shift. In 1738, the Baltimores and Penns reached a compromise on the border dispute, and Pennsylvania's political climate changed. Thomas Penn immediately set out to reform proprietary land policies. He issued a mandate requiring colonists who had not paid for the land to remit remaining balances within a short period or face legal proceedings. Simultaneously, he replaced several well-known and trusted proprietary officials with outsiders less sympathetic to the colonists' interests. In early 1739, news reached Pennsylvania that Britain was at war. Tensions between the Quaker-dominated assembly and the proprietors' supporters, led by prominent Anglicans, grew when the Quakers refused to allocate money for a militia. Proprietary officials tried to unseat the Quaker majority in the assembly so they could win funding for military efforts. As a result, the elections of the early 1740s became hotly contested, tumultuous affairs.[79]

By 1742, Wistar was no longer supporting proprietary policy, and he held sufficient power among the German-speaking community to influence their loyalties. In previous years, most of the immigrants had voted for the Quaker ticket in legislative elections. Many of the earliest arrivals belonged to religious groups who shared the Quakers' pacifist positions. The more recent arrivals, however, were Reformed and Lutheran and had fewer scruples against going to war. The proprietary faction worked hard to win their votes. Nevertheless, when Germans from the outlying regions arrived in Philadelphia for the 1742 election, they sided with the Quakers.[80]

Wistar, his brother John, and Christopher Sauer, another German-speaking immigrant, helped to ruin the tenuous coalition of support the proprietary party constructed. According to Richard Peters, an Anglican and one of the Penns' officials, Sauer "poyson'd all the Dutch" by publishing both a translation of the Militia Act for the Lower Counties and a table of fines for colonists delinquent in paying for their land. "The Dutch who came occasionaly to Town," he continued, "were told by the Wisters that numbers were in Jayle in the Lower Counties for not paying their Fines & . . . That the Proprs intended to make use of the Militia to eject such as could not pay of their Possessions." Peters was convinced that "these storys were greedily swallowed by those ignorant People" and then reinforced by Sauer when the immigrants returned home through Germantown.[81]

79. Tully, *William Penn's Legacy*, 3–32; Fogleman, *Hopeful Journeys*, 135–40; Schwartz, "*Mixed Multitude*," 159–73.

80. Tully, *William Penn's Legacy*, 32–38; Schwartz, "*Mixed Multitude*," 173–76. For a discussion of German immigrants and the franchise, see Fogleman, *Hopeful Journeys*, 31–39.

81. Richard Peters Letterbook, 1741–43, 28, Peters Papers, HSP; Parsons, "Bloody Election," 290–306.

Peters's assessment of Wistar's role was likely accurate. Between the fall elections in 1741 and those in 1742, Wistar had finalized land sales with fourteen of the Tulpehocken Germans who were buying their Fells' Manor land.[82] The sudden flurry of land transactions was no coincidence. Many of the Germans had migrated in search of inexpensive land and to escape oppressive taxes imposed by aristocratic landlords. As the Penns tightened their land policies, the immigrants became increasingly concerned about their tenuous hold on their properties. Furthermore, the Penns had been slow to react to violence against German colonists west of the Susquehanna only a few years earlier. In that case, people had been imprisoned and lost their lives in skirmishes over land titles. If war did reach the Tulpehocken Valley, a militia would not be able to protect property that the immigrants could prove no legal right to hold in the first place. The possible threat of being forcibly ejected from their farms encouraged them to complete legal land transactions, apply for naturalization, and use their rights to vote for those they thought would serve their interests best.[83]

By the early 1740s, Wistar had used his investments in Pennsylvania land to become more than a mediator. Combining his credit, capital, and connections to people in power with his ethnic identity and reputation among German-speaking immigrants, he fashioned a position for himself as a patron. Wistar's land speculation granted him wealth unheard of in Pennsylvania's merchant community or in the Palatinate's forestry department. When he died in 1752, Wistar bequeathed his wife and six children cash disbursements totaling £4,450 Pennsylvania currency, eleven city lots, and more than 5,000 acres of land. Each child received at least one city lot in Philadelphia and tracts in the surrounding counties. While many of Philadelphia's leading Quakers sought to leave legacies of land to all of their children, Wistar's bequests were unusual in their size and value.[84]

In part, Wistar's ability to position himself as a patron resulted from the luck of his timing. Philadelphia's economic conditions allowed for relatively easy social mobility for Anglo and European settlers in the 1720s, during Wistar's early years in the colony. The chaotic state of proprietary affairs provided him with ample room to maneuver. Had he arrived in the 1730s or 1740s, his experience likely would have been different. Nevertheless, Wistar's Palatine background was critical in shaping his actions in colonial Pennsylvania. The constricting nature of village life in Waldhilsbach, where his father struggled with

---

82. Berks County Deeds, A-1:5–9, 107–9; A-2:42–44, 392–94; A-5:103–6; 8:101–3; 16:16, 410–11; 18:93; 69:223; Lancaster County Deeds, C:318; E:187.

83. Fogleman, *Hopeful Journeys*, 125–42.

84. Philadelphia County Wills, bk. I, 493, microfilm copy, HSP.

his neighbors for every ounce of political or social status; his father's role as a forester, in which he constantly played man-in-the-middle; and Wistar's view of land as a marketable commodity fostered by his training as a forester and hunter—each informed Wistar's responses to Pennsylvania's circumstances. His European experience and knowledge shaped his persistent pursuit of property and patronage and his shrewd and savvy manipulation of his ethnic identity. In turn, Wistar's ethnic identity, individual decisions, and land purchases shaped the colony's landscape. His mediation between the proprietors and his fellow immigrants resulted in Pennsylvania German enclaves that stretched in an arc through Philadelphia's hinterland.

MY ESPECIALLY DEAR SIR AND MOST WORTHY FRIEND:

Your affectionate letters from March 4, May 24, 26, and 27 last past arrived in my hands through friends Thomas Meyer, Cunrad Baur, and Philip Ullrich (who all arrived here successfully). It was a joy to my heart to hear of the health of my worthy friend and his loved ones. It is my further wish that the Lord will keep you and bless you with good health for a long time. In contrast, however, it was heart-breaking and painful to learn of the death of my dear mother. I acknowledge with extremely grateful obligation not only the testimony of his sincere condolence, but also all of the love, service, provision, and help he showed her during her widowhood in a truly paternal way.

—CASPAR WISTAR to Georg Friederich Hölzer, December 1743

CHAPTER 7

Webs of Influence
TRANSATLANTIC TRADE AND PATRONAGE

Wistar began corresponding regularly with Georg Friederich Hölzer, a merchant in Neckargemünd, about the same time he started speculating in Pennsylvania land. Between 1730 and Hölzer's death in 1745, the two men fashioned commercial and communication channels that extended from the Neckar River Valley to the newly settled regions of Pennsylvania and New Jersey. [1] Wistar's rise to prominence within the German-speaking community resulted not only from his land speculation; he used his European connections to provide services for his fellow immigrants. He furnished them with commodities they were accustomed to using in Europe, facilitated their communication with friends and family at home, acted as a banker, assisted them in retrieving legacies, and helped them find jobs. Through his transatlantic trade networks, Wistar expanded his influence in the immigrant community. He used his business partnerships to carry out his role as a patron and patriarch in both Europe and British North America.

The connections Wistar and Hölzer created were fluid and did not depend on any single group of individuals. Wistar had arrived in Pennsylvania without links to established transatlantic communication networks or extended family members already living in North America. [2] He also faced particular risks when he traded with Europe because of his status as a foreigner. Consequently, Wistar and Hölzer relied on a variety of people participating in other networks that channeled information and goods back and forth across the Atlantic.

At the same time, Wistar's correspondence helped to create a German-speaking Atlantic world. He had migrated to Pennsylvania before ships carrying immigrants from Europe arrived regularly. By the early 1730s, however, Philadelphia, London, and Rotterdam merchants began to develop a "trade in strangers." They incorporated recruiting and transporting German-speaking immigrants

---

1. The correspondence between Wistar and Hölzer can be found in the Wistar Family Papers, HSP. Unless otherwise noted, the correspondence cited in this chapter is taken from the same collection.

2. For one example of later immigrants who arrived with transatlantic networks in tact, see Häberlein, "Communication," 156–71.

into their commercial endeavors.[3] Early arrivals, like Wistar, began to use the transportation system to communicate with family and friends in Europe and to import trade goods. They created a demand for frequent and predictable contact between Pennsylvania and the southwestern German territories. Although he never participated in the immigrant trade directly by purchasing shares in a ship, Wistar's exchanges with Hölzer both relied on and helped to shape the system that emerged by midcentury.

Wistar's connections also illustrate the interactive nature of the emerging German-Atlantic world. Hölzer's efforts on Wistar's behalf enabled the immigrant to assume his role as head of his European family from the other side of the ocean after his father's death in 1726. Likewise, Wistar provided Hölzer with new market opportunities as well as the ability to retrieve American legacies and debts on behalf of his own business associates and family members in the Neckar Valley. Thus the constantly shifting links that emerge from the correspondence of the two men allowed for profit and patronage to flow in both directions across the Atlantic.

In many ways, Wistar was a typical Philadelphia dry goods merchant. He began his career in transatlantic trade as an artisan and shopkeeper. Although he initially purchased material for his button-making business and hardware for his shop from local suppliers, he soon imported them directly from continental Europe.[4] Like other Philadelphia retailers, he also bought dry goods and hardware from Neat and Neave, prominent wholesalers in London.[5] In addition, Wistar's advance from a retailer to wholesale merchant mirrored the activities of other Philadelphia shopkeepers. He did an extensive trade—in the thousands of pounds—with retailers in the city and surrounding countryside. Like his Anglo-American contemporaries, he purchased merchandise on long-term English credit and offered short-term loans to the shopkeepers who bought his wares.[6]

Nevertheless, several factors distinguished Wistar's trade from Anglo-American commercial networks. His legal status as a German-speaking immigrant was the first difference that set him apart. The Navigation Acts of the

3. Wokeck, *Trade in Strangers*, 59–112.

4. Francis Richardson's Account Book, 1685–1721, 35, Henry Francis DuPont Winterthur Museum Library, Winterthur, Del.; Dec. 8, 1726, James Logan Ledger, 1720–27, Logan Papers, HSP; Wistar to Peter DeKoker, Rotterdam, Dec. 9, 1736; Wistar to Hölzer, Nov. 8, 1733; Hölzer to Wistar, June 1, 1740. For a description of Philadelphia's merchant community, see Doerflinger, *Vigorous Spirit*, 11–69.

5. Inventory of Caspar Wistar, Apr. 13, 1752, Wistar Family Papers, HSP; Doerflinger, *Vigorous Spirit*, 86–87.

6. Inventory of Caspar Wistar, Apr. 13, 1752, Wistar Family Papers, HSP; Doerflinger, *Vigorous Spirit*, 86–87. Wistar's brother John, who owed Wistar's estate more than £2,000 in bills and bonds, is one example of a retailer with a commercial network in the colony's back country; John Wister Ledger, 1747–70, Wister Family Papers, vol. 1, HSP.

seventeenth century allowed only British subjects to participate in transatlantic trade.[7] Guarding vigilantly against any lingering problems his status as a foreigner might create, Wistar and his supporters pushed for an exceptionally protective clause in his 1724 naturalization act. He would be "free and fully able and capable to trade, traffic, load, freight and transport all . . . manner of goods, wares and merchandises not by law prohibited to be imported or exported" as if he was one of "the natural liege people and subjects of the King of Great Britain born in this province of Pennsylvania."[8] Wistar's act was the first naturalization bill the Pennsylvania legislature passed including a trade clause.[9]

Despite the act's special precautions, however, transatlantic trade promised to be extremely risky for Wistar. The legitimacy of the act remained contested as central and provincial governments jockeyed for power. One of the discussions that had delayed the approval of Wistar's naturalization emanated from the crown's instructions to the Pennsylvania governor regarding private legislation. The crown directed that all private acts include a clause "suspending the Execution of such act until his Majesty's royal approbation shall be had thereof."[10] The governor approved Wistar's act only after the appropriate clause was added.[11] Clearly the crown intended to supersede colonial legislative decisions about naturalization.

Furthermore, British legal decisions confined the validity of legislative naturalization acts to the provinces in which they were granted. Provincial governments could confer the rights of natural-born British subjects only within their own jurisdiction, not within the empire. Therefore, when naturalized subjects moved to a different colony, they were required to repeat the process. Wistar obviously understood the limited nature of the Pennsylvania act. When he purchased property in New Jersey, he successfully petitioned that colony's legislature for naturalization.[12]

7. McCusker and Menard, *Economy*, 46–50; Lawrence Harper, *The English Navigation Laws: A Seventeenth-Century Experiment in Social Engineering* (New York: Columbia University Press, 1939; repr. 1973); Thomas Barrow, *Trade and Empire: The British Customs Service in Colonial America, 1660–1775* (Cambridge: Harvard University Press, 1967); Oliver M. Dickerson, *The Navigation Acts and the American Revolution* (Philadelphia: University of Pennsylvania Press, 1951), 1–30.

8. *Statutes at Large of Pennsylvania*, 3:424–26.

9. The two previous acts were passed in 1691 and 1709. However, the two acts contained many of the same names, since the 1691 act was never approved by the crown. *MPC*, vol. 2 *December 18, 1700 to May 16, 1717* (Philadelphia, 1852), 241, 248, 480, 488, 494; *Statutes at Large of Pennsylvania*, 2:298.

10. Quote is in *Votes*, 2:1579–80; *MPC*, 3:234.

11. *Votes*, 2:1583–84; *MPC*, 3:235.

12. In 1700 an order-in-council limited the jurisdiction of colonial acts to the colonies in which they were granted implying that naturalized aliens did not have the right to participate in transatlantic trade; James Kettner, *The Development of American Citizenship, 1608–1870* (Chapel Hill: University of North Carolina Press, 1978), 93–96. Wistar's New Jersey naturalization act is in Bernard Bush, *New Jersey Archives*, ser. 3, *Laws of the Royal Colony of New Jersey*, vol. 2 (Trenton: New Jersey State Library, Archives and History Bureau, 1982), 506.

While provincial officials interpreted his overseas business as legitimate, Wistar always risked accusations of illicit trade from imperial authorities.

Wistar also faced the constraints the Navigation Acts placed on trade from continental Europe. Imperial policy required merchants to transport European manufactured goods on English ships and to pass through an English port where imports were subject to special duties.[13] "Dangers are first in England," Wistar warned, "in that one is not supposed to bring such goods from other places." "The great danger of the big sea," he observed, was secondary to the hazards of trade.[14] The Navigation Acts forced Wistar to choose between illicit trade and paying higher costs for his European wares than his competitors paid for similar items imported from Great Britain.

During his earliest years of importing goods, Wistar smuggled merchandise into Pennsylvania in the trunks of German-speaking immigrants to avoid paying British duties. From the colony's beginning, settlers had transported new tools and supplies to sell for a profit along with their household goods. This strategy allowed them to liquidate assets in Europe and transfer their capital to British America in the form of manufactured commodities. Customs officials tended to look the other way when the merchandise belonged to a family's household.[15] Wistar clearly understood the illicit nature of his actions, however; he advised Hölzer to keep his transactions secret. To minimize losing all of his goods if English officials discovered them, Wistar directed Hölzer not to send "everything with one person" but to "put my rifles in the people's trunks" and "divide them as much as is possible." He promised to "gladly pay the people for their efforts and also serve them further in return for their trouble."[16]

But Wistar eventually was forced to change his strategy. As customs officials in Philadelphia began to tighten their control over incoming immigrant ships, they threatened to expose his illegal trade. In 1736, officials confiscated imported goods on the *Princess Augusta*, a ship carrying some of Wistar's merchandise. They were convinced that the large number of "household goods" the immigrants brought with them were, in fact, new wares they intended to sell for a profit. The volume of merchandise they confiscated suggests that a significant illicit commerce was evolving with the immigrant transportation system.[17]

Shortly after the confiscation, Wistar lamented to Hölzer that the customs officials "have become so bad that one can hardly unload things from the

13. "The Navigation Act of 1660" and "The Navigation Act of 1696," in *Documents of American History*, ed. Henry S. Commager, 3rd ed. (New York: F. S. Crofts, 1947), 32–34; 38–39.
14. Wistar to [Hölzer], n.d.
15. Beiler, "Smuggling Goods," 9–23.
16. [Wistar to Hölzer], [1731?]; the direct quote is from Wistar to Hölzer, Nov. 1, 1735.
17. Oct. 4, 1736, Records of the Court of Vice Admiralty held in Philadelphia, Pa., vol. 1, 1735–47, 65–107, Manuscript Division, Library of Congress, Washington, D.C.; Beiler, "Smuggling Goods," 9–23. I would like to thank Marianne Wokeck for directing me to the case of the ship *Princess Augusta*.

ship."[18] He told another correspondent that they "held watch on the ship day and night." Wistar claimed that the officials waited until the immigrant men went to the courthouse to take their oaths of allegiance, then they boarded the ship, went below deck, and confiscated tools and bedding. He observed with horror that "the evil-doers [customs officials] were so bad that they searched people's sacks and under women's clothes."[19]

Wistar was fortunate: one of his agents who had returned on the *Princess Augusta* managed to smuggle his mirrors off the ship before customs officials confiscated its contents. The remainder of his merchandise was supposed to have been on the ship but had been delayed in the Netherlands. "I was lucky that my barrel stayed there until Captain Stedman came," a relieved Wistar reported. "He loaded it and paid the duties and it was delivered to me in tact with the 350 scythes."[20] Wistar advised Hölzer to send all future supplies with ship captains who knew him and to make sure they paid the appropriate duties in London.[21] The increased chances of confiscation heightened Wistar's need to rely on trustworthy people to transact his business.

In addition to the risk his status as a naturalized foreigner created, the structure of Wistar's trade connections with continental Europe also differed from typical Philadelphia-British networks. Many of Pennsylvania's Quaker merchants relied on family members or business associates belonging to the Society of Friends to carry out commercial transactions in Great Britain.[22] Wistar's European family members were foresters, not merchants, and he had no Quaker ties to the Neckar Valley. Consequently, he depended predominantly on one European business partner, a childhood friend, to negotiate his transactions.

Hölzer, Wistar's primary partner, was born in 1692 and was the son of Neckargemünd's town clerk. He and Wistar had attended school together when they were boys.[23] In 1716, he married the daughter of a leading local family of tanners and merchants and became a shopkeeper in the market town. By the time of his death in 1745, Hölzer had become a town council member and an elder in the

---

18. Wistar to Hölzer, Nov. 20, 1736.

19. Wistar to Baltesar Langhaers, Nov. 25, 1736.

20. Ibid.

21. Wistar to Hölzer, Nov. 20, 1736. Whether in fact Wistar continued to pay duties is questionable. In 1737 Wistar asked Hölzer to instruct the rifle maker not to mark his rifles with "CW" and, if possible, to divide them and send them with different people. Wistar to Hölzer, Oct. 1, 1737.

22. Alison Olson, *Making the Empire Work: London and American Interest Groups, 1690–1790* (Cambridge: Harvard University Press, 1992), 7–8; Doerflinger, *Vigorous Spirit*, 58–62; Tolles, *Meeting House*, 85–108. See also Bernard Bailyn, *The New England Merchants in the Seventeenth Century* (Cambridge: Harvard University Press, 1979), 16–44; J. F. Bosher, "Huguenot Merchants and the Protestant International in the Seventeenth Century," *William and Mary Quarterly* 52 (1995): 77–100; Wilson, *Pious Traders*, 67–156.

23. Hölzer to Wistar, Feb. 23, 1742.

Reformed Church.[24] Throughout the fifteen or more years they corresponded, Wistar never returned to Europe and Hölzer never traveled to America; instead, the two men trusted others to transport letters, money, and goods across the Atlantic for them. The particular risks involved in trade between continental Europe and the British colonies increased the importance of finding reliable brokers and carriers. Furthermore, the business partners needed a significant corps of agents to offset the dangers created by Wistar's ambiguous legal status.

Family members proved the most trustworthy carriers between Hölzer and Wistar. Wistar's brother John arrived in Philadelphia in 1727 and likely brought merchandise with him from the Neckar Valley.[25] Ten years later, when his two sisters moved to Pennsylvania with their families, Wistar reported that he had received Hölzer's letter "along with all of the things" he had sent with them.[26] In 1742, Wistar's niece traveled crossed the Atlantic chaperoned by Wilhelm Ziegler, one of his agents who had gone to Germany the year before.[27] Hölzer instructed Wistar that he would find his brother-in-law's goods, "two copies of Rev. Widder's *Passion* sermons, as well as two reports from Frankfurt and two calendars from Saxony" in his niece's trunk. His rifles were marked and packed in Ziegler's chest.[28]

Wistar also relied on extended kinship connections for transacting business. His wife's cousin, Baltasar Langhaer, took letters and money to Krefeld for Wistar in 1734.[29] Heinrich Zimmerman, John Wister's brother-in-law, acted as Wistar's agent several times as well.[30] In both cases, family connections provided Wistar with legitimacy and an element of trust that proved critical when armed conflict threatened the agents' journeys.

24. In 1721, Hölzer was listed among the top class of shopkeepers (*Krämer*) in the tax lists and was taxed for property valued at 170 *Gulden*. Schätzungsbuch, 1721, Stadt Neckargemünd, Stadtarchiv Neckargemünd; NgRKB (1635–1749); NgLKB (1699–1760 and 1700–1769); Mannheim Reformierte Kirchenbuch (15, 16, 19), EOK.

25. Strassburger and Hinke, *Pennsylvania German Pioneers*, 1:7.

26. Ibid., 1:169, 170, 172. Wistar to Hölzer, Oct. 1, 1737.

27. Wilhelm Ziegler is not a close relative to Andreas Ziegler of Waldhilsbach, mentioned in Chapter 2.

28. Hölzer to Wistar, May 10, 1742.

29. Wistar to Hölzer, Nov. 7, 1734. Langhaer connected Wistar and Catharine to their extended family and to Hölzer between 1734 and 1736, when conflict kept news and merchandise from traveling to Pennsylvania. Wistar to Gerhard Johnson, Kriegsheim, Nov. 4, 1733; Wistar to Andreas Wynert and Jan van Emrath, Krefeld, Nov. 6, 1734; Wistar to Hölzer, Nov. 7, 1734; Hölzer to Baltasar Langhaer, Krefeld, Apr. 28, 1735; Wistar to his family, Waldhilsbach, Nov. 10, 1735; Wistar to [Hölzer], Nov. 10, 1735; Wistar to [Hölzer], [Nov. 20, 1736]; Wistar to Baltasar Langhaer, Krefeld, Nov. 25, 1736; Wistar to Baltasar Langhaer, Krefeld, Dec. 9, 1736; Jan von Emrath, Krefeld, to Wistar, June 1743; Strassburger and Hinke, *Pennsylvania German Pioneers*, 1:35, 36.

30. Wistar to Gerhard Johnson, Kriegsheim, Nov. 4, 1733; Wistar to Hölzer, Nov. 4, 1733; Johannes Schmick, Philadelphia, to Hölzer, Nov. 4, 1733; Wistar to Hölzer, Feb. 15, 1734; Wistar to his family, Waldhilsbach, Feb. 16, 1734; Wistar to Andreas Wynert and Jan van Emrath, Krefeld, Nov. 6, 1734.

Langhaer brought another advantage to Wistar and Hölzer: he linked them to members of Catharine Wistar's extended family in Krefeld and Kriegsheim, who participated in Mennonite commercial networks spanning the Rhine Valley.[31] After Langhaer traveled back to Krefeld, Wistar began to order merchandise through his relatives and their business associates.[32] In 1736 he thanked Peter DeKoker, a Rotterdam merchant connected to Mennonite commercial networks, for storing his barrel of scythes and shipping it with Captain Stedman. He sent DeKoker money to cover his costs and requested that "if there is any left over, would he be so good and send me borax for the remaining money?" Furthermore, Wistar asked DeKoker if he would forward any future shipments that arrived in Rotterdam to Captain Stedman.[33] Langhaer's family connections, therefore, granted Wistar entry into another religious commercial network during the period before the German Lutheran, Reformed, or Moravian churches established regular transatlantic communication channels.

Other participants in the same sectarian networks linked Wistar to immigrants willing to transport his merchandise. Jacob Schnebeli, a Mennonite merchant in Mannheim, was a liaison between Swiss and Palatine immigrants and the Mennonite Commission for Foreign Needs, an Amsterdam relief agency for religious refugees. Schnebeli's house in Mannheim became an information center for early settlers moving to Pennsylvania, especially those with connections to Germantown and Lancaster colonists.[34] By 1732, Hölzer was relying on Schnebeli to find immigrants willing to transport Wistar's merchandise in their chests.[35] Several years later when listing the people who had offered to bring

31. These were the same religious networks (mostly Mennonite) Penn had used to promote his colony. See Chapter 4 and Beiler, "Distributing Aid," 73–87. For examples of how these same connections functioned as a commercial network, see Dieter Hangebruch, ed., *Das Tagebuch der Brüder Claes und Abraham ter Meer, 1732–1756* (Krefeld: Verein für Heimatkunde e. V. Krefeld, 2002).

32. For additional examples of agents within this widespread religious network, see Wistar to Baltasar Langhaer, Krefeld, Nov. 25 and Dec. 9, 1736; Wistar to Peter DeKoker, Rotterdam, Dec. 9, 1736; Jan Van Emrath, Krefeld, to Wistar, June 1743; Johannes Zwengenberg, Krefeld, to Wistar, June 28, 1743. Baltasar Langhaer and Jan Van Emrath were German Quakers and Mennonites at Krefeld and Kriegsheim (respectively) who were related to Wistar by marriage. Johannes Zwengenberg was a Mennonite merchant at Krefeld. Peter de DeKoker was a merchant in Rotterdam who was sympathetic to Quakers, Mennonites, and Dunkers. See also Hangebruch, *Das Tagebuch*, 57, 59, 85, 173, 179, 181, 185, 191, 213, 245, 257, 273, 299, 309.

33. Wistar to Peter DeKoker, Holland, Dec. 9, 1736.

34. Beiler, "Distributing Aid," 73–87; Rosalind J. Beiler, "Information Networks and the Dynamics of Migration: Swiss Anabaptist Exiles and Their Host Communities," in *Religious Refugees in Europe, Asia and North America (6th–21st Centuries)*, ed. Susanne Lachenicht (Munster: Lit Verlag, 2007), 81–91.

35. Hölzer to Wistar, May 4, 1732; Strassburger and Hinke, *Pennsylvania German Pioneers*, 1:3, 59–66. For Schnebeli's participation, see the Dutch Mennonite *Commissie voor de Buitenlandsche Nooden* (Commission for Foreign Need), Gemeentearchif Amsterdam, Amsterdam, 565, A, #2263, #2280, #2281.

trade goods to America, Wistar asked Hölzer to greet Schnebeli and noted that he "could also serve me in this way as he circulates a lot among these people and knows many of them."[36]

Wistar also depended on ship captains who participated in the immigrant transportation system that was forming in the 1730s. Two Rotterdam merchant firms, John Stedman and Isaac and Zachary Hope, monopolized the ships that carried continental Europeans to Philadelphia.[37] After Captain Stedman rescued his barrel of scythes in 1736, Wistar requested all his European contacts to send merchandise with the captain whenever possible. He instructed Hölzer to have their agents take his things to "Captain Stedman, who will be in Holland [and] who is my good friend." He promised that Stedman would "take care of them and also pay the duties."[38] Wistar relied on other ship captains as well. He told Hölzer that if agents could not find Stedman, they "should tell one of the captains who will go along [to America] that the barrel is for me and he should pay the duties." Wistar promised to reimburse the captains Hölzer employed for their expenses when they arrived in Philadelphia. He assured his partner that "the captains who bring Germans here almost all know me."[39]

Stedman and others like him only traveled back and forth across the Atlantic. Wistar also needed someone to carry his commodities from Neckargemünd to Rotterdam if he was not going to rely on immigrants and illicit trade. To fill the gap, Wistar utilized Rhine shippers who also participated in the immigrant transportation system. In 1737, Wistar promised to send his brother Ludwig and Hölzer some furs with Captain Stedman the following spring. He asked his brother to arrange with the "ship people" who took immigrants to Rotterdam to convey the furs from there to Neckargemünd. "Otherwise I know of no other possibility to send them to you since the people who travel from here to Germany have too much to take with them."[40] Two years later Hölzer wrote that the Rhine shipper Dorzenbach had delivered the furs.[41]

"Newlanders" offered a final set of agents on whom Wistar and Hölzer depended for receiving news and delivering goods. During the 1730s and 1740s Europeans used the term "newlander" to refer to returning immigrants, many of whom carried commissions from friends, relatives, and business partners to

36. Wistar to Hölzer, Nov. 20, 1736.

37. Marianne S. Wokeck, "Promoters and Passengers: The German Immigrant Trade, 1683–1775," in *World of William Penn*, ed. Dunn and Dunn, 261–66.

38. Wistar to Hölzer, [Nov. 20, 1736].

39. Ibid.

40. Wistar to Johann Ludwig Wüster, Sept. 25, 1737.

41. Hölzer to Wistar, Apr. 1, 1739. Hölzer's accounts also included "shipper Horsch's" charges for taking goods from Neckargemünd to Mannheim; Hölzer to Wistar, June 1 and June 6, 1740. Horsch (Horst) was involved in transporting immigrants down the Neckar and Rhine rivers; GLA 77/5651.

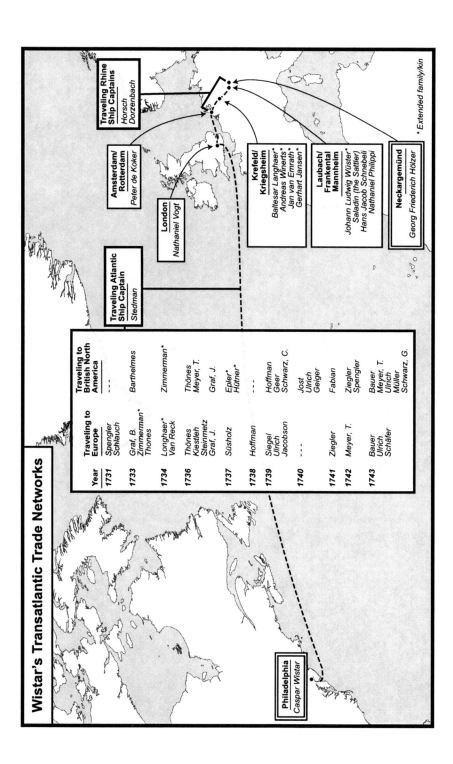

Wistar's Transatlantic Trade Networks

Philadelphia
Caspar Wistar

Traveling Atlantic Ship Captain
Stedman

London
Nathaniel Vogt

Amsterdam/Rotterdam
Peter de Koker

Traveling Rhine Ship Captains
Horsch
Dorzenbach

Krefeld/Kriegsheim
Baltesar Langhaer*
Andreas Winerts*
Jan van Emrath*
Gerhart Jansen*

Laubach/Frankental Mannheim
Johann Ludwig Wüster*
Saladin (the Sattler)
Hans Jacob Schnebeli
Nathaniel Philippi

Neckargemünd
Georg Friederich Hölzer

* Extended family/kin

Year	Traveling to Europe	Traveling to British North America
1731	Spengler Schlauch	- - -
1733	Graf, B. Zimmerman* Thones	Barthelmes
1734	Longhaer* Van Reck	Zimmerman*
1736	Thones Kiestleh Steinmetz Graf, J.	Thönes Meyer, T. Graf, J.
1737	Süsholz	Epler* Hütner*
1738	Hoffman	- - -
1739	Siegel Ulrich Jacobson	Hoffman Geer Schwarz, C.
1740	- - -	Jost Ulrich Geiger
1741	Ziegler	Fabian
1742	Meyer, T.	Ziegler Spengler
1743	Bauer Ulrich Schäfer	Bauer Meyer, T. Ulrich Müller Schwarz, G.

retrieve legacies, transact business, and recruit additional colonists.[42] Hölzer entertained using one in 1735 when he mentioned that the man with whom he had hoped to ship Wistar's goods failed to arrive.[43] Four years later Hölzer learned through the newlander Philipp Ulrich that the ship containing merchandise he sent to Wistar had wrecked off Rhode Island. On his return trip the following year and again several years later, Ulrich carried merchandise and letters between the Neckar Valley and Philadelphia.[44] Newlanders, with their knowledge of both America and Europe, became useful brokers for Wistar and Hölzer.

Thus the transatlantic partnership between Wistar and Hölzer depended on finding a significant number of reliable individuals to travel between them. All of the agents the two men chose brought their own resources to the transactions. Family members and friends supplied trust and loyalty; people like Langhaer, DeKoker, and Schnebeli provided legitimacy and a wide circle of contacts; ship captains granted them a means of transportation and a way to pay duties; and newlanders possessed contacts in both America and Europe. Although Wistar's trade channels could not have functioned without the resources his brokers offered, each of them profited from doing business with him. Family members received help getting established in America; Schnebeli's emigrants gained a patron in Pennsylvania; and ship captains and newlanders received commissions for transacting Wistar's business. The reciprocal benefits to all participants helped to bind the commercial transactions together and to minimize the dangers inherent in trade between continental Europe and British North America.

Wistar's transatlantic commercial connections brought him much more than wealth. No doubt he earned financial rewards, but his European trade was never as lucrative as his land speculation. Instead, his links to the Rhine and Neckar valleys allowed him to import commodities for highly specialized markets, retain his role as family patriarch, and furnish his fellow immigrants with specialized services that won him patronage.

The items Hölzer shipped to Wistar throughout the 1730s were not readily available in the colonies, especially in the newly settled areas of Pennsylvania. Hardware such as knives, scissors, needles, brass and iron goods, and copper

42. William T. O'Reilly, "'A Paragon of Wickedness': Newlanders and Agents in Eighteenth-Century German Migration," Working paper no. 96–25, International Seminar on the History of the Atlantic World, 1500–1800, Harvard University, 1996; Georg Fertig, "Transatlantic Migration from the German-Speaking Parts of Central Europe, 1600–1800: Proportions, Structures, and Explanations," in *Europeans on the Move: Studies on European Migration, 1500–1800*, ed. Nicholas Canny (Oxford: Clarendon Press, 1994), 228–31; Häberlein, *Vom Oberrhein*, 92–101; Roeber, *Palatines*, 95–132.

43. Hölzer to Baltasar Langhaer, Krefeld, Apr. 28, 1735.

44. For references to Ulrich, see Hölzer to Wistar, Apr. 1, 1739, June 1, 1740, Feb. 23, 1742, May 17, 1743; Wistar to Hölzer, Dec. 1743.

kettles made up a large portion of the commodities Wistar ordered. In addition, Hölzer sent him mirrors, eyeglasses, tobacco pipes, ivory combs, and "brabander" lace—all goods that were not made in the American colonies.[45] Wistar was also buying for a specialized and discriminating market. In 1733, he requested "100 dozen of the very best Augsberger eye glasses—only those, no others" and "3 pistoles" worth of "large mirrors" encased in different colored wood—those that Hölzer thought were "the nicest and best." Wistar wanted thirty dozen shirt clasps of all kinds "but most of them with hearts." And he asked Hölzer to send him three dozen pairs of "fine linen men's stockings" and three dozen pairs of "fine women's stockings with red or blue flecks."[46]

Wistar also ordered merchandise reflecting the religious and cultural preferences of some of the German-speaking immigrants. In one instance, he wanted "two big bibles like Machnet's," one dozen "Psalters," one dozen "New Testament books," and two dozen "ABC books." In addition to German-language literature used by radical Pietists, he asked Hölzer to send him hairpins "like those the Mennonite or Swiss women wear."[47] Wistar used his capital and his connections to Hölzer to supply the immigrants settling his land with the quality goods they were accustomed to using in Europe.

The most specialized commodities Wistar imported, however, were rifles custom made for the American market. Between 1731 and 1745, Hölzer supplied him with more than fifty rifles.[48] Wistar's European training under the elector's chief huntsman had given him firsthand knowledge of hunting rifles and their technology. The immigrant's Quaker affiliation did not deter him from importing firearms that he clearly viewed as hunting implements. Wistar received his first shipment of rifles from Hölzer sometime before 1731, and thereafter he sent special instructions on how to make and alter pieces for American consumers.[49]

---

45. Wistar to Hölzer, May 4, 1732, Nov. 8, 1733, Nov. 20, 1736, and Nov. 23, 1738.

46. Wistar to Hölzer, Nov. 8, 1733.

47. Ibid. Blasius Daniel Machnet was a member of the Community of True Inspiration in Europe who migrated to Pennsylvania in the 1720s. Gottlieb Scheuner, *Inspirations-History, 1714–1728*, trans. Janet W. Zuber (Amana, Iowa, 1977), 1–98. For a discussion of German-language book trade, see A. Gregg Roeber, "German and Dutch Books and Printing," in *History of the Book in America*, vol. 1, *The Colonial Book in the Atlantic World*, ed. Hugh Amory and David D. Hall (Cambridge: Cambridge University Press, 2000), 298–313. See also James Green, "The Book Trade in the Middle Colonies, 1680–1720," and "English Books and Printing in the Age of Franklin," in the same volume, 199–223, 248–97.

48. Hölzer to Wistar, May 4, 1732; Wistar to Hölzer, Nov. 20, 1736, Oct. 1, 1737; Hölzer to Wistar, [n.m.] 1739; June 1, 1740, May 10, 1742, May 17, 1743.

49. Hölzer to Wistar, May 4, 1732; Wistar to Hölzer, Nov. 20, 1736. Evidence that Wistar received his first shipment of rifles by May 1731 is in the account he gives to Hölzer of the rifles he sold for Hölzer. For examples of rifles ordered to specification, see Wistar to Johann Ludwig Wüster, Sept. 25, 1737; Wistar to Hölzer, Nov. 20, 1736, Oct. 1, 1737, and Nov. 17, 1737.

In particular, Wistar insisted that the barrels should be longer than normal "because the people [here] prefer rifles with barrels that are three feet and three to four inches long."[50] The modifications Wistar requested match those that Lancaster gunsmiths eventually made to the "Pennsylvania rifle" in the following decades.[51]

For several years, Wistar managed to dominate Pennsylvania's market for custom-made rifles. His success, however, depended on Hölzer's ability to procure highly skilled gunsmiths who produced quality work. Wistar sent his correspondent specific instructions about every detail of his pieces from the condition of the locks to the bore of the barrels and the way he wanted them rifled. He was adamant in his opinions of different gunsmiths' work. He observed in 1733 that the Rothenberger artisan's rifles were "good and well made." Concerning the pieces from the gunmaker in Suhl, however, Wistar did not wish to blame Hölzer, but he asked "if possible, please do not send me any more of his rifles. [I] would rather have no more rifles" than more made by him.[52]

In return for his brokerage and a promise to be discreet about the identity of the gunsmiths, Wistar gave Hölzer a share of the Pennsylvania market. In 1736, he reported that he had sold seven firearms totaling £20 Pennsylvania currency on Hölzer's behalf.[53] In spite of their attempts at secrecy, news of Wistar's best source of rifles eventually spread and threatened to destroy his market dominance. In 1743, Hölzer warned that "all of the newlanders who came through the area" wanted to purchase pieces from the gunsmith at Rothenberg, one of his key suppliers. In particular, "Hillegass from Sinsheim thought that he could snatch several of my friend's rifles but he received none."[54] Hölzer managed to fend off Hillegass, but he permitted one of Wistar's friends as well as his nephew to take pieces he had ordered for Wistar.

50. Wistar to Hölzer, Oct. 1, 1737.

51. Jerome H. Wood Jr., *Conestoga Crossroads: Lancaster, Pennsylvania, 1730–1790* (Harrisburg: Pennsylvania Historical and Museum Commission, 1979), 133; Henry J. Kauffman, *The Pennsylvania-Kentucky Rifle* (New York: Bonanza Books, 1960), 8–31. Wistar's importation of guns argues against Michael Bellesiles's contention that there was not a market in British North America "to justify the regular importation of firearms by merchants" during the colonial period. Bellesiles maintains that most guns were imported by colonial governments for military use. The modifications Wistar specified for the American market clearly indicate that the guns were intended for hunting rather than warfare. Bellesiles's interpretation has been questioned by early American scholars; however, if he is correct, the fifty guns Wistar imported over a fourteen-year period constitute a significant number. Michael Bellesiles, *Arming America: The Origins of a National Gun Culture* (New York: Alfred A. Knopf, 2000), 70–110, quote is on p. 81. For an overview of the controversy surrounding Bellesiles's interpretation, see Peter Hoffer, *Past Imperfect: Facts, Fictions, Frauds—American History from Bancroft and Parkman to Ambrose, Bellesiles, Ellis, and Goodwin* (New York: Public Affairs, 2004), 141–71.

52. Wistar to Hölzer, Oct. 28, 1733.

53. Wistar to Hölzer, Nov. 20, 1736.

54. Hölzer to Wistar, May 17, 1743.

In an effort to retain the sole patronage of the gunsmith at Rothenberg, Wistar pleaded with Hölzer to convince him of the benefits he had gained from their trade. "I trust that the gunsmith will consider that I have already done business with him for a long time and, through my worthy friend's [Hölzer's] commissions, I have allowed him to earn a pretty penny," he wrote. Wistar hoped that the gunsmith would supply him with high-quality, extra-long rifles in the future just as he had in the past. Furthermore, Wistar wanted the gunsmith to "allow all of his rifles to come to no one other than me."[55] The entrepreneur's control of a highly specialized commodity for the American market was dependent on Hölzer's successful brokerage and his continued exclusive access to the work of the gunsmith at Rothenberg.

Wistar's transatlantic trade connections allowed him to supply a specialized market, and they also brought him social benefits. Through his business relationship with Hölzer, Wistar managed to retain his role as patriarch of his European family. Hölzer likely assisted Wistar's nineteen-year-old brother John when he moved to Pennsylvania in 1727.[56] A number of families from Meckesheim, Neckargemünd, and villages close to Sinsheim arrived on the same ship as John. Many of them belonged to Reformed congregations and settled at Goshenhoppen.[57] As an elder in the Reformed Church in Neckargemünd, Hölzer likely knew of their migration. He probably helped John with his transportation arrangements.[58] He also assisted Wistar's young, single niece when she migrated alone to Pennsylvania in 1742. Hölzer extracted promises from his agent and another female friend to take special care "of the preservation of her honor, because she is a young woman."[59]

When political conflict cut their communication lines, Hölzer looked after Wistar's Palatine affairs and family. In 1733, French troops occupied Heidelberg and the area along the Rhine.[60] By the following year, Wistar and his brother

55. Wistar to Hölzer, Dec. 1743.

56. The American descendants of Johannes Wüster spell their name "Wister," those of Caspar Wüster use "Wistar." Eighteenth-century documents are not consistent. English-language documents use Wistar and Wister interchangeably while German-language documents maintain the original German name.

57. Strassburger and Hinke, *Pennsylvania German Pioneers*, 1:7–10; "Register," 1716, GLA 145/292. Hans Georg Welcker, Andreas Zimmerman, and Leonard Seltenreich were all from Meckesheim and were members of the Reformed Church there. Johann Georg Schwab, who was also on the same ship, was from Leimen and was a brother-in-law to Abraham Rhiem, the immigrant who loaned Wistar money in 1717. Another group of Reformed families migrated from Sinsheim and neighboring villages. German church records illustrate the family connections between these three areas. See Burgert, *Eighteenth-Century Emigrants*, 44, 45, 114–15, 158, 160–61, 166, 173, 183, 187, 220, 236, 250, 259, 264, 276, 277, 302, 323, 335, 350, 354, 363, 388, 392, 401, 406, 411, 412, 414.

58. Hölzer to Wistar, May 4, 1732. Hölzer refers in this letter to a bill he sent to Wistar in May 1731 for goods he had shipped prior to that date.

59. Hölzer to Wistar, May 10, 1742.

60. Holborn, *History*, 183–85.

had read "with saddened hearts" the "melancholy" reports in the newspapers of "war and the cry of war." They feared the French army would reach their widowed mother and siblings who remained in the Palatinate. Wistar wrote that he would be grateful if Hölzer "could serve my mother through advice or deeds." If his mother or other family members wanted to join him and his brother in Pennsylvania, they "wanted to do what was right for her" and to fulfill their "brotherly duty" to their siblings.[61]

From May 1733 until November 1736, Wistar received no news from Hölzer or his family. He repeatedly begged Hölzer to use the money he had sent for merchandise to move family members to safety if necessary.[62] As the silence from home grew longer, Wistar's pleas became more frantic. His formal salutations to Hölzer—the standard "My dear and worthy friend"—became increasingly emotional. In June 1734, he began with: "Much loved and worthy friend in Jesus, it was with saddened heart that I read in our newspaper of the present melancholy condition of our fatherland, where we hear here that there is nothing except the cry of war. The more we hear of war and the cry of war, the more we are caused to turn around and to begin a prudent life in Jesus."[63] By November 1735, Wistar was convinced that "the end of the world is near because our Savior said that before the end you will hear of war and war's cry." He exhorted Hölzer, therefore, to "seek the Lord while he is to be found and call on him because he is near."[64]

Finally, in late 1736, Wistar received Hölzer's news that all members of his family had survived the war. Hölzer had distributed the money Wistar and his brother sent to their family, and he had purchased merchandise to ship to Wistar. The following spring Hölzer assisted two of Wistar's sisters and their families in their journey to Pennsylvania. After their safe arrival, Wistar repeatedly expressed his gratitude for Hölzer's service. He promised to send Hölzer some American seeds and specimens and a bear skin in appreciation for his help.[65] In addition, Wistar offered to sell more merchandise for Hölzer in order to repay some of the "debt" he owed Hölzer for looking after his family.[66]

---

61. Wistar to Hölzer, Feb. 15, 1734.

62. Wistar to Hölzer, Feb. 2, 1734, June 19, 1734, Nov. 7, 1734, Nov. 11, 1735, and Nov. 20, 1736. See also letters from Wistar to his mother and brother and sisters, Feb. 16, 1734 and Nov. 10, 1735.

63. Wistar to Hölzer, June 19, 1734.

64. Wistar to Hölzer, Nov. 10, 1735.

65. Such "rarities" were status symbols among the nobility and merchants in Europe. John Bartram, from whom Wistar received the specimens, collected seeds for clients of English aristocrats. See Berkeley and Berkeley, *John Bartram.* See Thomas Müller-Bahlke and Klaus E. Göltz, *Die Kunst- und Naturalienkammer der Franckeschen Stiftungen* (Halle: Franckesche Stiftungen, 1998) for a contemporary example of how Europeans displayed American artifacts.

66. Wistar to Hölzer, Oct. 1, 1737.

Wistar also relied on Hölzer to care for his widowed mother after his siblings had all moved away from Waldhilsbach. Hölzer began to send regular reports of her health. In 1739, he wrote that he hoped family members would not mind if he gave their mother "a couple glasses of wine" in her old age.[67] Hölzer also interceded on her behalf when a neighbor tried to take advantage of her. He reassured Wistar that "as I already often have promised, I will take care of her as if she were my own mother so long as I live."[68] Shortly before Wistar's mother died in 1743, Hölzer sent him and his brother a copy of her will, and after her death he described in loving detail her funeral ceremony for family members in America. He wrote about the "consoling" sermon the pastor of the Reformed Church gave and commented on the large number of people from Neckargemünd who attended her burial in Gaiberg, where Reformed parishioners were buried. He claimed that he "had never seen such a funeral in a village."[69] Hölzer became, in effect, a surrogate son to the elderly woman whose children had moved away. He enabled Wistar to fulfill his duties as patriarch to his European family members.

Wistar also used his partnership with Hölzer to retrieve legacies his American family members inherited in Europe. Shortly after they immigrated, Hölzer began the time-consuming legal processes to collect inheritances for both of Wistar's sisters. In one case, Hölzer managed to obtain a meager sum of money, after much effort, which he sent to Wistar's brother-in-law in the form of rifles.[70] The other case proved even more difficult, however; by the time Hölzer subtracted all of the costs involved, the legacy of 1,000 *Gulden* had dwindled to almost nothing.[71]

In exchange, Wistar worked diligently to help Hölzer's friends and acquaintances who wanted to settle in the British colonies. In 1743 Hölzer introduced Georg Schwartz to Wistar and his brother. Schwartz was a young man who traveled to Pennsylvania, "to seek there, with God's help, his fortune." Since he had "neither relatives nor friends" in the British colonies, Hölzer asked Wistar to give the young man advice and help him find a trade.[72] Seven months later

67. Hölzer to Wistar, [n.m.] 13, 1739; Feb. 20, 1740.

68. Hölzer to Wistar, Feb. 23, 1742.

69. Hölzer to Wistar, May 17, 1743, and May 27, 1743. Anna Catharine Müller Wüster's will was dated Jan. 21, 1742. Wistar's parents remained a mixed marriage even in death. The Rev. Hillsbach Hölzer mentioned in his letter was the pastor of the Bammental Reformed Church whose congregation included parishioners in Gaiberg and Waldhilsbach from 1742 to 1764. Wüst, *Bammental*, 410. Wistar's father was buried in Neckargemünd, in the cemetery that belonged to the Lutheran Church built in 1717. NgLKB; Wüst, *Neckargemünd*, 396–98.

70. Hölzer to Wistar, Feb. 20, 1740, June 1, 1740, and Feb. 23, 1742.

71. Hölzer to Wistar, June 1 and June 6, 1740, June 15, 1741, Feb. 23 and May 10, 1742, and May 17, 1743.

72. Hölzer to Caspar and Johannes Wistar, May 26, 1743.

Wistar reported that "the young Schwartz, [who] arrived happily along with Claus Müller," had settled in Conestoga (Lancaster) and was "very inclined to learn shoemaking."[73] In 1753, perhaps a further testimony of Wistar's patronage, Schwartz took out a mortgage from Sebastian Graff, a prominent landowner and merchant in Lancaster. Graff was an acquaintance of Wistar's and one of the brokers who had carried goods and money back and forth across the Atlantic for him in the early 1730s.[74] In return for helping his European family members, Wistar assisted Hölzer's friends in finding jobs and land in Pennsylvania.

Wistar also worked to obtain legacies and retrieve debts on behalf of Hölzer's associates. In 1742, after Hölzer's brother-in-law died, Wistar attempted to collect an outstanding debt to the estate from a shoemaker who had immigrated to Germantown.[75] At another point, he assisted a European friend and business associate of Hölzer's in securing a legacy from a relative in Pennsylvania. The complex case involved a group of immigrants who had settled near Wistar's backcountry land. At one point, Wistar wrote in exasperation that he believed "it would be good to have [the executors of the estate] arrested" because they refused to pay the legacy.[76] In both cases, Wistar mustered all his influence and knowledge of the Pennsylvania German community to reward Hölzer for helping his family and associates in the Palatinate.[77] In dispensing aid to family and friends, the two men wove intricate webs of patronage that spanned the Atlantic.

Wistar's influence soon extended well beyond his relatives. He began to use his transatlantic partnership with Hölzer to retrieve legacies for other immigrants as well. In 1733, Wistar sent Hölzer a power of attorney for him to retrieve a legacy on behalf of Johannes Schmick from the Pastor and Elders at Grundau. As soon as Hölzer had collected the 200 *Gulden* in Europe, Wistar would advance the money to Schmick in Pennsylvania.[78] Schmick became impatient, however, when war interfered with the transaction. Wistar instructed Hölzer to write directly to Schmick, otherwise "he will think we wanted to betray him; he

73. Wistar to Hölzer, Dec. 1743. Schwartz remained in the borough of Lancaster where he became a saddle maker, joined the Moravian Church, married, and raised a family of ten children. Burgert, *Eighteenth-Century Emigrants*, 1: 335–36.

74. Lancaster County Deeds, D:49; Wood, *Conestoga Crossroads*, 12, 29, 32, 50, 174.

75. Letter of attorney, May 12, 1742, and Hölzer to Wistar, May 17, 1743.

76. Wistar, Philadelphia, to Jacob Reiff, Skippack, Apr. 5, 1743.

77. Jacob Reiff to Wistar, Aug. 14 and Oct. 8, 1742, Jan. 24 and Sept. 9, 1743; Wistar to Reiff, Apr. 5, 1743; Hölzer to Wistar, May 17, 1743; Christoph and Johann Baltasar Michel, Mannheim, to Wistar, May 29, 1743; Wistar to Hölzer, Dec. 1743.

78. Power of attorney, Johannes Schmick, Philadelphia, to Georg Frienderich Hölzer, Neckargemünd, Nov. 4, 1733.

was annoyed this year when he received no word and he thought I would pay him the money."[79]

By 1742, Hölzer was reporting on five different inheritance cases he was working on for Wistar.[80] In one case, Hölzer sold property for Hans Peter Zuber, a former acquaintance of Wistar's from Gaiberg. He wrote that he had finally concluded the transaction but "only after a great deal of difficulty." Had an old friend of Wistar's not "lent his support and gotten involved in the affair," Hölzer believed it would have been even harder.[81] He warned that if Zuber was not happy with the price he had received, "I cannot help him. I did what I could from my whole heart and worked very hard on his behalf, to which the whole village of Gaiberg and the district of Dilsberg can attest." In the meantime, the economy had so deteriorated that Hölzer believed he would have done even more poorly had he waited to sell the property.[82] In Zuber's case, as in all of the others, Wistar and Hölzer went to great lengths to identify all the people involved in their transactions and their relationship to each of the partners.[83]

Wistar also extended his sphere of influence by providing credit to fellow immigrants. As early as 1733 he was attempting to retrieve money from the family members of Heinrich Hiestand at Ibersheimer Hoff in the Palatinate. He had loaned Hiestand 130 *Gulden*, 2 *Kopfstück* (£14 sterling) after his arrival in Pennsylvania. It took Wistar nine years to recover the sum from Hiestand's associates in the Palatinate, and the process involved numerous people and connections in America and the Rhine and Neckar valleys.[84] In addition to other debts he retrieved from Europe, Wistar's inventory listed bonds, mortgages, and book debts valued at £23,209 Pennsylvania currency due to his estate at his death. The overwhelming majority of the names listed on the bonds were German.[85]

79. Wistar to Hölzer, Nov. 7, 1734.
80. Power of attorney, Hans Peter and Anna Magdalena Zuber to Wistar, June 4, 1741; Hölzer to Wistar, Feb. 23, May 5, 1742, May 17, 1743; Wistar to Hölzer, Dec. 1743.
81. Hölzer to Wistar, Feb. 23, 1742.
82. Hölzer to Wistar, May 17, 1743.
83. Wistar's retrieval of legacies was not unique. By the late 1740s, agents in other secular trade networks carried commissions to the German southwest territories to obtain inheritances; Roeber, *Palatines*, 95–132. Wistar's correspondence with Hölzer is too fragmentary to know how many inheritances they worked on. Only scraps of Wistar's letterbook for the period from circa 1731 to 1738 and Hölzer's letters to Wistar from 1739 to 1744 remain. Between 1733 and 1744 Hölzer worked to retrieve at least six legacies although most of them were for Wistar's relatives or acquaintances. Hölzer's death in 1745 curtailed Wistar's use of his services. Whether Wistar had other associates who assisted him from then until his own death in 1752 is impossible to know given the extant records.
84. Wistar to Hölzer, Oct. 28, Nov. 4, 1733, June 19, 1734, Nov. 10, 1735; Hölzer to Wistar, Feb. 23, May 10, 1742.
85. At the time of his death, the outstanding bonds due to Wistar totaled 15,841 Pennsylvania pounds and the book debts totaled 3,285 Pennsylvania pounds. Inventory of the Goods and Chattels personal of Caspar Wistar, Apr. 13, 1752, Wistar Family Papers, HSP.

Whether providing them with instant cash or extending credit so they could purchase his land, Wistar's connections offered critical services to immigrants trying to make a new start.[86]

His success in using his commercial networks to assist fellow immigrants established Wistar's transatlantic reputation as a trustworthy and dependable patron. In one case, John Theobald Endt, a merchant in Germantown, recommended that a European friend send his American niece's legacy to Pennsylvania to invest because the interest rate was so much higher than in Krefeld. Endt recommended Wistar as one of four trustees who should be assigned to oversee the investment. Wistar's reputation for handling money responsibly and for helping immigrants establish themselves in America raised his influence among Pennsylvanians and their European families.[87]

Name recognition and a dependable, if fluid, transatlantic network helped to turn Wistar's house and shop into a communication center for Pennsylvania Germans. In 1737, Durst Thommen, a Swiss immigrant who settled near Wistar's land, wrote to his European friends that "if anyone should want to report or write to me, they should [send their] report to Philadelphia at Caspar Wister's or John Wister's, where I will be sure to receive it."[88] Wistar and his brother, who by this time was also a Philadelphia shopkeeper and shared Wistar's business connections, provided an informal postal service for the immigrant community.[89]

Thus, when Wistar and his brother managed to use their persuasive power to turn the immigrant vote in 1742, their influence was based on much more than their knowledge of the Penns' land policies. In fact, Wistar had constructed a series of fluid transatlantic trade and communication channels that he used to provide merchandise, credit, and other services to newly arrived settlers. He had created relationships of mutual obligation and dependence that stretched from the newly settled regions of Pennsylvania to the Neckar River valley.[90]

86. Fogleman, *Hopeful Journeys*, 69–99.

87. Durnbaugh, *Brethren in America*, 55. The original letter is not reprinted in its complete form in Durnbaugh. In the original he notes: "durch den ersten Vorschlag den ich gethan habe, an Ihn meinen werthen Freund, als neml. Arent Hassert, welcher nun auch zum Ruhe gegangen ist, u. Caspar Wistar, welcher auch gestorben, u. Christoph Sower u. Ich. Wir wolten gute haußhalter gewesen seyn über das Geld, als treue Vätter." Best. 80/4/ Nr. 33a, Stadtarchiv Krefeld. I would like to thank James Duffin, who generously shared this letter with me.

88. Durst Thommen to the government of Basel, Oct. 3, 1737, in Leo Schelbert, "Von der Macht des Pietismus," *Baseler Zeitschrift für Geschichte und Altertumskunde* 75 (1975): 105. "Wan mich jemand berichten oder schreiben wolte, so berichte man auff Philadelfia in deß Caspar Wisters oder Johanas Wister, da werde ichs ordenlich bekommen."

89. Aaron S. Fogleman, "Hopeful Journeys: German Immigration and Settlement in Greater Pennsylvania, 1717–1775" (Ph.D. diss., University of Michigan, 1991), 165–66.

Trade between continental Europe and the British American colonies posed special risks to German-speaking immigrants like Wistar. To minimize the hazards of his status as a naturalized subject and the expense of importing merchandise from Europe, he based his exchanges on a fluid set of relationships bound by reciprocity and trust. His commercial transactions were anchored on each side of the Atlantic by the resources he and Hölzer had at their disposal. A constantly changing group of agents, each bringing specific assets to the exchanges, traveled between the two merchants. By relying on brokers with their own sets of contacts, Wistar and Hölzer succeeded in making all of the connections required to carry on trade with suppliers in continental Europe. Wistar's commercial and communication networks raised his social status and allowed him to function as a patriarch and patron within the German-speaking Atlantic community.

90. The rich set of correspondence between Wistar and Hölzer offers a rare opportunity to hear their voices and catch glimpses of their family and business relationships. But there is much we cannot tell. The letters furnish tantalizing suggestions of other connections for which we have no further evidence. Wistar may have communicated regularly with his wife's family members living in Krefeld, Neuwied, and Kriegsheim. He may have continued importing merchandise from Europe, using his connections to retrieve legacies after Hölzer's death in 1745, but if he did so, no evidence survives. By the mid-1740s, other German-speaking immigrants had established communication channels. Clergy in the Lutheran, Reformed, and Moravian churches and other prominent individuals and entrepreneurs played similar mediation roles for the immigrant community in the middle decades of the eighteenth century. For examples of these networks, see Müeller-Bahlke, "Communication at Risk," 139–55, and Häberlein, "Communication," 156–71.

TO THE NEW JERSEY LEGISLATURE:

The Petition of Caspar Wistar, Proprietor of the Glassworks ... Humbly Sheweth That Your Petitioners have at a very great Expense and Risque, erected the Said Glass Works the first in America, That the Making of Glass within this Province is, as your Petitioners conceive, a Considerable Advantage to the Country, not only as it saves the Money that must otherwise be sent abroad for that Commodity but as it brings Cash in, for Quantities exported to other Colonies, much of which is expended here in defraying the Charges of the Works, to the no small Benefitt of the Inhabitants, ... That it is no Unusual Thing in Wise Governments, to encourage new Manufactures, by Granting Bounties And Immunities to those who Introduce them.

—PETITION OF Caspar Wistar and glassmakers, January 29, 1752

CHAPTER 8

Creative Adaptations

THE UNITED GLASS COMPANY AND WISTARBURG, NEW JERSEY

By 1738, Wistar had accumulated enough capital through his button-making business, land speculation, and merchant activities to invest in a new enterprise. On January 13 of that year, he signed a lease with John Ladd for the use of 18,000 cords of wood from a fifty-acre plot of land in Salem County, New Jersey.[1] Nine months later, four glassmakers arrived in Philadelphia aboard the ship *Two Sisters*. Shortly thereafter, Wistar contracted with the German-speaking artisans to form the United Glass Company. They agreed to teach Wistar and his son the art of making glass in return for one-third of the company's profits. Wistar, for his part, promised to pay for the glassmakers' transatlantic voyage, provide housing for them, and furnish the capital for establishing the glassworks in exchange for the remaining profits.[2]

Wistar's enterprise was the first long-lived, successful glass manufactory in British North America.[3] Indeed, both Wistar and his son Richard believed their operation to be the first of its kind.[4] Several attempts to manufacture glass had been made in the seventeenth century, but none had succeeded for more than a short period of time.[5] The United Glass Company outlived both Wistar and his son; Catharine, Wistar's widow, and his grandchildren continued to oversee the glassworks until 1782.[6]

1. Ladd Papers, Stewart Collection, Rowan University, Glassboro, N.J. (hereafter Ladd Papers).

2. R. M. Acton, "A Short History of the Glass Manufacture in Salem County, New Jersey," *PMHB* 9 (1885): 344–45; Joseph S. Sickler, *The History of Salem County, New Jersey* (Salem, 1939), 93.

3. Palmer, "Wistarburg," 1; Helen McKearin, *Two Hundred Years of American Blown Glass* (New York: Crown Publishers, 1950), 7–13.

4. Jan. 29, 1752, Petition of Caspar Wistar, Martin Halter, and William Wentzel to the New Jersey Legislature, NJA; Petition of Richard Wistar to the Earl of Loudoun, General of His Majesty's Forces in North America, 1756 or 1757, Huntington Library, San Marino, Calif. (reproduced in Palmer, "Wistarburg," 8).

5. Palmer, "Wistarburg," 21–23.

6. The final year of the United Glass Company's production is disputed; several scholars maintain that production stopped during the Revolution. Palmer notes that the works was finally deserted in 1778; "Wistarburg," 2. Although the enterprise may have been deserted when war reached New Jersey, production continued into the 1780s. Wistar's son Richard tried to sell the enterprise in 1780 but failed to find an interested buyer. The glassworks continued to function after his death in 1781. His son described a day's work at the enterprise late that year. In March 1782, Richard's heirs leased the

In addition to its longevity, historians have noted the novel nature of Wistar's contract with the glassmakers; their agreement established a company that resembled a modern corporation.[7] Similarly, Wistarburg, the village that grew up around the operation, functioned more like a nineteenth-century factory town than an eighteenth-century rural market center. In traditional historical accounts, the United Glass Company foreshadows the exceptional nature of industrial development in the United States.[8]

From a twenty-first-century perspective, Wistar's business organization may have been unique in the British American colonies. Viewed from within its contemporary transatlantic world, however, the New Jersey glassworks represents both the continuity of European practices and adaptations to an American environment. Government regulation of the economy and natural resources created a different set of circumstances in the Palatinate from those in the mid-Atlantic colonies. Nevertheless, Wistar and his partners exploited business and organizational strategies resembling those of their European counterparts. The nature of Wistar's United Glass Company did not differ dramatically from eighteenth-century European glass-making communities.

At the same time, Wistar's New Jersey enterprise demonstrates the growing diversity of the colonial American economy. As the eighteenth century progressed, American markets became more integrated into emerging British Atlantic trade.[9] Colonists increasingly demanded and could afford the same consumer goods Europeans were purchasing. Businesses like Wistar's United Glass Company began producing a broader array of products for the growing American market.[10] It is no accident, then, that Wistar's eighteenth-century glassworks succeeded.

Wistar first learned about the natural resources required for making glass as a hunter's apprentice in the Palatinate.[11] While working in the elector's

---

property to Adam Brinneholtz. Catharine Wistar, Caspar's widow, lived until 1786 and according to Caspar's will, was to receive a share in the profits from the glassworks. In 1793, the property was legally divided between Richard Wistar's heirs and subsequently sold in parcels. *Pennsylvania Journal,* Oct. 11, 1780; N.J. Wills, Gloucester County, 1374, NJA; Thomas Wistar, Wistarburgh, to Caspar Wistar, Philadelphia, Dec. 28, 1781, Henry Godard Leach Collection, HSP; lease, Richard Wistar's heirs to Adam Brinneholtz, Mar. 1782, Wyck Papers, American Philosophical Society, Philadelphia; Philadelphia County Wills, bk. I, 493, microfilm copy, HSP; Salem County Deeds, A:266, NJA.

    7. Palmer, "Wistarburg," 66.

    8. Sickler, *History of Salem County,* 94.

    9. Hancock, *Citizens of the World;* Butler, *Becoming America;* McCusker and Menard, *Economy.*

    10. T. H. Breen, "An Empire of Goods," in *Colonial America,* ed. Stanley Katz, John M. Murrin, and Douglas Greenberg (New York: McGraw-Hill, 1993); Richard Bushman, *The Refinement of America: Persons, Houses, Cities* (New York: Alfred A. Knopf, 1992); Cary Carson, Ronald Hoffman, and Peter Albert, eds., *Of Consuming Interests: The Style of Life in the Eighteenth Century* (Charlottesville: University Press of Virginia, 1994).

    11. Historians have questioned how Wistar, a hunter's apprentice in Europe and a brass button maker in Pennsylvania, knew about glass-making resources and technology. They challenged family

forestry administration, he helped to monitor the timber used by various forest industries. One of those operations was Peterstal, a glassworks founded by Johann Peter Wentzel in 1710 and located several miles from Wistar's home.[12] Glassmakers relied on large amounts of wood to fuel the furnaces needed to melt sand, potash (unpurified wood ashes), and other ingredients for the glass batch.[13] During Wistar's apprenticeship, his master collected fees from the proprietors at Peterstal for the lumber they cut. Consequently, Wistar would have been familiar with the glassworks, its operation, and the kind of timber and sand needed to produce glass.[14] Simeon Grießmeyer, one of the partners of the United Glass Company, represents the direct links between Wistar's enterprise and Peterstal. Grießmeyer's father and uncle were journeymen at Wentzel's manufactory when he was born in 1715.[15] In addition, Hölzer's suggestion in 1740 that Wistar might obtain additional glassmakers from the site at Peterstal suggests that both men were familiar with Wentzel's enterprise.[16] The Palatine manufactory, therefore, was a model for Wistar's United Glass Company and presents a good comparison of the government's control of resources as well as business and labor organizations in the two places.

On January 3, 1710, Johann Peter Wentzel, a master glassmaker from Württemburg, petitioned the elector of the Palatinate for permission to establish a glassworks near Heidelberg. Wentzel proposed to build his operation on the site of a 1680s glass manufactory.[17] The entrepreneur claimed that the area behind

---

traditions that maintain Wistar recognized the appropriate sand for making glass while traveling on business through New Jersey. Arlene Palmer, "Glass Production in Eighteenth-Century America: The Wistarburgh Enterprise," *Winterthur Portfolio* 11 (1976): 77. For family traditions, see Davids, *Wistar Family*, 4; Rubincam, "Wistar-Wister Family," 143; Jordan, *Colonial and Revolutionary Families*, 1:258; and Haines, *Some Notes*, 5.

12. Documentation for the Peterstal glassworks is abundant, but very little has been written about the enterprise. Manuscripts in GLA 229/82943 document the history of several glass manufactories on or close to the site from the mid-seventeenth through the nineteenth centuries; however, local histories are nearly silent on the enterprise's history. *Stadt- und Landkreise*, 1:318; *Stadt- und Landkreise*, 2:1070–72; Reinhard Hoppe, *Dorfbuch der Gemeinde Ziegelhausen mit Ortsteil Peterstal* (Heidelberg, 1940), 39–42.

13. Palmer, "Wistarburg," 32–51.

14. Mar. 10, 1713, GLA 229/82943, 2:145–48; "Short Report"; 1702, GLA 77/1197.

15. Aug. 8, 1715, Kirchenbuch Stift Neuburg, 1700–1806, Katholische Kirchenbuchamt, Heidelberg; GLA 229/82943, 2:121–31; Léon Maurice Crismer, "Origines et Mouvements des Verriers Venus en Belgique au XVIIIe Siècle," *Annales du 7e Congrès International d'Étude Historique du Verre* (Liege, 1978), 338–42, 351.

16. June 1, 1740, Georg Friederich Hölzer to Caspar Wistar, Wistar Family Papers, HSP.

17. Hendrich Van der Wahl was a wood merchant from Holland who had invested his capital in a glassworks at Ziegelhausen. Van der Wahl hired his brother-in-law to oversee the enterprise, and in 1686 he underwrote the costs for a Venician glassmaker to come to Ziegelhausen to make "fine crystal glass." For Van der Wahl's glass manufactory and those that preceded it at Ziegelhausen and Schönau,

the old furnace could be used for a new works without destroying the elector's game. The region, he noted, was "an abominable wilderness" with "stony ridges and cliffs overgrown with old beechwood." The wild area also included "burnt-out houses," for French troops had destroyed the region seventeen years earlier.[18] Wentzel believed his glassworks would help to clear the "wilderness," and he suggested that he, with his three copartners and their workers and families, would help to repopulate the area. He maintained it was in the interest of the government to support his proposal.

Wentzel understood the cameralist economic policies of the government, which were designed to turn natural resources into revenue while protecting them from entrepreneurs and the aristocracy seeking individual profits. The elector, like other princes seeking to rebuild their territories, looked to foreign artisans in trades not dominated by guilds to help turn state lands into profitable commodities.[19] For this reason, Wentzel's petition included the conditions under which he wished to establish the glassworks. His requests signaled the beginning of his negotiations to acquire the closely protected resources necessary for his enterprise.[20] The process he went through stands in stark contrast to Wistar's efforts twenty-eight years later.

The perquisites Wentzel asked for fell into three general categories: the acquisition of timber and ashes; tax and rent reductions; and the means to provide food for his workers and their families. The most important of Wentzel's requests was for timber. Since the proposed site was in a state-owned forest, the elector's forestry department tightly controlled the use of wood. The glassmakers needed timber to fuel the furnaces and to make potash. Consequently, Wentzel asked for wood to build the original structures at the glassworks and for fueling the furnaces. In addition, he requested permission for his potash burners to use the dead wood in the forest and to purchase house ashes from villagers in the surrounding districts at a discounted price.[21]

Second, Wentzel sought tax exemptions and special privileges as a renter. He argued that since the glasshouse would require a large outlay of capital, he should receive several rent-free years. He also wanted special privileges for himself and his workers that included exemption from the compulsory labor, military

see GLA 229/82943, 1. Ebeling, *Der Holländerholzhandel*, 97–99, outlines the role of the Van der Wahls in the lumber and commercial networks along the Rhine River and their connections to banking families in Frankfurt.

18. Jan. 3, 1710, GLA 229/82943, 2:1–4.

19. "Neue Impulse," 163; Gawthrop, *Pietism*, 26–33.

20. GLA 229/82943, 2:5–7.

21. Jan. 3, 1710, GLA 229/82943, 2:1–7. For an eighteenth-century description of the process of glassmaking, see Johann Samuel Hallens, *Werkstäte der heutigen Künste, oder die neue Kunsthistorie*, vol. 3 (Brandenburg and Leipzig, 1764), 141–61. Palmer also outlines the process in "Wistarburg."

service, and the quartering of soldiers required of most Palatine subjects. Finally, Wentzel requested that he and his partners be made hereditary tenants of the glassworks so that his heirs could inherit the right to continue his enterprise.[22]

Third, Wentzel requested special rights to provide food and provisions for his workers and their families. Wentzel was not a Palatine subject, nor would status as a hereditary tenant provide him with full citizenship. Consequently, he needed to negotiate his specific rights with the government. He asked for permission to farm the land his workers cleared, to enclose grazing pastures at the site, and to fatten swine on communal property (rights usually auctioned off to citizens of the village). He also requested that he be allowed to purchase as much food and drink as his workers would consume.[23]

Establishing his operation, however, was not as simple as listing the terms for investing his capital. A group of advisors rendered their opinions on Wentzel's usefulness to the government's interests. Karl von Venningen, the head of the forestry administration concluded, "The establishment of a Glasshouse would be more useful than harmful to the woods and game, especially if some fields and meadows could be cleared."[24] But he thought that some of Wentzel's conditions might hurt the state's resources if not limited. For example, he recommended that the glassmakers be restrained to a specific district; "otherwise," he said, "they will want to cut down half of the woods."[25] He also thought that if their grazing rights were not restricted, "they will want to maintain a whole herd of cattle and want to graze it far and wide."[26] In his advice, von Venningen sought to keep Wentzel from obtaining too many of the government's valuable resources.

The final agreement Wentzel signed with the government contained many of his original conditions, but he was forced to make concessions. The contract added limitations to Wentzel's consumption of timber and potash. For example, he and his workers could cut timber from the glasshouse district for fuel but at his own expense and for the exclusive use of the furnaces. Government officials wanted to make sure Wentzel did not sell timber from state lands to Holland wood merchants, a lucrative trade and source of revenue for the state. Wentzel also was required to replant his district so that by the time the last plot was cleared, the first would be ready to cut again. The forestry department was to monitor both timber cutting and potash production at the site.[27]

Wentzel's contract specified the taxes and tithes he would pay in return for the privilege of making glass on state lands. He was made hereditary tenant and

22. Jan. 10, 1710, GLA 229/82943, 2:5–7.
23. Ibid.
24. Jan. 9, 1710, GLA 229/82943, 2:16–21.
25. Ibid.
26. Ibid.
27. May 1, 1710, GLA 229/118077.

received two rent-free years, but thereafter he was required to pay an annual rent (180 *Gulden*) and all of the other legal fees hereditary tenants usually paid. The contract also stipulated that Wentzel and his workers would pay annual tithes on the fields and meadows they cleared and farmed.[28] Finally, Wentzel was allowed to import food and drink for his workers if he paid the appropriate duties and did not charge any fees to those who consumed his provisions.[29] Clearly the government intended to monitor closely Wentzel's enterprise and its use of the state's forest. As long as the glassworks promoted government interests by supplying revenues, repopulating the area, and clearing unused land, it was viewed as an asset.

In contrast to Wentzel, Wistar signed no contract with the government in order to establish his glassworks in Salem County, New Jersey. In fact, he received no permission from the government at all to begin his enterprise. Colonial administrators first noticed Wistar's glassworks in 1740, one year after he had started making glass. A customs official reported to the Commissioners for Trade and Plantations in London that "there has lately been Erected a Glass work" near Salem "by one Casper Wester a Palatine, and is brought to perfection so as to make Glass."[30] Government officials did not view Wistar's glassworks as a threat nor did they initially attempt to control it in any way.[31]

Instead of petitioning the government for the use of timber and land, as Wentzel had done, Wistar purchased more than 100 acres of woodland from Clement Hall and Amos Penton and leased 18,000 cord of wood and 50 acres of land for "a plantation" from John Ladd Jr. in January 1738. His agreement with Ladd allowed Wistar to cut the specified amount of wood over a twenty-five-year period in exchange for £300 proclamation money. Wistar was to pay the first £100 upon executing the lease and make payments of £33:6:8 for the next six years.[32] Whereas Wentzel paid a yearly rent to the government during his lifetime, Wistar paid off his lease to a private individual in six years. The Palatine government restricted Wentzel from obtaining timber outside of the glasshouse district, an area that soon proved too small for Wentzel's needs. On the other side of the ocean, Wistar and his son Richard purchased additional woodland

---

28. Ten *Kreutzer* per *Morgen* for planted fields and fifteen *Kreutzer* per *Morgen* for meadow.

29. GLA 229/118077.

30. Charles Carkesse to Thomas Hill, July 31, 1740, in *Documents Relating to the Colonial, Revolutionary, and Post-Revolutionary History of the State of New Jersey*, ed. William A. Whitehead et al., *The Archives of the State of New Jersey, 1631–1800*, 1st series, 31 vols. (Newark, 1800–1906) (hereafter *Colonial N.J. Documents*), 6:98.

31. This lack of interest changed after 1763; Arlene Palmer, *The Wistars and Their Glass, 1739–1777* (Millville, N.J.: Wheaton Village Museum, 1989), 7–10.

32. Deed, Clement Hall to Caspar Wistar, Jan. 7, 1738; Deed, Amos Penton to Caspar Wistar, Jan. 23/24, 1738, Wistar Family Papers (576), Salem County Historical Society, Salem, N.J.; Agreement, John Ladd and Caspar Wistar, Jan. 13, 1738, Ladd Papers.

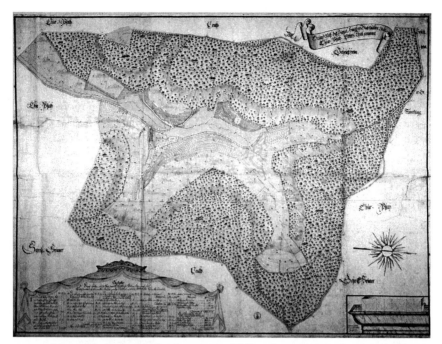

FIG. 13 Map of the Peterstal Glasshouse tract. H Ziegelhausen Nr. 9. Courtesy of the Generallandesarchiv Karlsruhe.

from neighboring New Jersey landholders when they needed more fuel. By the time of Richard's death in 1781, the "Glasshouse tract" included more than 2,000 acres of land.[33]

If New Jersey's government did not place restrictions on Wistar's use of timber, Wistar nevertheless practiced measures to preserve his woodland similar to those stipulated in Wentzel's contract. In 1747, Benjamin Franklin sent a detailed description of Wistar's glassworks to a merchant interested in establishing a similar enterprise in Connecticut. He claimed that Wistar cut one-thirtieth of his timber each year and replanted it immediately thereafter. His Palatine apprenticeship taught Wistar the importance of preserving his source of fuel.[34]

The one natural resource Wistar had difficulty finding was the right clay for constructing the company's ovens and pots for cooking the glass batch. On January 25, 1739, one month after he had signed the contract with the four master

33. Wistar Family Papers (576), Salem County Historical Society, Salem, N.J. Richard Wistar's will states that it contained more than 1,500 acres. Will of Richard Wistar, Oct. 5, 1780, probated Jan. 3, 1782, New Jersey Wills, Gloucester County, 1374. When the division of property was filed on May 30, 1791, it contained a total of 2,054 acres. See Salem County Deeds, A:266, NJA.

34. Franklin to Thomas Darling, Feb. 10, 1746/7; Leonard W. Labaree, ed., *The Papers of Benjamin Franklin*, vol. 3 (New Haven: Yale University Press, 1961), 109.

glassmakers, Wistar wrote to Hölzer in Neckargemünd, asking him to send clay from Coblenz for the glass furnace. Hölzer promised to do his best to find the right clay and send it the following year with Captain Stedman. Wistar, however, failed to mention it again and Hölzer never sent it.[35] Apparently he found another source for the clay. In 1747, Franklin reported that Wistar had been buying clay in England but had finally found a source somewhere in the colonies.[36] The American clay caused problems, however; New Jersey's Governor Jonathan Belcher noted Wistar's complaints that "the Clay for the Furnace Bottoms was but poor and often gave way to their great damage."[37] In his petition to the New Jersey legislature in 1752, Wistar wrote that the glassmakers "frequently meet with great Losses by the breaking of their Potts, not having yet been able to find any Clay that will Stand the fire."[38] Wentzel, in contrast, seemed to have no problem obtaining clay from Coblenz. An inventory of materials at the Peterstal glasshouse taken in 1713, included 300 clumps of "Coblenzer clay" assessed at 22 *Gulden* 30 *Kreuzer.*[39]

Just as the process for acquiring the appropriate resources for making glass differed between the two places, so did the tax obligations of the two enterprises. Wentzel received two years of free rent, but from the beginning he had to pay a series of taxes, tithes, and duties on supplies and land to a variety of authorities. But Wistar did not pay any provincial taxes on his glasshouse tract for the first twelve years of the company's operation. The New Jersey colonial government supported itself by issuing bills of credit rather than through general taxes. Consequently, from 1735 to 1751 the legislature levied no taxes.[40]

The year 1751, however, proved to be a turning point; that year the legislature agreed on a provincial tax bill. A preliminary assessment valued the United Glass Company at £1,000 New Jersey currency.[41] In response to the proposed legislation, Wistar and his partners petitioned for tax-exempt status for the glassworks. Like Wentzel, they pointed to the advantages the enterprise brought to New Jersey. Not only did the glassworks keep money in the colony that would otherwise be sent abroad to purchase glass, it also brought cash into the province

35. For a description of the way in which the ovens were constructed, see Palmer, "Wistarburg," 43–44. The relationship between Hölzer and Wistar is outlined in Chapter 5. Hölzer to Wistar, Feb. 20 and June 1, 1740, Wistar Family Papers, HSP.

36. Franklin to Darling, Feb. 10, 1747; *Papers of Benjamin Franklin*, ed. Labaree, 3:110.

37. Belcher to Alford, Aug. 24, 1752, *Colonial N.J. Documents*, 8:110.

38. Petition to the Legislature, Jan. 29, 1752, NJA.

39. Mar. 10, 1713; GLA 229/82943, 2:145–48. This account included fees paid to Wistar's master, the chief hunter of Bruchhausen, and was taken during Wistar's tenure as a hunter's apprentice. Wistar may have known about the Coblenzer clay from his apprenticeship, although it is more likely that the glassmakers who helped him set up his glassworks in 1739 suggested Coblenz as a source of clay.

40. Peter Wacker, "The New Jersey Tax-Ratable List of 1751," *NJ History* 107 (1989): 24–25.

41. Wacker, "New Jersey Tax-Ratable," 33.

through its exports of glass to nearby colonies. Furthermore, the company fueled the local economy by purchasing ashes and provisions for workers from neighboring farmers. After maintaining that it "is no unusual Thing in Wise Governments, to encourage new Manufactures, by Granting Bounties And Immunities to those who Introduce them," the partners asked to be relieved from the extra tax proposed by the new bill.[42] Whether or not Wistar received tax exemption status from the taxes levied beginning in 1752 remains unclear. Nevertheless, the United Glass Company enjoyed at least twelve years of production without the burden of paying extensive government fees.[43]

A final area of difference in government regulation at Peterstal and Wistarburg concerns provisioning their workers. Wistar did not worry about receiving permission to graze cattle for food for his workers. Nor did he have to purchase communal rights from neighboring villagers to fatten hogs. Instead, he bought more than 1,000 bushels of grain and 10,000 weight of pork each year from local farmers. Whereas Wentzel argued with his neighbors over closely controlled traditional usage rights, Wistar's enterprise created income for surrounding inhabitants who were working to improve their land.[44]

The government's involvement in the glass-making communities at Peterstal and Wistarburg differed significantly. Whereas state officials monitored every step of the process in Wentzel's operation from before its inception to its demise, Wistar's glassworks went virtually unnoticed until after it was well established. A series of insolvent partners, restrictions on cutting wood, high taxes and rents, and war severely hindered glass production at Peterstal.[45] In New Jersey, unregulated access to timber and sand and low taxes encouraged Wistar's enterprise, which flourished until war interfered in the 1770s.

42. Petition to Legislature, Jan. 29, 1752, NJA.
43. The Salem County tax on the glassworks rose from twenty shillings in 1746 to three pounds in 1749. Palmer, *Wistars and Their Glass*, 8.
44. GLA 229/82943, 2:81–85, 189–233; Petition to Legislature, Jan. 29, 1752, NJA. For a description of Wistar's glassworks property in 1780, see advertisement in *Pennsylvania Journal*, Oct. 11, 1780. At that point it was advertised as including "about 250 Acres of cleared Land within fence, 100 whereof is mowable meadow, which produces hay and pasturage sufficient for the large stock of cattle and horses employed by the Manufactory. There is Stabling sufficient for 60 head of cattle, with a large Barn Granary, and Waggon-house. The unimproved Land is well wooded, and 200 Acres more of meadow may be made." Reproduced in Palmer, *Wistars and Their Glass*, 6.
45. By 1719, Ludwig Reinhard von Juncken obtained three-quarters share of the glassworks. When he died in 1734, his widow claimed that government restrictions on cutting timber had halted glass production between 1728 and 1734 and that the 7,000 *Gulden* they had invested in the works was a total loss. Following von Jungken's death, Wentzel obtained control of all shares in the manufactory. After he died in 1743, his widow and children continued to run the enterprise until 1758. GLA 229/82943, 3:542–47; GLA 229/118126; GLA 229/118061; Klaus Irmscher and Rosalind Beiler, "Die Wanderungsbewegungen der Glasmacher Wenzel aus Gründau-Breitenborn im Deutschen Südwesten, Erste Teil," *Genealogie* 9/10 (1998): 274–96.

Although government involvement in the daily operations of the two glass-works differed significantly, the business strategies of their entrepreneurs had much in common. Wistar's contractual arrangements with his partners may have been unique in the British colonies, but internal contracts were common among glassmakers in Europe.[46] In setting up his company, Wistar transferred European practices to his American context.

Wentzel established his original Palatine glassworks in company with three other glassmakers—Johann Christoph Wentzel, Leonhard Friederich Wentzel, and Johann Heinrich Wentzel.[47] Within a year of beginning production, Johann Peter accused Johann Christoph Wentzel of embezzling money from the sale of glass they produced jointly. Accusations evolved into threats and physical brawls. Before long the journeymen and workers at the furnace threatened to leave the site. A government commission resolved the dispute in Johann Peter Wentzel's favor and production struggled on. In 1712, Johann Martin Gottfried Hermanni purchased the three partners' shares of the company and divided ownership of the glassworks equally with Johann Peter Wentzel.[48]

To prevent any similar disputes with his new partner, Wentzel signed an agreement with Hermanni explicitly outlining the terms of their partnership. Hermanni, who was not a glassmaker, became the primary investor in the company. Wentzel was responsible for overseeing the daily operation of the manufac-tory, and he received a special salary for his on-site supervision. As the primary investor, Hermanni agreed to deposit 500 *Gulden* in cash in the partnership's fund, which was to remain there for three years without interest. The partners also hired a joint factor who acted as a bookkeeper and business manager for the firm.[49]

Like Wentzel's contract with Hermanni, Wistar's 1738 agreement with the glassmakers in New Jersey centered around a primary investor, skilled artisans, and a factor. As the primary investor, Wistar agreed to pay for his partners' transportation costs, provide capital for living quarters, and pay the start-up

46. For examples of guild agreements and other contracts signed between glassmakers, see Stefan Krimm, *Die mittelalterlichen und frühneuzeitlichen Glashütten im Spessart* (Aschaffenburg, 1982), 226–36; N. Daniel Schwalm, ed., "The Glass Works near Stephanshof," *Johannes Schwalm the Hessian* 1 (1980): 36–38.

47. Hoppe, *Ziegelhausen Dorfbuch*, 41, mistakenly states that these men were brothers from Isenburg in Hesse. See also Walter Gundlach, "Zur Geschichte der Glashütten im Laubacher und Büdinger Wald und ihrer Glasmeister," *Hessische Familienkunde* 11 (1973) 7:290. For the family connections of the four partners, see Irmscher and Beiler, "Die Wanderungsbewegungen ," 274–96.

48. GLA 229/82943, 2:75–101.

49. GLA 229/82943, 2:105–15. Hermanni never contributed the promised capital. Within a short period of time, only Wentzel's half of the manufactory was operating and Hermanni's workers were planning to leave because he had not purchased the supplies they needed to make glass. When his creditors began to threaten the enterprise, Hermanni's distant relative tried to bail him out. In 1719, however, the government sold his half of the lease to Major von Juncken. From that point until 1728, the glassworks at Peterstal managed to produce glass. GLA 229/82943, 2.

costs of the company. In return, he received the exclusive rights to his partners' skills—they promised to teach only him and his son the art of glass-making. Like the glassworks at Peterstal, the United Glass Company had a factor who was the bookkeeper and general business manager.[50]

Wistar also adopted a similar organizational structure to that of the Peterstal operation. Both enterprises were arranged as individual companies within a larger company. At Peterstal, Wentzel and Hermanni oversaw their own ovens and their own workers. Each partner was responsible for furnishing his workers with food, tools, and supplies—including timber, potash, and sand. Each man also paid his own workers' wages. The two men, however, shared the general administrative costs of the company. Government fees, building and repair costs, and wages for wood- and glasscutters came out of the joint partnership's fund. Wentzel and Hermanni agreed to calculate the income and expenses of the partnership after each blast of the furnace and to share equally in the profits or losses.[51]

The structure of the United Glass Company at Wistarburg was similar, although a bit more complex. Like Wentzel and Hermanni, Wistar and the four glassmakers established small companies within a single larger company. The "whole" company covered the costs for maintaining the ovens and buildings and for making potash. Wistar carried two-thirds of the costs of the "whole" company while the four glassmakers jointly paid one-third of its expenses. The "whole" company also had three subsidiary "particular" companies. Each of the "particular" companies centered around the glassmakers themselves. Johann Wilhelm Wentzel and Caspar Halter each had his own company in partnership with Wistar. Each man paid one-third of the costs and received one-third of the profits from his own company's production. The remaining two glassmakers, Simeon Grießmeyer and Johan Martin Halter, shared a third "particular" company with Wistar. Together they paid one-third of the costs and shared one-third of the profits from their specific company.[52]

At Wistarburg, as at Peterstal, the "particular" companies revolved around individual ovens where the glassmakers worked. In 1744, Wistar confirmed the conditions of his original agreement with his partners. Upon liquidation of the company, the glassmakers would each retain ownership of the ovens and tools from their specific companies.[53] The two kettles in the potash house and all

50. Acton, "Short History," 344–45; Adeline Pepper, *The Glass Gaffers of New Jersey and Their Creations from 1739 to the Present* (New York, 1971), 20–21; Philadelphia County Wills, bk. I, 493, microfilm copy, HSP; Caspar Wistar, Account Book G, 1743–69, Wistar Family Papers, HSP (hereafter Account Book G).

51. GLA 229/82943, 2:145–48.

52. Account Book G.

53. The oven and tools that Wistar purchased from the glassmakers probably refers to the £85 he paid each one in 1741.

TABLE 6 Business Organization of Glassworks at Peterstal and Wistarburg

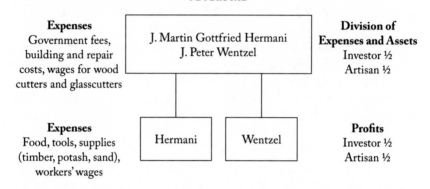

PETERSTAL

Expenses
Government fees,
building and repair
costs, wages for wood
cutters and glasscutters

J. Martin Gottfried Hermani
J. Peter Wentzel

**Division of
Expenses and Assets**
Investor ½
Artisan ½

Expenses
Food, tools, supplies
(timber, potash, sand),
workers' wages

Hermani   Wentzel

Profits
Investor ½
Artisan ½

WISTARBURG

Expenses
Building and repair
costs, potash production,
wages for wood cutters
and glass cutters

Caspar Wistar
J. Wilhelm Wentzel, J. Caspar
Halter, J. Martin Halter,
Simeon Grießmeyer

**Division of
Expenses and Assets**
Investor ⅔
Artisans ⅓

Expenses
Food, tools,
wages

C. Wistar
J. W. Wentzel

C. Wistar
J. C. Halter

C. Wistar
J. M. Halter
S. Grießmeyer

Profits
Investor ⅔
Artisans ⅓

the other iron tools purchased by and used for the "whole" company were to be divided between Wistar and the glassmakers with Wistar receiving two parts and the glassmakers one part. Thus each of the artisans owned the ovens and tools of their specific companies and paid the wages of the workers under them. The tools and implements for making potash and cutting timber belonged to the "whole" company.[54]

Finally, just as Wentzel and Hermanni agreed to settle their accounts at the end of each year's blast, so Wistar and the four glassmakers at Wistarburg calculated their expenses and profits annually. The first firing of the United Glass Company's ovens began in the fall of 1739 and continued through the spring of

54. Account Book G.

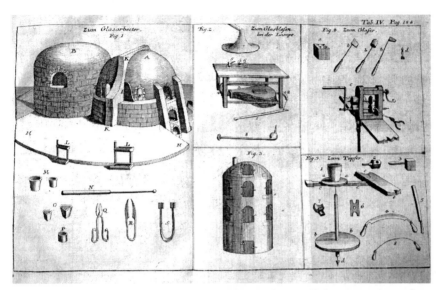

FIG. 14 Glass-making furnace and tools. From Johann Samuel Halle, *Werkstate der heutigen Kunste, oder die neue Kunsthistorie*. Brandenburg and Leipzig: Johann Benedlin Halle und Johann Samuel Halle, 1764, vol. 3, p. 188. Courtesy of the Frank H. Stewart Room, Campbell Library, Rowan University, Glassboro, N.J.

the following year. Because of the summer heat, the blasts generally lasted from October to May. Wistar and the glassmakers (like Wentzel and Hermanni) usually closed out their accounts in May, immediately following the end of the blast, or in the fall, before the new firing began.[55]

Wistar's original contract with the four glassmakers continued until his death, but the specific arrangements of the company shifted as it grew. In 1748, Simeon Grießmeyer, one of the original glassmakers, died and his widow and heirs continued to maintain his part of the contract.[56] Between Grießmeyer's death and 1751, transitions in the organization of the glassworks occurred as several new glassmakers arrived at Wistarburg. From 1751 on, Johann Wilhelm Wentzel and Johann Martin Halter were the only two of the original glassmakers who remained in the partnership. Caspar Halter, if he remained at the glassworks, no longer shared directly in its profits as a partner. The accounts for 1751/52 were listed as the first blast, which implies a new contract between the proprietors of the enterprise.[57]

55. GLA 229/82943, 2:105–16; Account Book G.
56. May 25, 1748, Letters of administration, New Jersey Wills, Salem County, 828, NJA. Christian Crattinger was most likely making glass in his place.
57. At the same time, a new factor took over the record keeping at the glassworks; Account Book G.

The United Glass Company witnessed further changes in 1752 after Caspar Wistar died and his son Richard took over his part of the partnership. Nevertheless, the general structure remained the same. Like its European counterpart, the United Glass Company continued to operate as a series of companies within a company and the Wistars continued as the primary investors who marketed the glassmakers' products. In establishing his glassworks, Wistar transferred the business organization of European entrepreneurs to his American context.

In contrast, the labor organizations of the British American and Palatine glassworks illustrate both the transfer and adaptation of European forms to a new environment. At the two sites, villages emerged in the "wilderness" as workers arrived to support the enterprises. Both Wentzel and Wistar became patrons within their respective communities. Nevertheless, conditions in New Jersey fostered new forms of labor not available in the Palatinate.

The villages that grew up around the two glassworks were made up of people who earned their living from the companies. Both Wentzel and Wistar relied most heavily on skilled artisans for the production of their glass. At Peterstal, Wentzel, who was a master glassmaker, had achieved the highest level of European training. In addition, journeymen and apprentices helped him to produce glass. By 1713, at least eight journeymen worked at Hermanni's oven, and Wentzel likely had a similar number of skilled artisans assisting him.[58]

Skilled glassmakers also played a central role at Wistarburg. Two of Wistar's original partners were probably master glassmakers. Benjamin Franklin reported that the company had begun with only two glassmakers but they had trained four men for a total of six skilled artisans by 1747.[59] Although all four of the original glassmakers were partners in the enterprise, the status of Johann Martin Halter and Simeon Grießmeyer as journeymen at the beginning of the venture likely dictated their joint "particular" company.[60] Wistar's partnership revolved around the original glassmakers, but clearly other men worked and trained under them. The two men who rounded out the six glassmakers Franklin reported in 1747 were "Engel" and "Heinrich," whose wages all four of the original partners contributed to in 1745 and 1746.[61] Additional German-speaking immigrants also worked as glassmakers at Wistarburg, either as journeymen or apprentices.[62]

58. GLA 229/82943, 2:145–48.
59. Benjamin Franklin to Thomas Darling, Mar. 27, 1747, in *Papers of Benjamin Franklin*, ed. Labaree, 3:114.
60. Account Book G. If he was a journeyman at the beginning of the partnership, Johann Martin Halter was a master glassmaker by the time of his death in 1767. Gloucester County Historical Society, *Records of the Friesburg Emanual Lutheran Church* (Woodbury, N.J., 1984), 94–95.
61. Accounts for 1745/46, Account Book G.
62. Accounts for 1746/47, 1747/48, 1750/51, Account Book G.

In addition to skilled artisans, other kinds of workers contributed to the enterprises at Peterstal and Wistarburg. Both companies hired woodcutters and driers, glass cutters, potash burners, and carters. Whereas Wentzel relied on wage laborers for such tasks, Wistar supplemented wage laborers with indentured servants. In 1752, Wistar claimed that sixty people, many of whom were servants, earned a living from the glassworks.[63] Receipts for the costs of transatlantic voyages, servant indentures, account book entries, and newspaper advertisements for runaway servants from the glassworks confirm Wistar's use of indentured labor.[64] Indentured servitude represented a new form of labor in America where transportation expenses were an equally important component of the costs of training servants.

Slavery was a second form of labor unavailable to Wentzel that Wistar could have used in the glassworks. Although there is no record that slaves worked at the United Glass Company, contemporary Quakers in New Jersey and Pennsylvania did use slaves to operate iron furnaces and do farm work. An oral tradition about Wistar records his decision not to purchase slaves. "A Cargo of Slaves arriving in the river Delaware, he [Wistar] thought it might be an object to purchase some for laborers in his Glass works, and saw the Captain of the vessel on the subject." Having returned home to dinner without making a decision, "the family soon perceived that something was the matter; he remained silent & thoughtful, without eating, which was very unusual." After some time passed, Wistar "rose from the table and left the house, but soon returned with his accustomed cheerfulness, & resuming his seat at table, said 'now I have done with them,' and commenced his meal."[65]

Wistar's contemporaries confirm family traditions about his decision not to buy slaves. In 1734 (four years before he founded the United Glass Company), Wistar accompanied Baron Philip Georg Friederich von Reck from Philadelphia to Trenton and the two men discussed opportunities for immigrants in the colonies. Wistar told von Reck "in elaborate terms how difficult it is to get ahead in this country because servants are not to be had and it is not Christian to buy Negroes."[66] In spite of his choice not to purchase African bound laborers, slavery, like indentured servitude, was an American form of labor unavailable to Palatine entrepreneurs like Wentzel.

Laborers in the two villages were similar, however, in their dependence on the entrepreneurs for food and housing. Wentzel's negotiations with the government

63. Petition to Legislature, Jan. 29, 1752, NJA.
64. Receipt Book of Caspar Wistar, 1747–84, Am .941, HSP; Account Book G; "Account of Servants," *PMHB* 30 (1906): 434; *PMHB* 32 (1908): 368.
65. Brown, "Interesting Records."
66. Jones, *Detailed Reports*, 1:119–20. Interestingly, Wistar showed no apparent scruples about dispossessing Native Americans of their lands.

reveal how he obtained provisions for his employees, but not his system for distribution. New Jersey's United Glass Company purchased food in bulk from neighboring farmers. Wistar ran a general store at the glassworks, and his son owned a grist mill nearby. In his store, Wistar's employees and partners purchased goods on credit against the profit of the glass they would make that year. At the end of each blast, the company's factor added the annual expenditures in the store into the accounts between Wistar and the four partners.[67] Whether through credit or in accordance with the terms of a contract, workers at both Peterstal and Wistarburg depended on Wentzel and Wistar to provide food and housing.

By the time of their deaths, Wentzel's in 1743 and Wistar's in 1752, both men were viewed by others as patrons to the new villages of dependent laborers that had grown up around their enterprises.[68] Wentzel, in spite of ongoing problems with his partners, neighboring villagers, and the government, managed to keep the glassworks functioning sporadically until his death. In 1737, he paid to have a Catholic chapel built for his family and workers.[69] From then on, the village surrounding Wentzel's glassworks was known as "Peterstal"—Peter's valley.[70]

One of the few historians to chronicle Wentzel's enterprise points to the negative image of patronage he had among his neighbors. Petitioners from the bordering district accused him and his partner of "little by little, single-handedly taking into their protection all kinds of riff-raff and rabble, among whom were Jews and many criminals who were expelled from other places or were exiles who found no other haven." Furthermore, Wentzel and his partner "made [the rabble] their subjects and collected protection money from them."[71] Wentzel's chroniclers emphasized a view of him as a money-hungry patron who was attempting to establish his own little fiefdom at Peterstal.

In perhaps similar ways, Wistar came to be recognized as the patron for the village that grew up around the United Glass Company. The best indication of his status is the name of the village. Just as Peterstal was named after Wentzel, so Wistarburg received the name of its proprietor. While none of Wistar's neighbors complained that he was becoming a petty lord, he did, in fact, establish a community of dependent laborers. The people at the glassworks relied on Wistar

67. Petition to the Legislature, Jan. 29, 1752, NJA; Account Book G.
68. Wentzel died on Aug. 25, 1743; Peterstal Katholische Kirchenbuch, 1738–1810; Katholische Kirchenbuchamt, Heidelberg. Wistar died in Philadelphia on March 21, 1752, of dropsy; family Bible records, HSP; Brown, "Interesting Records."
69. Peterstal was used on the title page of the church records which were begun in 1738. Katholische Kirchenbuchamt, Heidelberg. For Wentzel's petition to the bishop of Worms, see documents from June 5, and July 14, 1737, GLA 229/40993. Wentzel lists the number of workers and inhabitants at the glasshouse at sixty.
70. Hoppe, *Ziegelhausen Dorfbuch*, 40–41; *Stadt- und Landkreise*, 2:1071; GLA 229/82943, 3.
71. Quoted in Hoppe, *Ziegelhausen Dorfbuch*, 41.

and his family for their housing, food, and supplies. Many of the workers were indentured servants, who depended on Wistar for their most basic needs.

The chroniclers of Wistarburg's history tell the story of Wistar's patronage in a different light from those of Peterstal. In his *History of Salem County*, Joseph Sickler notes that Wistar's general store was also the center of community life for the village. "From the old chronicles come stories of winter sleighing parties coming to the store for their balls, dances, entertainments and other diversions of those pre-Revolutionary days."[72] Instead of a leftover vestige of feudalism, whose neighbors condemned him for extracting dues from his vagabond workers, Wistar was portrayed as a benevolent, paternalist proprietor, whose neighbors and dependents participated in the benefits of his generosity.

The two perspectives historians offer, however, reveal more about twentieth-century interpretations than eighteenth-century realities.[73] True, Wistar experienced fewer government restrictions in New Jersey than Wentzel in the Palatinate. Ultimately Wentzel's heirs were forced out of business, and glassmaking died out as an industry in the region. Although the United Glass Company stopped producing glass in the early 1780s, new enterprises flourished in nineteenth-century South Jersey, where timber and sand remained easily accessible and unregulated. Nevertheless, the business strategies of American glassmakers and the internal structures of their organizations and communities varied little from those of their European counterparts. The companies within a company that appear so unique to Wistar's enterprise were simply a continuation of business organizations in continental Europe. The United Glass Company, like the glassworks at Peterstal, relied on investors, skilled artisans, and factors to carry out production. And perhaps most telling, Wistar, like Wentzel, became a patron to a village of dependent families that grew up in the "wilderness."

Placing the glass-making community at Wistarburg within its eighteenth-century transatlantic context dispels the image of the colonial American enterprise as exceptional. It reveals that European artisans and entrepreneurs brought with them knowledge and experience, which they adapted to their new environments. At the same time, Wistarburg demonstrates the opportunity eighteenth-century America's growing economy offered to savvy individuals like Wistar who shrewdly and aggressively used those adaptations to turn the "wilderness" into marketable commodities.

---

72. Sickler, *History of Salem County,* 94. Sickler was a contemporary of Hoppe, who emphasized Wentzel's attempt to become a feudal lord–like patron. Whereas Hoppe and subsequent historians have minimized the economic role that the Peterstal glassworks played, Sickler and historians of American glass have praised Wistar's enterprise as the beginning of a booming industry.

73. It is instructive that both Hoppe's (1940) and Sickler's (1939) accounts were written in the midst of World War II and likely reflected their respective views of their countries' pasts.

When I first came to this land, I hauled ashes in a wheel barrow; my brother helped to burn charcoal here and we were content with our lives. Now the Lord has trusted us with something more; [we] are, once again, content.

—CASPAR WISTAR to Johann Ludwig Wüster, 1737

It does not matter how much or little [one] brings here, for I have seen people, who in Germany were well off and also brought some money with them, who became poor here and [I] have also seen those who had nothing become rich here.

—CASPAR WISTAR to Georg Friederich Hölzer, 1737

On March 16 in Philadelphia, the very well-known Caspar Wistar died of dropsy in his fifty-sixth year. He served his family and relatives well; in addition, he made many friends with his uncountable worldly riches, which he generously distributed to the poor and of which he could have given away even more. With all of his great fortune, he lived modestly and was concerned about upholding the freedom of the country. He was not corruptible and did not act according to the will of others.

—CHRISTOPHER SAUER, *Pennsylvania Berichte*, April 1, 1752

Conclusion

By the time of his death in 1752, Wistar had completed his rise from a lowly day laborer who hauled ashes for a soap maker to a leadership position among his fellow German immigrants in Pennsylvania. His steps to the pinnacle included apprenticing as a brass button maker, working his way into the Quaker community in Philadelphia, obtaining legitimacy as a British subject, investing in real estate, building transatlantic trade connections, and founding a glass-making village. In the process, he established himself comfortably among Philadelphia's merchant elite and became a patron to the colony's Germans.

Wistar succeeded in his entrepreneurial pursuits in part because of his European legacies. His family's positions as Palatine foresters and his hunter's apprenticeship provided him with specialized knowledge and insight that he integrated into his endeavors in British America. Because of his training, he recognized opportunities to turn natural resources like timber, sand, and land into marketable commodities. He knew about hunting technology and capitalized on his transatlantic business connections to supply a specialized American market for rifles. Wistar also used his father's strategies when positioning himself within Pennsylvania's local political and social hierarchies. Like Wüster, the young man recognized the importance of religious affiliation for legitimation, sought the patronage of economic and political leaders, and married someone with the appropriate social status and kinship networks. And, like his grandfather and father, he played man-in-the-middle while pursuing wealth and security for his family. Through his land speculation and by providing credit to fellow newcomers, he negotiated between the interests of the provincial government, Anglo-Americans, and German-speaking immigrants.

Wistar's success also resulted from the luck of his timing. He arrived in Philadelphia at an opportune moment—with enough time to establish himself before large numbers of German-speaking and Scots-Irish settlers began arriving in the late 1720s. The uncertain status of the colonial government following Penn's death also created conditions that Wistar used to his benefit. He took advantage of Pennsylvania's particular circumstances in the 1730s and 1740s to mediate between various colonial interests while pursuing wealth.

Wistar's mediation, however, also depended on his character. It is difficult to access his personality. We know who his business associates were, but not his friends. Nor does the record reveal how Wistar behaved toward others; we do not know whether he was a sycophant to those in power or how he treated his dependents. The writer of his obituary believed he was generous, modest, and incorruptible, and his descendants portrayed him as a morally upright man.[1] What we do know is that he was a good judge of character. In choosing business partners, selecting agents to represent his interests, and assessing immigrants' credibility, he picked people he determined to be trustworthy. Evidently he made wise decisions, because his endeavors were met with success more often than failure. Others viewed Wistar as dependable and trustworthy too. Pennsylvania's proprietors relied on him to communicate their interests to his fellow immigrants. German-speaking settlers trusted his judgments about the provincial government's policies. And some of them thought he was a careful investor. In addition to the knowledge he brought with him and his good timing, Wistar's ability to assess others and his own reputation were critical for his success.

By the time he died, Wistar also had completed his immigrant journey. In spite of his fears when he left home that he would never be seen or heard from again, Wistar managed to fashion ongoing links to his family and friends in the Palatinate. He did so by relying on every possible means available. Young men who were relatives or who were connected to his in-laws carried letters and money to his family members and to Hölzer; ship captains transported gifts for those who helped him to the Rhine Valley; and newlanders made travel arrangements for his extended family. Through his partnership with Hölzer, Wistar insured that his widowed mother received adequate care, and he supplied money to move his European family members to safety during war. Wistar successfully maintained contact with his home through a flexible set of connections to the Neckar Valley.

Again, timing was critical. Having arrived without links to family or friends, Wistar had to establish his own place in Pennsylvania's society before he could fulfill his familial obligations as the oldest son. By the time his father died in 1726, Wistar had become a naturalized Pennsylvanian and married the daughter of well-established Germantown Quakers with their own family ties to the Rhine Valley. In the next two decades he used the growing immigrant population and the transportation system that brought them to the colony not only to establish a leadership position but also to maintain his position as the patriarch of his transatlantic family.

Ultimately, the sacrifice of his mothers' approval and the risk he took of never seeing family and friends again paid off in the legacies he left behind. He was able

---

1. Sauer, obituary for Caspar Wistar, *Pennsylvania Berichte,* Apr. 1, 1752, HSP; Haines, *Some Notes;* Moon, *Morris Family,* 1:356–63.

to provide his children with the economic and social stability that his father had failed to secure in Waldhilsbach. Whereas he and his siblings left the region to earn their living, of Wistar's six children who survived to adulthood all but one married Anglo-American spouses with extensive kinship networks, and all remained in the mid-Atlantic area. Richard married Sarah Wyatt, the daughter of prominent New Jersey Quakers.[2] Margaret married Reuben Haines, the stepson of a well-established Philadelphia brewer who inherited the family business.[3] Katherine married Isaac Greenleafe, a prominent Philadelphia merchant.[4] Rebecca married Samuel Morris, the grandson of Anthony Morris (the wealthy Quaker politician whose will her father had witnessed in 1721).[5] Sarah, who remained unmarried, amassed her own fortune by the late eighteenth century.[6] And Caspar married Mary Franklin, a Quaker from Long Island.[7] They all settled and raised their own families in Philadelphia, New Jersey, or New York. By the end of the eighteenth century Wistar's children and grandchildren were prominent merchants, professionals, and philanthropists in the mid-Atlantic region.

In contrast to his own siblings, all of Wistar's children were raised in a single religious confession: they were all Quakers. Although Wistar himself never became a "weighty" Friend (a minister or elder), several of his children married into leading Quaker families.[8] Richard's mother-in-law was a "public Friend"—a traveling minister—who was well respected in Philadelphia's Quaker community. He and his sons were actively involved in prison relief in the 1770s and 1780s.[9] When Rebecca married Samuel Morris, she became a part

2. Hinshaw, *Encyclopedia*, 2:111, 113.

3. Feb., Mar., and Apr. 1760, Philadelphia Monthly Meeting, Women's Meeting Minutes, 1757–67, pp. 48, 50, 52–53, Friends Historical Library of Swarthmore College, Swarthmore, Pa.; Hinshaw, *Encyclopedia*, 2:538, 690.

4. Sept. and Oct. 1753, Philadelphia Monthly Meeting, Women's Meeting Minutes, 1728–56, p. 256–57, Friends Historical Library of Swarthmore College, Swarthmore, Pa.; Hinshaw, *Encyclopedia*, 2:536.

5. Hinshaw, *Encyclopedia*, 2:602.

6. Documents concerning Sarah Wistar (1738–1815) are in Wistar Family Papers and Wistar, case 14, box 17, Gratz Collection, HSP.

7. Hinshaw, *Encyclopedia*, 2:690.

8. Wistar does not appear in the records of the Philadelphia Ministers and Elders, Friends Historical Library of Swarthmore College, Swarthmore, Pa. He was appointed one time (along with Anthony Benezet) to see that a marriage was carried out in 1745. Philadelphia Monthly Meeting, 1745–55, p. 9. He also assisted Anthony Morris and Jeremiah Elfreth in mediating a dispute in 1747. Philadelphia Monthly Meeting, 1745–55, pp. 44, 47–48. And in one instance in the same year he brought a business dispute of his own to the monthly meeting for arbitration. Philadelphia Monthly Meeting, 1745–55, pp. 30–32, Friends Historical Library of Swarthmore College, Swarthmore, Pa.

9. Willard Heiss, ed., *Quaker Biographical Sketches of Ministers and Elders, and Other Concerned Members of the Yearly Meeting of Philadelphia, 1682–1800* (Indianapolis, Ind.: pub. by the editor, 1972), 170, 690; Rubincam, "Wistar-Wister Family," 145–47; Joshua L. Baily, "Address at the Centennial Celebration of the Erection of Twelfth Street Meeting-House, Tenth Month 25, 1912," *Quaker History* 18 (1917): 56–60.

of a long-established Philadelphia family who counted numerous Quaker ministers among its members, although Samuel's position on the War for Independence threatened his status within the Society of Friends.[10] Caspar's wife Mary
belonged to a well-established Quaker family from Long Island.[11] In contrast to
his parents and his siblings, Wistar, his wife, and their children shared the same
religious affiliation throughout his American lifetime.

Thus the world Wistar inhabited when he died in 1752 differed significantly
from the one he had left behind in 1717. The Pennsylvania proprietors' control of
their land paled in comparison to the Palatine elector's bureaucracy that closely
monitored the state's forests. Philadelphia's expansion provided room for social
and economic mobility unavailable in Waldhilsbach. And the colony's version of
religious diversity allowed for more unity within his own family than had been
possible for that of his father's in the peculiar circumstances of the Palatinate at
the turn of the seventeenth century.

Nevertheless, the European knowledge and responses Wistar brought with
him wrought changes in his new environment. He and his fellow immigrants
were not always aware of the ways their decisions altered the world around
them. Nor were they the only impetus for change. But their reactions to their
American contexts helped to reshape them.

One of the ways Wistar's European background changed the Pennsylvania landscape was through his land speculation. The unavailability of land in
Waldhilsbach and the restrictions his father faced acquiring social and economic
security influenced Wistar's attempts to invest heavily in real estate. He purchased large tracts of unimproved Pennsylvania acreage and resold it to other
immigrants who were just as eager as he to buy land. His speculation among
fellow German-speaking newcomers contributed to the ethnic enclaves that
dotted the colony's landscape by the 1740s and 1750s.

Wistar's purchases also furthered the process of "taming the wilderness"—of
imposing European notions of order on the land. As a forester's apprentice,
he understood how to turn natural resources into commodities. He recognized
the difference between the "wilderness" of Pennsylvania and the well-ordered,
controlled forests and farms of the Palatinate. Through his investments in real
estate, iron-making, and glass-making, he brought European-style control to the
American landscape. The order Wistar helped to impose, however, was neither
that of a Palatine forest nor of a compact European village. Instead, his transactions created a landscape dotted by independent, scattered family farms and
enterprises run on property owned by individuals rather than the government.

10. Moon, *Morris Family,* 1:420–56.
11. Ibid., 1:364, 372.

Similarly, Wistar's communication and trade channels both evolved with and were instrumental in creating a German-Atlantic world. When he first left Waldhilsbach in 1717, the German population in Pennsylvania was still rather small. By the time of his death, however, German-speaking settlers made up more than 30 percent of the colony's population.[12] Wistar's transatlantic activities helped to increase migration. After he moved to Pennsylvania, Wistar not only maintained contact with his family and friends, he also provided incentives for others to move to the British colonies. He sent back reports that encouraged relatives and friends to migrate. Even when conditions for immigrants deteriorated and Wistar became less enthusiastic about Pennsylvania's opportunities, he did not advise all of his fellow Europeans to remain at home. Instead he provided the information immigrants needed for making careful decisions about whether or not to travel to British America.

Furthermore, in acting as a mediator for fellow immigrants, Wistar helped to make their new circumstances more familiar. By extending credit, serving as a postman, supplying German books and merchandise, helping to retrieve legacies, and acting as a legal guardian, he enabled German speakers to feel more secure in their unfamiliar surroundings. If immigrants could obtain land easily and transplant some aspects of their culture to Pennsylvania, British America would not seem so foreign. Thus Wistar's individual decisions and actions helped to shape an emerging German-Atlantic world.

Finally, Wistar's United Glass Company of Salem County, New Jersey, provides an example of the new technologies and business organization immigrants brought to the American colonies. Wistar was not a glassmaker and did not possess the necessary skills to start his New Jersey glassworks; however, he knew from his apprenticeship in the Palatinate what resources were needed for making glass. He used that limited knowledge and his access to capital to supply a commodity for which he saw a market. In the process of establishing the glassworks, Wistar and his partners adapted European business and labor organizations to fit the environment of New Jersey. Once again, Wistar's decisions based on old-world knowledge in the context of the colony's fluid political and economic structures helped to reshape his surroundings. The United Glass Company was the first enterprise of what was to become a major industry in southern New Jersey by the middle of the nineteenth century.

12. The percentage of German immigrants in Pennsylvania is calculated on the number of immigrants arriving in Philadelphia between 1727 and 1750 and Pennsylvania's estimated total population. Marianne Wokeck, "The Flow and Composition of German Immigration to Philadelphia, 1727–1776," *PMHB* 105 (1981): 260; United States Bureau of the Census, *Historical Statistics of the United States, Colonial Times to 1957* (Washington, D.C., 1960), 756.

By examining Wistar's Atlantic world, therefore, the details of cultural change begin to emerge. Individuals moving from Europe to British America in the eighteenth century encountered significantly different worlds upon their arrival. In the process of adapting to those new environments, they capitalized on their past experience and knowledge. Like Wistar, many immigrants did not necessarily wish to replicate all of their European circumstances in the British colonies—they left, for the most part, in search of something better. Nevertheless, their innovative adaptations and integration of European ways into their new worlds helped to reshape their American environments.

APPENDIXES

APPENDIX 1 Andreas Wüster Genealogy

Andreas Wüster = Anna ?
b. c. 1627 Crailsheim?
d. 7/30/1692 Neunkirchen

1663–1680 Forstknecht
1681–1692 Oberförster

Anna Magdalena = Hans Conrad Müller
bapt. 1665   s. of forstknecht
(NkRKB)   for Sinsenheim
                    m. 1686 (NkRKB)

Maria Catharina
bapt. 1669
(NkRKB)
d. 1670
(NkRKB)

Hans Caspar = Anna Catharina Müller
bapt. 1671   bapt. 1671
(NkRKB)   (BRKB)
d. 1/15/1726   m. 1695 (BRKB)
(NgLKB)

Anna Sibila = ?
bapt. 1676
(NkRKB)
[lived west of
Rhine 1743–52]
(Short Report)

Maria Catharina = Hans Philipp Hofmann
bapt. 1673   s. of Philipp Albecht
(NkRKB)   Hoffman
                      m. 1695 (NkRKB)

                    = Hans Philipp Lentz
                      from Oberschwarzach
                      m. 1713 (NkRKB)

Anna Maria
bapt. 1679
(NkRKB)
d. 1686
(NkRKB)

Maria Helena = ?
bapt. 1684
(NkRKB)
[m. Deschler?]
[lived west of Rhine]
1743–52] (Short Report)

Johannes Christopher
bapt. 1682
(NkRKB)

Johann Adam
bapt. 1687
(NkRKB)

Sources: BRKB = Bammental reformierte Kirchenbuch, EOK
            NgLKB = Nechargemünd lutherische Kirkenbuch, EOK
            NkRKB = Neunkirchen reformierte Kirchenbuch, EOK
            Short Report = "Ein kortzer Bericht von Caspar Wistar," HSP

APPENDIX 2 Hans Caspar Wüster Genealogy

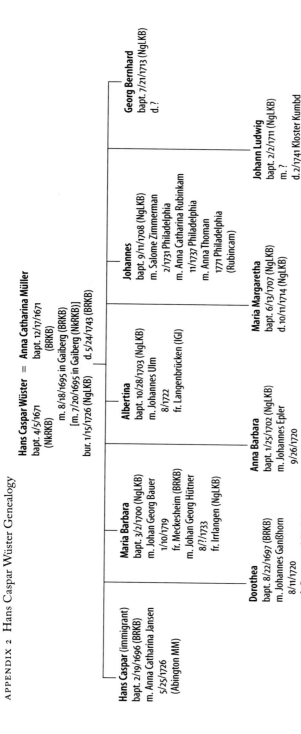

Hans Caspar Wüster = **Anna Catharina Müller**
bapt. 4/5/1671   bapt. 12/17/1671
(NkRKB)   (BRKB)
m. 8/18/1695 in Gaiberg (BRKB)
[m. 7/20/1695 in Gaiberg (NkRKB)]
bur. 1/15/1726 (NgLKB)   d. 5/24/1743 (BRKB)

Hans Caspar (immigrant)
bapt. 2/19/1696 (BRKB)
m. Anna Catharina Jansen
5/25/1726
(Abington MM)

Maria Barbara
bapt. 3/2/1700 (NgLKB)
m. Johan Georg Bauer
1/10/1719
fr. Meckesheim (BRKB)
m. Johan Georg Hütner
8/?/1733
fr. Irrlangen (NgLKB)

Dorothea
bapt. 8/22/1697 (BRKB)
m. Johannes Ganßhorn
8/11/1720
fr. Bammental (NgKKB)

Anna Barbara
bapt. 1/25/1702 (NgLKB)
m. Johannes Epler
9/26/1720
fr. Gaiberg (BRKB)

Albertina
bapt. 10/28/1703 (NgLKB)
m. Johannes Ulm
8/1722
fr. Langenbrücken (IGI)

Johannes
bapt. 9/11/1708 (NgLKB)
m. Salome Zimmerman
2/1731 Philadelphia
m. Anna Catharina Rubinkam
11/1737 Philadelphia
m. Anna Thoman
1771 Philadelphia
(Rubincam)

Maria Margaretha
bapt. 6/13/1707 (NgLKB)
d. 10/11/1714 (NgLKB)

Johann Ludwig
bapt. 2/2/1711 (NgLKB)
m. ?
d. 2/1741 Kloster Kumbd
(Short Report)

Georg Bernhard
bapt. 7/21/1713 (NgLKB)
d. ?

Sources: Abbington MM = Abington Monthly Meeting, Pennsylvania, transcripts, HSP
             BRKB = Bammental reformierte Kirchenbuch, EOK
             IGI = International Genealogical Index (Genealogical Society of the Church of the Latter-Day Saints, Utah; microfiche copies at the Historical Society of Pennsylvania,
             Philadelphia, Pa.)
             NgLKB = Neckargemünd lutherische Kirchenbuch, EOK
             NgKKB = Neckargemünd katholische Kirchenbuch, Katholische Pfarramt, Goldene Anchor, Neckargemünd
             NgRKB = Neckargemünd reformierte Kirchenbuch, EOK
             NkRKB = Neunkirchen reformierte Kirchenbuch, EOK
             Rubincam = Milton Rubincam, "The Wistar-Wister Family: A Pennsylvania Family's Contributions Toward American Cultural Development," *PA History* 20 (1953): 142–64.
             Short Report = "Ein kortzer Bericht von Caspar Wistar," HSP

APPENDIX 3 Caspar Wistar Genealogy

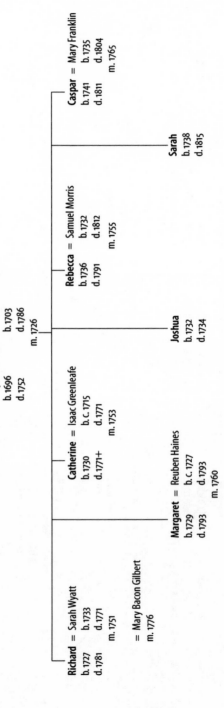

Caspar Wistar = **Catherine Jansen**
b.1696   b.1703
d.1752   d.1786
       m. 1726

Richard = Sarah Wyatt
b.1727   b.1733
d.1781   d.1771
       m. 1751

= Mary Bacon Gilbert
       m. 1776

Catherine = Isaac Greenleafe
b.1730   b.c.1715
d.1771+   d.1771
          m. 1753

Margaret = Reuben Haines
b.1729   b.c.1727
d.1793   d.1793
          m. 1760

Joshua
b.1732
d.1734

Rebecca = Samuel Morris
b.1736   b.1732
d.1791   d.1812
          m. 1755

Sarah
b.1738
d.1815

Caspar = Mary Franklin
b.1741   b.1735
d.1811   d.1804
          m. 1765

Source: Richard Wistar Davids, *The Wistar Family: A Genealogy of the Descendants of Caspar Wistar, Emigrant in 1717* (Philadelphia, 1896).

Manuscripts
German Sources
Archiv der Franckesche Stiftung, Halle:
    Hauptarchiv
Archiv des Evangelischen Oberkirchenrates Karlsruhe, Karlsruhe:
    Luthern and Reformed Church records for Bammental, Dilsberg, Gaiberg,
        Mannheim, Mauer, Meckesheim, Neckargemünd, Neunkirchen, Wiesenbach,
        Waldhilsbach
Badisches Generallandesarchiv, Karlsruhe:
    Amtsprotokolle, Abt. 61/5463, 5465, 5467, 5468, 5469, 5470, 5471, 5474, 5479, 9861, 9862,
        9864
    Pfalz Generalia, Abt. 77/1182, 1197, 1732, 1738, 1739, 1740, 1805, 1818, 1865, 4227, 4311, 4330,
        4363
    Dilsberg Amt, Abt. 135
    Heidelberg Amt, Abt. 145/45, 50, 183, 292, 364
    Official Records, Abt. 229/30951 (Gaiberg), 40993 (Heiligkreutzsteinau), 71466
        (Neckargemünd), 82943 (Peterstal), 109145, 109147 (Waldhilsbach), 118061,
        118077, 118126 (Ziegelhausen)
International Genealogical Index (Genealogical Society of the Church of the Latter-
    Day Saints, Utah; microfiche copies at the Historical Society of Pennsylvania,
    Philadelphia):
    Catholic Church records for Dilsberg, Langenbrücken
    Reformed Church records for Meckesheim
Katholische Kirchenbuchamt Pfarramt, Heidelberg:
    Catholic Church records for Neuburg, Peterstal
Katholische Pfarramt, Neckargemünd:
    Catholic Church records for Neckargemünd, 1635–1750
Staatsbibliothek zu Berlin—Preussischer Kulturbesitz, Berlin:
    Francke Nachlaβ
Stadtarchiv Krefeld, Krefeld:
    Best. 80/4/Nr. 33a
Stadtarchiv Neckargemünd, Neckargemünd:
    Neckargemünd Schätzungsbuch, 1721

American Sources

American Philosophical Society, Philadelphia:
   Wyck Collection
Campbell Library, Rowan University, Glassboro, N.J.:
   Stewart Collection, Ladd Papers
Historical Society of Pennsylvania, Philadelphia:
   Am .941, Caspar Wistar, Receipt Book, 1747–84
   Cadwalader Papers
   Gratz Collection, Wistar Papers
   Henry Godard Leach Collection
   Logan Papers
   Marriage Certificates
   Norris Papers
   Penn Papers, Official Correspondence
   Penn Papers, Penn Manuscripts, Correspondence of the Penn Family, vol. 18, 1732–67
   Penn Papers, Pennsylvania Journals
   Penn Papers, Thomas Penn Letter Books
   Pennsylvania Berichte
   Pennsylvanisher Staatsbote
   Peters Papers
   Philadelphia County Wills
   Society Miscellaneous Collection
   Wistar Family Papers, 1717–1848
   Wister Family Papers, vol. 1, John Wister Ledger
Lancaster Mennonite Historical Society, Lancaster, Pa.:
   Papers of *Commissie voor de Buitenlandsche Nooden,* Archives of the Dutch Menno-
      nite Church, Gemeentearchief, Amsterdam, microfilm copy
Library of Congress, Manuscript Division, Washington, D.C.:
   Records of the Court of Vice Admiralty
Museum of American Glass, Wheaton Arts, Millville, N.J.:
   Lease and Release, Caspar Wistar
New Jersey State Archives, Trenton, N.J.:
   Wills, Inventories, and Probate Records
   Bureau of Archives and History, Petitions
Pennsylvania State Archives, Harrisburg, Pa.:
   RG-17, Records of the Land Office, Patent Books, Commission Books, Copied
      Surveys
   Pennsylvania County Deeds, microfilm copies
Salem County Historical Society, Salem, N.J.:
   Wistar Family Papers (576)
   Wistar Family File
Widener Library, Harvard University, Cambridge, Mass.:
   American Weekly Mercury
   Pennsylvania Gazette
Winterthur Museum and Country Estate, Winterthur, Del.:
   Diary of Christopher Wiegner
   Delaware Deeds
   Francis Richardson's Account Book

Published Primary Sources

"Account of Servants Bound and Assigned Before James Hamilton, Mayor of Philadelphia." *Pennsylvania Magazine of History and Biography* 30 (1906): 427–36; 32 (1908):
351–67.

Barker, Burt Brown, contributor. *Henckel Family Records* 3 (1928): 90–116; 4 (1929): 118–30;
6 (1931): 212–30; 8 (1932): 314–40.

Bender, Harold S., ed. "Palatinate Mennonite Census Lists, 1664–1774." *Mennonite Quarterly Review* 14 (1940): 5–40.

Berkeley, Edmund, and Dorothy Smith Berkeley, eds. *The Correspondence of John Bartram,
1734–1777.* Gainesville: University Press of Florida, 1992.

Bush, Bernard, ed. *New Jersey Archives,* ser. 3., *Laws of the Royal Colony of New Jersey.* Trenton: New Jersey State Library, Archives and History Bureau, 1982.

Castleman, Richard. *The Voyage, Shipwreck, and Miraculous Escape of Richard Castle-
man, Gentlemen, with a Description of Pensylvania and the City Philadelphia 1726, in
The Voyages and Adventures of Captain Robert Boyle, in Several Parts of the World, by
W. R. Chetwood.* London, 1728.

Chur-Fürstlicher Pfaltz Forst-und Wald- auch Weid-werks Jagd- und Fischerey- Ordnung.
Heidelberg: Hof u. Universitäts Buchdrucker, Johann Meyer, 1711.

Commager, Henry S., ed. *Documents of American History.* 3rd ed. New York: F. S. Crofts,
1947.

[Duche, Jacob]. *Caspipina's Letters, Containing Observations on a Variety of Subjects, Literary, Moral, and Religious.* Bath, England, 1777.

Dunn, Richard S., and Mary Maples Dunn, eds. *The Papers of William Penn.* Vol. 1,
1644–1679. Philadelphia: University of Pennsylvania Press, 1981.

———. *The Papers of William Penn.* Vol. 3, *1685–1700.* Philadelphia: University of Pennsylvania Press, 1986.

———. *The Papers of William Penn.* Vol. 4, *1708–1718.* Philadelphia: University of Pennsylvania Press, 1987.

Durnbaugh, Donald. "Two Early Letters from Germantown." *Pennsylvania Magazine of
History and Biography* 84 (1960): 219–33.

Gloucester County Historical Society. *Records of the Friesburg Emanual Lutheran Church.*
Woodbury, N.J., 1984.

Guldin, Samuel. "Diary of Samuel Guldin, Relating to His Journey to Pennsylvania,
June to September, 1710." *Journal of the Presbyterian Historical Society* 14 (1930): 28–41,
64–73.

Haines, Caspar Wistar. *Some Notes Concerning Caspar Wistar Immigrant and on the Origin
of the Wistar and Wister Families.* Presented at the celebration of the 200th anniver-
sary of the marriage of Caspar Wistar and Catherine Jansen, May 25, 1726. Philadelphia, 1926.

Hallens, Johann Samuel. *Werkstäte der heutigen Künste, oder die neue Kunsthistorie.* Vol. 3.
Brandenburg and Leipzig, 1764.

Hangebruch, Dieter, ed. *Das Tagebuch der Brüder Claes und Abraham ter Meer, 1732–1756.*
Krefeld: Verein für Heimatkunde e. V. Krefeld, 2002.

Hazard, Samuel, ed. *Pennsylvania Archives,* ser. 1, *Selected and Arranged from Original
Documents in the Office of the Secretary of the Commonwealth.* Vol. 1, *1664–1747.* Philadelphia: Joseph Severns, 1852.

Kelsey, R. W., ed. and trans. "An Early Description of Pennsylvania: Letter of Christopher
Sower, Written in 1724, Describing the Conditions in Philadelphia and Vicinity, and

the Sea Voyage from Europe." *Pennsylvania Magazine of History and Biography* 45 (1921): 243–54.

Kochertal, Josua. *Außführlich- und umständlicher Bericht von der berühmten Landschafft Carolina In dem Engelländischen America gelegen.* Frankfurt, 1709.

Labaree, Leonard W., ed. *The Papers of Benjamin Franklin.* New Haven: Yale University Press, 1959–.

MacKinney, Gertrude, and Charles F. Hoban, eds. *Pennsylvania Archives,* 8th ser., 8 vols., *Votes and Proceedings of the House of Representatives of the Province of Pennsylvania, 1682–1776.* Harrisburg, 1931–35.

Minutes of the Provincial Council of Pennsylvania from the Organization to the Termination of the Proprietary Government. Vol. 2, *December 18, 1700, to May 16, 1717.* Philadelphia: Joseph Severns, 1852.

Minutes of the Provincial Council of Pennsylvania from the Organization to the Termination of the Proprietary Government. Vol. 3, *May 31, 1717, to January 23, 1735–6.* Philadelphia: Joseph Severns, 1852.

Mitchel, James T., and Henry Flanders, eds. *The Statutes at Large of Pennsylvania from 1682–1801.* Vol. 2, *1700–1712.* Harrisburg: State Printer of Pennsylvania, 1893.

———. *The Statutes at Large of Pennsylvania from 1682–1801.* Vol. 3, *1712–24.* Harrisburg: State Printer of Pennsylvania, 1895.

———. *The Statutes at Large of Pennsylvania from 1682–1801.* Vol. 4, *1724–1744.* Harrisburg: State Printer of Pennsylvania, 1897.

Mittelberger, Gottlieb *Gottlieb Mittelberger's Journey to Pennsylvania in the Year 1710 and Return to Germany in the Year 1754.* Translated and edited by Oscar Handlin and John Clive. Cambridge: Harvard University, Press, 1960.

Myers, Albert Cook, ed. *Narratives of Early Pennsylvania, West New Jersey and Delaware, 1680–1707.* New York: Barnes and Noble, 1912.

Nicolson, Marjorie, ed. *Conway Letters: The Correspondence of Anne, Viscountess Conway, Henry More, and Their Friends, 1642–1684.* New Haven: Yale University Press, 1930.

Pastorius, Francis Daniel. *Umständige Geographische Beschreibung Der zu allerletzt erfundenen Provintz Pensylvaniae, In denen End-Gräntzen Americae In der West-Welt gelegen Durch Franciscum Danielem Pastorium, J. U. Lic. und Friedens-Richtern daselbsten. Worbey angehencket sind einige notable Begebenheiten, und Bericht-Schreiben an dessen Herrn Vatern Melchiorem Adamum Pastorium, Und andere gute Freunde.* Frankfurt and Leipzig, 1700.

Pennsylvania Archives, 2nd ser., *Minutes of the Board of Property of the Province of Pennsylvania.* Vol. 19. Harrisburg, 1876–93.

Staatlichen Archivverwaltung Baden-Württemberg. *Die Stadt- und die Landkreise Heidelberg und Mannheim: Amtliche Kreisbeschreibung.* Vol. 1, *Allgemeiner Teil.* Karlsruhe: G. Braun GmbH, 1966.

———. *Die Stadt- und die Landkreise Heidelberg und Mannheim: Amtliche Kreisbeschreibung.* Vol. 2, *Die Stadt Heidelberg und die Gemeinden des Landkreises Heidelberg.* Karlsruhe: G. Braun GmbH, 1968.

Strassburger, Ralph B., and William Hinke, eds. *Pennsylvania German Pioneers: A Publication of the Original Lists of Arrivals in the Port of Philadelphia from 1727–1808.* Vol. 1, *1727–1775.* 1934; repr. Baltimore: Genealogical Publishing, 1980.

Thomas, Gabriel. *An Historical and Geographical Account of the Province and Country of Pensilvania.* London, 1698.

United States Bureau of the Census. *Historical Statistics of the United States, Colonial Times to 1957.* Washington, D.C., 1960.

Votes and Proceedings of the House of Representatives of the Province of Pennsylvania. Vol. 1. Philadelphia, 1752.

Whitehead, William A., et al., eds. *The Archives of the State of New Jersey, 1631–1800.* 1st ser., 31 vols. *Documents Relating to Colonial and Revolutionary, and Post-Revolutionary History of New Jersey.* Newark: New Jersey Historical Society, 1880–1906.

Wistar, Caspar. "Letter to Fellow Countrymen." December 4, 1732. Reprinted in *The Perkiomen Region, Past and Present* 2 (Nov. 15, 1899): 119–20.

Wistar, Isaac Jones. *Autobiography of Isaac Jones Wistar, 1827–1905.* Philadelphia, 1914.

Wister, Jones. *Jones Wister's Reminiscences.* Philadelphia: J. B. Lippincott, 1920.

Secondary Literature

Acton, R. M. "A Short History of the Glass Manufacture in Salem County, New Jersey." *Pennsylvania Magazine of History and Biography* 9 (1885): 343–46.

Allen, David G. *In English Ways: The Movement of Societies and the Transferal of English Local Law and Custom to Massachusetts Bay in the Seventeenth Century.* Chapel Hill: University of North Carolina Press, 1981.

Allmann, Joachim. *Der Wald in der frühen Neuzeit. Eine mentalitäts-und sozialgeschichtliche Untersuchung am Beispiel des Pfälzer Raumes, 1500–1800.* Berlin: Duncker and Humblot, 1989.

Armitage, David. "Three Concepts of Atlantic History." In *The British Atlantic World, 1500–1800.* Edited by David Armitage and Michael J. Braddick. New York: Palgrave Macmillan, 2002.

Baily, Joshua L. "Address at the Centennial Celebration of the Erection of Twelfth Street Meeting-House, Tenth Month 25, 1912." *Quaker History* 18 (1917): 56–60.

Bailyn, Bernard. *Atlantic History: Concept and Contours.* Cambridge: Harvard University Press, 2005.

———. *The New England Merchants in the Seventeenth Century.* Cambridge: Harvard University Press, 1979.

———. *The Peopling of British North America: An Introduction.* New York: Random House, 1986.

———. *Voyagers to the West: A Passage in the Peopling of America on the Eve of the Revolution.* New York: Random House, 1986.

Barrow, Thomas. *Trade and Empire: The British Customs Service in Colonial America, 1660–1775.* Cambridge: Harvard University Press, 1967.

Bauer, Erich. *Der Soonwald: Auf den Spuren des Jägers aus Kurpfalz.* Stuttgart: DRW-Verlag, 1974.

Beiler, Rosalind J. "Bridging the Gap: Cultural Mediators and the Structure of Transatlantic Communication." In *Atlantic Communications: The Media in American and German History from the Seventeenth to the Twentieth Century.* Edited by Norbert Finzsch and Ursula Lehmkuhl. Oxford: Berg, 2004. Pages 45–64.

———. "Distributing Aid to Believers in Need: The Religious Foundations of Transatlantic Migration." *Pennsylvania History* 64 Supplemental Issue (1997): 73–87.

———. "Information Networks and the Dynamics of Migration: Swiss Anabaptist Exiles and Their Host Communities." In *Religious Refugees in Europe, Asia, and North*

America Sixth–Twenty-first Centuries. Edited by Susanne Lachenicht. Munster: Lit
    Verlag, 2007. Pages 81–91.

———. "Smuggling Goods or Moving Households? The Legal Status of German-
    Speaking Immigrants in the First British Empire." In *Menschen zwischen zwei Welten:
    Auswanderung, Ansiedlung, Akkulturation.* Edited by Walter G. Rödel and Helmut
    Schmahl. Trier: WVT Wissenschaftlicher Verlag Trier, 2002. Pages 9–23.

———. "The Transatlantic World of Caspar Wistar: From Germany to America in the
    Eighteenth Century." Ph.D. diss., University of Pennsylvania, 1994.

Bellesiles, Michael. *Arming America: The Origins of a National Gun Culture.* New York:
    Alfred A. Knopf, 2000.

Bender, Harold S. "The Founding of the Mennonite Church in America at Germantown,
    1683–1708." *Mennonite Quarterly Review* 7 (1933): 238–46.

Benrath, Gustav Adolf. "Die konfessionellen Unionsbestrebungen des Kurfürsten Karl
    Ludwig von der Pfalz." *Zeitschrift die Geschichte des Oberrheins* 116 (1968): 187–252.

Benz, Richard. *Heidelberg: Schicksal und Geist.* Konstanz: J. Thorbecke, 1961.

Bosher, J. F. "Huguenot Merchants and the Protestant International in the Seventeenth
    Century." *William and Mary Quarterly* 52 (1995): 77–100.

Brecht, Martin. "August Hermann Francke und der Hallische Pietismus." In *Geschichte des
    Pietismus.* Vol. 1, *Das Pietismus vom siebzehnten bis zum frühen achtzehnten Jahrhun-
    dert.* Edited by Martin Brecht. Göttingen: Vandenhoeck and Ruprecht, 1993.

———. "Philipp Jakob Spener, sein Programm und dessen Auswirkungen." In *Geschichte
    des Pietismus.* Vol. 1, *Das Pietismus vom siebzehnten bis zum frühen achtzehnten Jahr-
    hundert.* Edited by Martin Brecht. Göttingen: Vandenhoeck and Ruprecht, 1993.

Brecht, Martin, Klaus Deppermann, Ulrich Gäbler, and Hartmut Lehmann, eds.
    Geschichte des Pietismus. Göttingen: Vandenhoeck and Ruprecht, 1993–2004.

Breen, T. H. "An Empire of Goods." In *Colonial America: Essays in Politics and Social
    Development.* 4th. ed. Edited by Stanley Katz, John M. Murrin, and Douglas Green-
    berg. New York: McGraw-Hill, 1993.

———. *The Marketplace of Revolution: How Consumer Politics Shaped American Indepen-
    dence.* New York: Oxford University Press, 2004.

Breen, T. H., and Timothy Hall. "Structuring Provincial Imagination: The Rhetoric and
    Experience of Social Change in Eighteenth-Century New England." *American
    Historical Review* 103 (1998): 1411–39.

Bridenbaugh, Carl and Jessica. *Rebels and Gentlemen: Philadelphia in the Age of Franklin.*
    New York: Oxford University Press, 1962.

Bronner, Edwin B. "Quaker Landmarks in Early Philadelphia." *Transactions of the Ameri-
    can Philosophical Society,* n.s., 43, pt. 1 (1953): 210–12.

———. "Village into Town, 1706–1746." In *Philadelphia: A 300-Year History.* Edited by
    Russell Weigley. New York: W. W. Norton, 1982.

———. *William Penn's "Holy Experiment": The Founding of Pennsylvania, 1681–1701.* 1962;
    repr. Westport, Conn.: Greenwood Press, 1978.

Burgert, Annette K. *Eighteenth-Century Emigrants from German-Speaking Lands to North
    America.* Vol. 1, *The Northern Kraichgau.* Breinigsville, Pa.: Pennsylvania German
    Society, 1983.

Bushman, Richard. *The Refinement of America: Persons, Houses, Cities.* New York: Alfred A.
    Knopf, 1992.

Butler, Jon. *Becoming America: The Revolution Before 1776.* Cambridge: Harvard University Press, 2000.

Carretta, Vincent. *Equiano the African: Biography of a Self-Made Man.* Athens: University of Georgia Press, 2005.

Carson, Cary, Ronald Hoffman, and Peter Albert, eds. *Of Consuming Interests: The Style of Life in the Eighteenth Century.* Charlottesville: University Press of Virginia, 1994.

Claussen, W. Edmunds. *Wyck: The Story of an Historic House, 1690–1970.* Philadelphia, 1970.

Collins, Margaret H., and Ellinor C. Aird. *The Collins Family.* Vol. 3, *Ancestors of the Distaff Side of the First Five Generations of the Collins Family in America.* Ardmore, Pa.: Collins, 1980.

Cressy, David. *Coming Over: Migration and Communication Between England and New England in the Seventeenth Century.* Cambridge: Cambridge University Press, 1987.

Crismer, Léon Maurice. "Origines et Mouvements des Verriers Venus en Belgique au XVIIIe Siécle." *Annales du 7e Congrès International d'Étude Historique du Verre.* Liege, 1978. Pages 321–58.

Cronon, William. *Changes in the Land: Indians, Colonists, and the Ecology of New England.* New York: Hill and Wang, 1983.

Davids, Richard Wistar. *The Wistar Family. A Genealogy of the Descendants of Caspar Wistar, Emigrant in 1717.* Philadelphia, 1896.

Davis, W. W. H. *The History of Bucks County, Pennsylvania from the Discovery of the Delaware to the Present Time.* New York: Lewis Publishing, 1905. Chap. 32, Dec. 12, 2003. Available at ftp://ftp.rootsweb.com/pub/usgenweb/pa/bucks/history/ local/davis/ davis30.txt.

Denniston, Elmer. *Genealogy of the Stukey, Ream, Grove, Clem and Denniston Families.* Harrisburg: Denniston, 1939.

Deppermann, Andreas. *Johann Jakob Schütz und die Anfänge des Pietismus.* Tübingen: Mohr Siebeck, 2002.

Deppermann, Klaus. "Pennsylvanien als Asyl des frühen deutschen Pietismus." *Pietismus und Neuzeit* 10 (1982): 190–212.

Diamondstone, Judith. "Philadelphia's Municipal Corporation, 1701–1776." *Pennsylvania Magazine of History and Biography* 90 (1966): 183–201.

Dickerson, Oliver M. *The Navigation Acts and the American Revolution.* Philadelphia: University of Pennsylvania Press, 1951.

Dipper, Christof. *Deutsche Geschichte, 1648–1789.* Frankfurt/Main: Suhrkamp, 1991.

———. "Volksreligiosität und Obrigkeit im 18. Jahrhundert." In *Volksreligiosität in der modernen Sozialgeschichte.* Edited by Wolfgang Schieder. Göttingen: Vandenhoeck and Ruprecht, 1986.

Distefano, Judy Mann. "A Concept of Family in Colonial America: The Pembertons of Philadelphia." Ph.D. diss., Ohio State University, 1970.

Doerflinger, Thomas. *A Vigorous Spirit of Enterprise: Merchants and Economic Development in Revolutionary Philadelphia.* New York: W. W. Norton, 1987.

Doutrich, Paul. "Cresap's War: Expansion and Conflict in the Susquehanna Valley." *Pennsylvania History* 53 (1986): 89–104.

Dunn, Richard S. "Penny Wise and Pound Foolish: Penn as a Businessman." In *The World of William Penn.* Edited by Richard S. Dunn and Mary Maples Dunn. Philadelphia: University of Pennsylvania Press, 1986.

————. "Servants and Slaves: The Recruitment and Employment of Labor." In *Colonial British America: Essays in the New History of the Early Modern Era.* Edited by Jack P. Greene and J. R. Pole. Baltimore: Johns Hopkins University Press, 1984.

Durnbaugh, Donald. *The Brethren in Colonial America.* Elgin, Ill.: Brethren Press, 1967.

————. *European Origins of the Brethren.* Elgin, Ill.: Brethren Press, 1958.

Dutrizac, Charles. "Local Identity and Authority in a Disputed Hinterland: The Pennsylvania-Maryland Border in the 1730s." *Pennsylvania Magazine of History and Biography* 115 (1991): 35–61.

Ebeling, Dietrich. *Der Holländerholzhandel in den Rheinlanden: Zu den Handelsbeziehungen zwischen den Niederlanden und dem westlichen Deutschland im 17. und 18. Jahrhundert.* Stuttgart: Franz Steiner Verlag, 1992.

Eckardt, Hans Wilhelm. *Herrschaftliche Jagd, bäuerliche Not, und bürgerliche Kritik: Zur Geschichte der fürstlichen und adligen Jagdprivilegien vornehmlich im südwestdeutschen Raum.* Göttingen: Vandenhoeck and Ruprecht, 1976.

Engel, Kate Carté. "'Commerce that the Lord could Sanctify and Bless': Moravian Participation in Transatlantic Trade, 1740–1760." Working paper no. 03009, International Seminar on the History of the Atlantic World, Harvard University, August 2003.

Faust, Albert B. *The German Element in the United States.* 2 vols. New York: Steuben Society of America, 1927.

Fenske, Hans. "International Migration: Germany in the Eighteenth Century." *Central European History* 13 (1980): 332–47.

Fertig, Georg. *Lokales Leben, atlantische Welt: Die Entscheidung zur Auswanderung vom Rhein nach Nordamerika im 18. Jahrhundert.* Osnabrück: Universitätsverlag Rasch, 2000.

————. "Transatlantic Migration from the German-Speaking Parts of Central Europe, 1600–1800: Proportions, Structures, and Explanations." In *Europeans on the Move: Studies on European Migration, 1500–1800.* Edited by Nicholas Canny. Oxford: Clarendon Press, 1994. Pages 228–31.

Fischer, David H. *Albion's Seed: British Folkways in America.* New York: Oxford University Press, 1989.

Fisher, Elizabeth W. "'Prophesies and Revelations': German Cabbalists in Early Pennsylvania." *Pennsylvania Magazine of History and Biography* 109 (1985): 299–333.

Flinn, Michael W. *The History of the British Coal Industry.* Vol. 2, *1700–1830: The Industrial Revolution.* Oxford: Clarendon Press, 1984.

Fogleman, Aaron S. "Hopeful Journeys: German Immigration and Settlement in Greater Pennsylvania, 1717–1775." Ph.D. diss., University of Michigan, 1991.

————. *Hopeful Journeys: German Immigration, Settlement, and Political Culture in Colonial America, 1717–1775.* Philadelphia: University of Pennsylvania Press, 1996.

————. "Migrations to the Thirteen British North American Colonies, 1700–1775: New Estimates." *Journal of Interdisciplinary History* 22 (1992): 691–709.

————. "Progress and Possibilities in Migration Studies: The Contributions of Werner Hacker to the Study of Early German Migration to Pennsylvania." *Pennsylvania History* 56 (1989): 318–29.

Gable, Ann Hinkle. *The Pastoral Years of Rev. Anthony Henckel, 1692–1717.* Camden, Maine: Penobscot Press, 1991.

Gagliardo, John. *Germany Under the Old Regime, 1600–1790.* London: Longman, 1991.

Gawthrop, Richard. *Pietism and the Making of Eighteenth-Century Prussia.* Cambridge: Cambridge University Press, 1993.

Glatfelter, Charles H. *Pastors and People: German Lutheran and Reformed Churches in the Pennsylvania Field, 1717–1793.* Vol. 2, *The History.* Breinigsville, Pa.: Pennsylvania German Society, 1981.

Goebel, Julius, ed. "Briefe Deutscher Auswanderer aus dem Jahr 1709." *Deutsch-Amerikanische Geschichtsblätter* 12 (1912).

———, ed. "Neue Dokumente zur Geschichte der Massenauswanderung im Jahre 1709." *Deutsch-Amerikanische Geschichtsblätter* 13 (1913).

Goebel, Max. *Geschichte des christlichen Lebens in der rheinisch-westphälischen evangelischen Kirche,* Vol. 2, *Das siebenzehnte Jahrundert.* Coblenz: Karl Bädeker, 1862.

Gough, Deborah Mathias. *Christ Church, Philadelphia: The Nation's Church in a Changing City.* Philadelphia: University of Pennsylvania Press, 1995.

Grabbe, Hans-Jurgen. "Das Ende des Redemptioner-Systems in den Vereinigten Staaten." *Amerika-Studien* 29 (1984): 277–96.

Graham, Robert Earle. "The Taverns of Colonial Philadelphia." *Transactions of the American Philosophical Society,* n.s., 43 (1953): 318–25.

Green, James. "The Book Trade in the Middle Colonies, 1680–1720." In *History of the Book in America.* Vol. 1, *The Colonial Book in the Atlantic World.* Edited by Hugh Amory and David D. Hall. Cambridge: Cambridge University Press, 2000.

———. "English Books and Printing in the Age of Franklin." In *History of the Book in America.* Vol. 1, *The Colonial Book in the Atlantic World.* Edited by Hugh Amory and David D. Hall. Cambridge: Cambridge University Press, 2000.

Greene, Jack. *Pursuits of Happiness: The Social Development of Early Modern British Colonies and the Formation of American Culture.* Chapel Hill: University of North Carolina Press, 1988.

Grubb, Farley. "Incidents of Servitude in Trans-Atlantic Migration." *Explorations in Economic History* 22 (1985): 316–39.

———. "The Market Structure of Shipping German Immigrants to Philadelphia." *Pennsylvania Magazine of History and Biography* 111 (1987): 27–48.

———. "Servant Auction Records and Immigration into the Delaware Valley, 1745–1831: The Proportion of Females Among Immigrant Servants." In *A Demographic History of the Philadelphia Region, 1600–1860.* Edited by Susan E. Klepp. *Proceedings of the American Philosophical Society* 133, no. 2 (1989): 190–214.

Gundlach, Walter. "Zur Geschichte der Glashütten im Laubacher und Büdinger Wald und ihrer Glasmeister." *Hessische Familienkunde* 11 (1973): 266–90.

Häberlein, Mark. "Communication and Group Interaction Among German Migrants to Colonial Pennsylvania: The Case of Baden-Durlach." In *In Search of Peace and Prosperity: New German Settlements in Eighteenth-Century Europe and America.* Edited by Hartmut Lehmann, Hermann Wellenreuther, and Renate Wilson. University Park: The Pennsylvania State University Press, 2000.

———. *Vom Oberrhein Zum Susquehanna: Studien zur badischen Auswanderung nach Pennsylvania im 18. Jahrhundert.* Stuttgart: W. Kohlhammer Verlag, 1993.

Hancock, David *Citizens of the World: London Merchants and the Integration of the British Atlantic Community, 1735–1785,* Cambridge: Cambridge University Press, 1995.

Hans, Alfred. *Die Kurpfälzische Religionsdeklaration von 1705. Ihre Entstehung und Bedeutung für das Zusammenleben der drei im Reich tolerierten Konfessionen.* Mainz : Selbstverlag der Gesellschaft für mittelrheinische Kirchengeschichte, 1973.

Harper, Lawrence. *The English Navigation Laws: A Seventeenth-Century Experiment in Social Engineering.* New York: Columbia University Press, 1939; repr. 1973.

Harris, P. M. G. "The Demographic Development of Colonial Philadelphia in Some
    Comparative Perspective." *Proceedings of the American Philosophical Society* 133 (June
    1989): 262–304.
Hausrath, Hans. "Zur Geschichte der kurpfälzischen Forstorganisation." In *Forstwissen-
    schaftliches Centralblatt.* Edited by Hermann von Fürst. Berlin: Verlagsbuchhandlung
    Paul Parey, 1908. Page 451.
Häusser, Ludwig. *Geschichte der Rheinischen Pfalz nach ihren politischen, kirchlichen und
    literarischen Verhältnissen.* Heidelberg: J. C. B. Mohr, 1845.
Heiss, Willard, ed. *Quaker Biographical Sketches of Ministers and Elders, and Other Con-
    cerned Members of the Yearly Meeting of Philadelphia, 1682–1800.* Indianapolis: pub. by
    the editor, 1972.
Heuvel, Christine van den. *Beamtenschaft und Territorialstaat: Behördenentwichklung
    und Sozialstruktur der Beamtenschaft im Hochstift Osnabrück, 1550–1800.* Osnabrück:
    Kommissionsverlag H. Th. Wenner, 1984.
Hinshaw, William W. ed. *Encyclopedia of American Quaker Genealogy.* Vol. 2, *Records and
    Minutes of Four of the Oldest Monthly Meetings Which Ever Belonged to the Philadelphia
    Yearly Meeting of Friends.* 1938; repr. Baltimore: Genealogical Publishing, 1994.
Hoffer, Peter. *Past Imperfect: Facts, Fictions, Frauds—American History from Bancroft and
    Parkman to Ambrose, Bellesiles, Ellis, and Goodwin.* New York: Public Affairs, 2004.
Holborn, Hajo. *A History of Modern German, 1648–1840.* Princeton: Princeton University
    Press, 1964.
Hoppe, Reinhard. *Dorfbuch der Gemeinde Ziegelhausen mit Ortsteil Peterstal.* Heidelberg,
    1940.
Horle, Craig, Joseph Foster, and Jeffrey Scheib et al., eds. *Lawmaking and Legislators in
    Pennsylvania: A Biographical Dictionary.* Vol. 2, *1750–1756.* Philadelphia: University of
    Pennsylvania Press, 1997.
Horle, Craig, and Marianne Wokeck et al., eds. *Lawmaking and Legislators in Pennsylva-
    nia: A Biographical Dictionary.* Vol. 1, *1682–1709.* Philadelphia: University of Pennsyl-
    vania Press, 1991.
Hsia, R. Po-Chia. *Social Discipline in the Reformation: Central Europe, 1550–1750.* London:
    Routledge, 1989.
Hull, William. *William Penn and the Dutch Quaker Migration to Pennsylvania.* Swarth-
    more, Pa.: Swarthmore College, 1935.
Ibach, Earl W. *The Hub of the Tulpehocken.* N.p.: Earl W. Ibach, 1976.
Irmscher, Klaus, and Rosalind Beiler. "Die Wanderungsbewegungen der Glasmacher
    Wenzel aus Gründau-Breitenborn im Deutschen Südwesten, Erste Teil." *Genealogie*
    9/10 (1998): 274–96.
Janney, Samuel M. *The Life of William Penn: With Selections from His Correspondence and
    Autobiography.* Philadelphia: Lippincott, Grambo, 1852.
Jennings, Francis. *The Ambiguous Iroquois Empire: The Covenant Chain Confederation of
    Indian Tribes with English Colonies from Its Beginnings to the Lancaster Treat of 1744.*
    New York: W. W. Norton, 1984.
———. "Brother Miquon: Good Lord!" In *The World of William Penn.* Edited by
    Richard S. Dunn and Mary Maples Dunn. Philadelphia: University of Pennsylvania
    Press, 1986. Pages 195–214.
———. "Incident at Tulpehocken." *Pennsylvania History* 35 (1968): 335–39.

———. "The Scandalous Indian Policy of William Penn's Sons: Deeds and Documents of the Walking Purchase." *Pennsylvania History* 37 (1970): 19–39.

Jensen, Arthur. *The Maritime Commerce of Colonial Philadelphia.* Madison: The State Historical Society of Wisconsin for the Department of History, University of Wisconsin, 1963.

Jones, George, ed. *Detailed Reports on the Salzburger Emigrants Who Settled in America, Edited by Samuel Urlsperger.* Vol. 1, *1733–1734.* Athens: University of Georgia Press, 1968.

———. *The Georgia Dutch: From the Rhine and Danube to the Savannah, 1773–1783.* Athens: University of Georgia Press, 1992.

Jones, Henry Z., Jr. *The Palatine Families of New York: A Study of the German Immigrants Who Arrived in Colonial New York in 1710.* 2 vols. Universal City, Calif.: Henry Z. Jones, 1985.

Jordan, John W., ed. *Colonial and Revolutionary Families of Pennsylvania.* Vol. 1. 1911; repr. Baltimore: Genealogical Publishing, 1978.

Kann, Mark E. *A Republic of Men: The American Founders, Gendered Language, and Patriarchal Politics.* New York: New York University Press, 1998.

Katz, Stanley, John M. Murrin, and Douglas Greenberg, eds. *Colonial America: Essays in Politics and Social Development.* 4th ed. New York: McGraw-Hill, 1983.

Kauffman, Henry J. *The Pennsylvania-Kentucky Rifle.* Harrisburg: Bonanza Books, 1960.

Kaufmann, Thomas. "Einleitung." In *Interkonfessionalität-Transkonfessionalität-binnenkonfessionelle Pluralitaät. Neue Forschungen zur Konfessionalisierungsthese.* Edited by Kaspar von Greyerz, Manfred Jakubowski-Tiessen, Thomas Kaufmann, and Hartmut Lehmann. Gütersloh: Mohn, 2002.

Keiper, Johann. *Pfälzische Forst- und Jagdgeschichte mit einem forstlichen und geschichtlichen Übersichtskärtchen.* Speyer: Pfälzische Gesellschaft zur Förderung der Wissenschaften, 1930.

Kettner, James H. *The Development of American Citizenship, 1608–1870.* Chapel Hill: University of North Carolina Press, 1978.

Kimmel, Michael S. *Manhood in America: A Cultural History.* New York: Free Press, 1996.

Klepp, Susan E. "Demography in Early Philadelphia, 1690–1860." *Proceedings of the American Philosophical Society* 133 (June 1989): 85–111.

Klepp, Susan E., and Billy G. Smith, eds. *The Infortunate: The Voyage and Adventures of William Moraley.* University Park: The Pennsylvania State University Press, 1992.

Knittle, Walter A. *Early Eighteenth-Century Palatine Emigration: A British Government Redemptioner Project to Manufacture Naval Stores,* 1937; repr., Baltimore: Genealogical Publishing, 1970.

Kollnig, Karl. *Wandlungen im Bevölkerungsbild des pfälzischen Oberrheingebietes.* Heidelberg: Carl Winters Universitätsbuchhandlung, 1952.

Krimm, Stefan. *Die mittelalterlichen und frühneuzeitlichen Glashütten im Spessart.* Aschaffenburg: Geschichts- und Kunstverein Aschaffenburg, 1982.

Landsman, Ned. *Scotland and Its First American Colony, 1683–1765.* Princeton: Princeton University Press, 1985.

Lehmann, Hartmut, Herman Wellenreuther, and Renate Wilson, eds. *In Search of Peace and Prosperity: New German Settlements in Eighteenth-Century Europe and America.* University Park: The Pennsylvania State University Press, 2000.

Lemay, J. A. Leo, and P. M. Zall, eds. *Benjamin Franklin's Autobiography: An Authoritative Text, Backgrounds, Criticism.* New York: W. W. Norton, 1986.

Lemon, James. *The Best Poor Man's Country: A Geographical Study of Early Southeastern Pennsylvania.* Baltimore: Johns Hopkins University Press, 1972.

Lenz, Rüdiger. *Kellerei und Unteramt Dilsberg: Entwicklung einer regionalen Verwaltungsinstanz im Rahmen der kurpfälzischen Territorialpolitik am unteren Neckar.* Stuttgart: W. Kohlhammer Verlag, 1989.

Lloyd, Mark F. "The Johnson Jansen Family and Their Houses in Eighteenth Century Germantown." *Germantown Crier* 33, no. 2 (1981): 36–43.

Lotz-Heumann, Ute. "The Concept of 'Confessionalization': A Historiographical Paradigm in Dispute." *Memoria y Civilizacion* 4 (2001): 93–114 .

MacMaster, Richard K. *Land, Piety and Peoplehood: The Establishment of Mennonite Communities in America, 1683–1790.* Scottdale, Pa.: Herald Press, 1985.

Martin, Asa E. "Lotteries in Pennsylvania Prior to 1833." *Pennsylvania Magazine of History and Biography* 47 (1923): 309–13.

McCusker, John J. *Money and Exchange in Europe and America, 1600–1775.* Chapel Hill: University of North Carolina Press, 1978.

McCusker, John J., and Russell Menard. *The Economy of North America, 1607–1789.* Chapel Hill: University of North Carolina Press, 1985.

McKearin, Helen, and George S. McKearin. *Two Hundred Years of American Blown Glass.* 1950; repr., New York: Crown, 1966.

McMahan, Michael. "'Public Service' versus 'Mans Properties': Dock Creek and the Origins of Urban Technology in the Eighteenth-Century Philadelphia." In *Early American Technology: Making and Doing Things from the Colonial Era to 1850.* Edited by Judith A. McGaw. Chapel Hill: University of North Carolina Press, 1994.

Michel, Paul. "Täufer, Mennoniten und Quäker in Kriegsheim bei Worms." *Der Wormsgau* 7 (1965/66): 41–52.

Moon, Robert C. *The Morris Family of Philadelphia: Descendants of Anthony Morris.* Philadelphia: R. C. Moon, 1898.

Morse, Emily, and Winifred McLachlan. *The Swope Family Book of Remembrance: A History of the Origins of the First Schwab, Schwob, Swope Families in Early Lancaster County, Pennsylvania, and Some of Their Descendants.* Vol. 2, *Jost Schwob.* Provo, Utah: J. Theron Smith, 1972.

Müller, Thomas J. *Kirche zwischen zwei Welten: Die Obrigkeitsproblematik bei Heinrich Melchior Mühlenberg und die Kirchengründung der deutschen Lutheraner in Pennsylvania.* Stuttgart: Franz Steiner Verlag, 1994.

Müller-Bahlke, Thomas. "Communication at Risk: The Beginnings of the Halle Correspondence with the Pennsylvania Lutherans." In *In Search of Peace and Prosperity: New German Settlements in Eighteenth-Century Europe and America.* Edited by Hartmut Lehmann, Hermann Wellenreuther, and Renate Wilson. University Park: The Pennsylvania State University Press, 2000.

Müller-Bahlke, Thomas, and Klaus E. Göltz. *Die Kunst- und Naturalienkammer der Franckeschen Stiftungen.* Halle: Franckesche Stiftungen, 1998.

Munger, Donna. *Pennsylvania Land Records: A History and Guide for Research.* Wilmington, Del.: Scholarly Resources, 1991.

Nash, Gary B. "City Planning and Political Tensions in the Seventeenth Century: The Case of Philadelphia." *Proceedings of the American Philosophical Society* 112 (1968): 60–64.

———. "The Early Merchants of Philadelphia: The Formation and Disintegration of a Founding Elite." In *The World of William Penn*. Edited by Richard S. Dunn and Mary Maples Dunn. Philadelphia: University of Pennsylvania Press, 1986.

———. *Quakers and Politics: Pennsylvania, 1681–1726*. 1968; rev. ed. Boston: Northeastern University Press, 1993.

———. *Urban Crucible: Social Change, Political Consciousness, and the Origins of the American Revolution*. Cambridge: Harvard University Press, 1978.

Nash, Gary B., and Billy G. Smith. "The Population of Eighteenth-Century Philadelphia." *Pennsylvania Magazine of History and Biography* 99 (1975): 362–68.

Oberholtzer, Ellis P. *Philadephia: A History of the City and Its People*. Philadelphia: S. J. Clarke Publishing, 1912.

Olson, Alison. *Making the Empire Work: London and American Interest Groups, 1690–1790*. Cambridge: Harvard University Press, 1992.

O'Reilly, William T. "'A Paragon of Wickedness': Newlanders and Agents in Eighteenth-Century German Migration." Working paper no. 96–25, International Seminar on the History of the Atlantic World, 1500–1800, Harvard University, 1996.

Otterness, Philip. *Becoming German: The 1709 Palatine Migration to New York*. Ithaca: Cornell University Press, 2004.

Palmer, Arlene. "Glass Production in Eighteenth-Century America: The Wistarburgh Enterprise." *Winterthur Portfolio* 11 (1976): 25–101.

———. "The Wistarburg Glassworks of Colonial New Jersey." Master's thesis, University of Delaware, 1973.

———. *The Wistars and Their Glass, 1739–1777*. Millville, N.J.: Wheaton Village Museum, 1989.

Parsons, William T. "The Bloody Election of 1742." *Pennsylvania History* 36 (1969): 290–306.

Penney, Norman. *My Ancestors*. Bishopsgate, E. C. Ashford, Kent; Printed for private circulation by Headley Brothers, 1920.

Pennypacker, Samuel W. *Historical and Biographical Sketches*. Philadelphia: Robert A. Tripple, 1883.

———. *The Settlement of Germantown*. 1899; repr. [New York]: B. Blom 1970.

Pepper, Adeline. *The Glass Gaffers of New Jersey and Their Creations from 1739 to the Present*. New York, 1971.

Pfister, Hans Ulrich. *Die Auswanderung aus dem Knonauer Amt, 1648–1750: Ihr Ausmass, ihre Strukturen und ihre Bedingungen*. Zurich: H. Rohr, 1987. Pages 257–77.

Reinhard, Wolfgang. *Geschichte der Staatsgewalt: Eine vergleichende Verfassungsgeschichte Europas von den Anfängen bis zur Gegenwart*. Munich: Verlag C. H. Beck, 2002, 125–209.

———. "Reformation, Counter-Reformation, and the Early Modern State: A Reassessment." *Catholic Historical Review* 75 (1989): 383–404.

———. "Zwang zur Konfessionalisierung? Prolegomena zu einer theorie des konfessionellen Zeitalters." *Zeitschrift für hisorische Forschung* 10 (1983): 257–77.

Reinhard, Wolfgang, and Heinz Schilling, eds., *Die katholische Konfessionalisierung*. Munster and Gütersloh: Mohn, 1995.

Renkewitz, Heinz. *Hochmann von Hochenau 1670–1721: Quellen Studien zur Gescheichte des Peitismus*. Vol. 5, *Arbeiten zur Geschichte des Pietismus*. Witten: Luther-Verlag, 1969.

Roeber, A. Gregg. "German and Dutch Books and Printing." In *History of the Book in America*. Vol. 1, *The Colonial Book in the Atlantic World*. Edited by Hugh Amory and David D. Hall. Cambridge: Cambridge University Press, 2000.

————. "In German Ways? Problems and Potentials of Eighteenth-Century German Social and Emigration History." *William and Mary Quarterly* 44 (October 1987): 750–74.

————. "The Origin and Transfer of German American Concepts of Property and Inheritance." *Perspectives in American History,* n.s., 3 (1986): 115–71.

————. "'The Origin of Whatever Is Not English Among Us': The Dutch-Speaking and the German-Speaking Peoples of Colonial British America." In *Strangers Within the Realm: Cultural Margins of the First British Empire.* Edited by Bernard Bailyn and Philip D. Morgan. Chapel Hill: University of North Carolina Press, 1991.

————. *Palatines, Liberty and Property: German Lutherans in Colonial British America.* Baltimore: Johns Hopkins University Press, 1993.

Rolland, Susanne Mosteller. "From the Rhine to the Catawba: A Study of Eighteenth-Century Germanic Migration and Adaptation." Ph.D. diss., Emory University, 1991.

Rotundo, Anthony E. *American Manhood: Transformations in Masculinity from the Revolution to the Modern Era.* New York: Basic Books, 1993.

Rubincam, Milton. "The Wistar-Wister Family: A Pennsylvania Family's Contributions Toward American Cultural Development." *Pennsylvania History* 20 (1953): 142–64.

Rublack, H.-Ch., ed., *Die lutherische Konfessionalisierung in Deutschland.* Gütersloh: Mohn, 1992.

Sabean, David W. *Power in the Blood: Popular Culture and Village Discourse in Early Modern Germany.* Cambridge: Cambridge University Press, 1984.

————. *Property, Production, and Family in Neckarhausen, 1700–1870.* Cambridge: Cambridge University Press, 1990.

Sachse, Julius, *The German Pietists of Provincial Pennsylvania, 1694–1708.* 1895; repr. New York: AMS Press, 1970.

————. "Pennsylvania: The German Influence in Its Settlement and Development." *Pennsylvania German Society Proceedings and Addresses* 14 (1905): 8–12.

————. *Pennsylvania: The German Influence in Its Settlement and Development: A Narrative and Critical History.* Pt. 27, *The Diarium of Magister Johannes Kelpius.* Lancaster, Pa.: Pennsylvania-German Society, 1917.

————. "Title Pages of Books and Pamphlets That Influenced German Emigration to Pennsylvania." *Pennsylvania German Society Proceedings and Addresses* 7 (1897): 201–56.

Sachse, Julius, ed. and trans. *Falkner's Curieuse Nachricht von Pensylvania: The Book That Stimulated the Great German Emigration to Pennsylvania.* Philadelphia: Pennsylvania German Society, 1905.

Schaab, Meinrad. "Die Wiederherstellung des Katholizismus in der Kurpfalz im 17. und 18. Jahrhundert." *Zeitschrift die Geschichte des Oberrheins* 114 (1966): 147–205.

————. *Geschichte der Kurpfalz.* Vol. 2, *Neuzeit.* Stuttgart: W. Kohlhammer Verlag, 1992.

Scharf, J. Thomas. *History of Delaware, 1609–1888.* Vol. 2. Philadelphia: L. J. Richards, 1888.

Schelbert, Leo. *The Swiss Migration to America: The Swiss Mennonites.* New York: Arno Press, 1980.

————. "Von der Macht des Pietismus: Dokumentarbericht zur Auswanderung einer Basler Familie im Jahre 1736." *Baseler Zeitschrift für Geschichte und Altertumskunde* 75 (1975): 90–119.

Scheuner, Gottlieb. *Inspirations-History, 1714–1728.* Translated by Janet W. Zuber. Amana, Iowa, 1977.

Schilling, Heinz, ed. *Die reformierte Konfessionalisierung in Deutschland—Das Problem der "Zweiten Reformation."* Gütersloh: Mohn, 1986.

———. "Konfessionelle und politische Identität." In *Nationale und ethnische Minderheiten und regionale Identitäten in Mittelalter und Neuzeit.* Edited by A. Czacharowski. Thorn, 1994.

Schmidt, Julius. *Chronik von Gaiberg-Waldhilsbach. Zugleich ein Beitrag Pfälzer Kirchenge-schichte.* Heidelberg, 1901.

Schnurmann, Claudia. *Atlantische Welten: Engländer und Nederländer im amerikanisch-atlantischen Raum, 1648–1713.* Cologne: Böhlau Verlag, 1998.

Schuchmann, Heinz. "Notes on the Origins of Joshua Kocherthal." Translated by Frederick S. Weiser. *Concordia Historical Institute Quarterly* 41 (1968).

———. "Der 1708 nach Amerika ausgewanderte Pfarrer Josua Kocherthal hieß ursprünglich Josua Harrsch." *Pfälazische Familien u. Wappenkunde: Biographie, Genealogie, Heraldik,* Supplement: *Mitteilungen zur Wanderungsgeschichte der Pfälzer,* November 6, 1967.

Schwalm, N. Daniel, ed. "The Glassworks near Stephanshof." *Johannes Schwalm the Hessian* 1 (1980): 36–38.

Schwartz, Sally. *"A Mixed Multitude": The Struggle for Toleration in Colonial Pennsylvania.* New York: New York University Press, 1987.

Scribner, Bob. "Communities and the Nature of Power." In *Germany: A New Social and Economic History.* Vol. 1, *1450–1630.* Edited by Bob Scribner. London: Arnold, 1996. Pages 294–98.

Shepherd, William R. *History of Proprietary Government in Pennsylvania.* New York: Columbia University Press, 1896.

Shirk, Willis. "Wright's Ferry: A Glimpse into the Susquehanna Backcountry." *Pennsylvania Magazine of History and Biography* 120 (1996): 67–69.

Shoemaker, Robert. "Christ Church, St. Peter's, and St. Paul's." *Transactions of the American Philosophical Society,* n.s., 43 (1953): 11.

Sickler, Joseph S. *The History of Salem County, New Jersey.* Salem, N.J.: Sunbeam Publishing, 1939.

Slaughter, Thomas. "Crowds in Eighteenth-Century America: Reflections and New Directions." *Pennsylvania Magazine of History and Biography* 115 (1991): 13–18.

Smith, Abbot E. *Colonists in Bondage: White Servitude and Convict Labor in America, 1607–1776.* 1947, repr. New York: W. W. Norton, 1971.

Smith, Billy G. *The "Lower Sort": Philadelphia's Laboring People, 1750–1800.* Ithaca: Cornell University Press, 1990.

Smith, Samuel. *The History of the Colony of Nova-Caesaria, or New Jersey.* New York, 1772.

Snyder, Martin. *City of Independence: Views of Philadelphia Before 1800.* New York: Praeger, 1975.

Sommer, Elizabeth. *Serving Two Masters: Moravian Brethren in Germany and North Carolina, 1727–1801.* Lexington: University Press of Kentucky, 2000.

Steele, Ian K. *The English Atlantic, 1675–1740: An Exploration of Communication and Community.* New York: Oxford University Press, 1986.

Stoeffler, F. Ernest. *The Rise of Evangelical Pietism.* Leiden: E. J. Brill, 1971.

Tatum, George B. *Penn's Great Town: 250 Years of Philadelphia Architecture Illustrated in Prints and Drawings.* Philadelphia: University of Pennsylvania Press, 1961.

Thompson, E. P. *Whigs and Hunters: The Origin of the Black Act.* New York: Pantheon Books, 1975.

Thompson, Peter. *Rum Punch and Revolution: Taverngoing and Public Life in Eighteenth-Century Philadelphia.* Philadelphia: University of Pennsylvania Press, 1999.

Tolles, Frederick B. *Meeting House and Counting House.* 1948; repr. New York: W. W. Norton, 1963.

Trueblood, D. Elton. *Robert Barclay.* New York: Harper and Row, 1968.

Tully, Alan. *William Penn's Legacy: Politics and Social Structure in Provincial Pennsylvania, 1726–1755.* Baltimore: Johns Hopkins University Press, 1977.

Völker-Rasor, Annette, ed. "Neue Impulse innerhalb des Faches Wirtschafts- und Sozialgeschichte: Alte Themen, Neue Akzente." In *Frühe Neuzeit.* Munich: Oldenbourg Verlag, 2006.

von Hippel, Wolfgang. *Auswanderung aus Südwestdeutschland: Studien zur württembergischen Auswanderung und Auswanderungspolitik im 18. und 19. Jahrhundert.* Stuttgart: Klett-Cotta, 1984.

Wacker, Peter O. "The New Jersey Tax-Ratable List of 1751." *New Jersey History* 107 (1989): 23–47.

Wallace, Anthony F. C. *King of the Delawares: Teedyuscung, 1700–1763.* 1949; repr. Syracuse: Syracuse University Press, 1990.

Wallace, Paul A. W. *Conrad Weiser, 1696–1760: Friend of Colonist and Mohawk.* 1945; repr. Baltimore: For Wennawoods Publishing by Gateway Press, 1996.

Wallmann, Johannes ed. *Briefe aus der Frankfurter Zeit, 1666–1686.* Vols. 1–4. Tübingen: Mohr and Siebeck 1992–2005.

Walter, Friedrich. *Geschichte des Theaters und der Musik am kurpfälzischen Hoffe.* Leipzig: Verlag von Breitkopf und Härtel, 1898.

Ward, W. R. *The Protestant Evangelical Awakening.* Cambridge: Cambridge University Press, 1992.

Watson, John. *Annals of Philadelphia and Pennsylvania in the Olden Time.* Philadelphia, 1857.

Wendel, Thomas. "The Keith-Lloyd Alliance: Factional and Coalition Politics in Colonial Pennsylvania." *Pennsylvania Magazine of History and Biography* 92 (1968): 289–305.

Whaley, Joachim. "A Tolerant Society? Religious Toleration in the Holy Roman Empire, 1648–1806." In *Toleration in Enlightenment Europe.* Edited by Ole Peter Grell and Roy Porter. Cambridge: Cambridge University Press, 2000.

Whisker, James Biser. *Pennsylvania Workers in Brass, Copper and Tin, 1681–1900.* Lewiston, N.Y.: Edwin Mellen Press, 1993.

Wilson, Renate. *Pious Traders in Medicine: A German Pharmaceutical Network in Eighteenth-Century North America.* University Park: The Pennsylvania State University Press, 2000.

Wokeck, Marianne S. "The Flow and Composition of German Immigration to Philadelphia, 1727–1776." *Pennsylvania Magazine of History and Biography* 105 (1981): 249–78.

———. "Promoters and Passengers: The German Immigrant Trade, 1683–1775." In *The World of William Penn.* Edited by Richard S. Dunn and Mary Maples Dunn. Philadelphia: University of Pennsylvania Press, 1986.

———. *Trade in Strangers: The Beginnings of Mass Migration to North America.* University Park: The Pennsylvania State University Press, 1999.

Wolff, Mabel P. *The Colonial Agency of Pennsylvania, 1712–1757.* Lancaster, Pa., 1933.

Wood, Jerome H., Jr. *Conestoga Crossroads: Lancaster, Pennsylvania, 1730–1790.* Harrisburg: Pennsylvania Historical and Museum Commission, 1979.

Wroth, Lawrence. "The Story of Thomas Cresap, a Maryland Pioneer." *Maryland Historical Magazine* 9 (1914): 1–37.

Wüst, Günther. *Bammental: Geschichte einer Elsenztalgemeinde.* Heidelberg: Heidelberger Verlagsanstalt, 1983

———. *1000 Jahre Neckargemünd, 988–1988: Beiträge zur Geschichte einer Neckartalgemeinde.* Neckargemünd: Burgermeisteramt, 1988.

———. *Waldhilsbach: Ein Beitrag zur Ortsgeschichte.* Neckargemünd: Druckerei Odenwälder, 2000.

Zahedieh, Nuala. "Economy." In *The British Atlantic World, 1500–1800.* Edited by David Armitage and Michael J. Braddick. New York: Palgrave Macmillan, 2002.

Zeeden, Ernst Walter. *Konfessionsbildung.* Stuttgart: Klett-Cotta, 1985.

Pietists
as emigrants, 7, 73–75, 145
in Palatinate, 76, 77–78, 83
in Philadelphia, 51, 98
poaching, 24–25
politics
New Jersey, 177
Palatinate, 29–30, 49
Philadelphia, 5, 29–30, 89, 108, 120 n. 40
religious affiliation and, 52–53, 58–59, 66, 69, 101, 106, 173
potash, 158, 159
Presbyterian church, Philadelphia, 97, 98
Protestant churches, 55, 57, 59, 62, 66, 68, 84. *See also individual Protestant denominations*

Quakers
CW's affiliation with, 1, 5, 8, 51, 69, 101–2, 106–8, 145, 173
in CW's family, 175–76
as merchants, 49, 106, 139
in Palatinate, 55, 75, 83
in Philadelphia, 53, 94, 96–98, 120 n. 40, 130, 131
use of slaves by, 169

Rauscher family, 78 n. 32
Reck, Philip Georg Friedrich von, 126, 169
Reformed church
in Amt Dilsberg, 61
clergy, 153 n. 90
CW's family affiliation with, 51, 53, 55, 58–59, 62, 65–67, 68
emigrants from, 7, 83, 130, 141, 147
in Palatinate, 35, 36 n. 21, 52, 54–56, 77, 84, 149
in Philadelphia, 69, 98
as state church, 56, 57, 60
religious affiliations. *See also individual religious denominations*
in colonies, 83, 84, 141
commercial networks through, 78, 141
in Palatinate, 51–69, 83, 84, 97
in Philadelphia, 92, 94, 96–98, 131
politics and, 52–53, 58–59, 66, 69, 101, 106, 173

social status from, 49, 58, 69, 89, 101, 106, 108, 173
Religious Declaration of 1705, 60
reputation-building, CW's, 5, 9, 101–2, 115, 124–26, 152, 174. *See also* social status
Rhiem, Abraham, 70, 78 n. 33, 79, 102, 147 n. 57
rifles, CW's importing of, 5, 138, 139 n. 21, 140, 145–47, 149, 173
Rith, Catharine, 123 n. 50
Rutter, John, 106
Rutter, Thomas, 106

Salem County, New Jersey. *See* Wistarburg, New Jersey
Sauer, Christopher, 90, 130
Schäfer family, 39 n. 27
Schmick, Johannes, 150
Schnebeli, Jacob, 141–42, 144
Schriessheim (Germany), 23
Schurmann, Anna Maria von, 74 n. 15
Schütz, Johann Jakob, 74–75
Schwab, Johann Georg, 147 n. 57
Schwab, Jost, 78 n. 33
Schwäbisch-Hallischen Rezess, 56, 57, 58, 59
Schwartz, Georg, 149–50
Scots-Irish immigrants, 110, 113, 114, *128,* 173
self-made man, image of, 2–3, 4, 89
Seltenreich, Leonard, 147 n. 57
ship captains, 139, 142, 144, 174
"Short Report of Caspar Wistar, A" (memoir), 1–4, 12, 28, 70, 88, 89
Sickler, Joseph, 171
Simultankirchen, 58, 67 nn. 45 and 51
Skull, Nicholas, 118 n. 28
slavery, 169
smuggling, CW's, 102 n. 58, 138–39
soap-making, 88, 100
social status, 89, 131–32, 176. *See also* reputation-building
marriage and, 38–39, 49
religious affiliation affecting, 49, 58, 69, 89, 101, 106, 108, 173
Society of Friends. *See* Quakers
Some Account of the Province of Pennsylvania (Penn), 72–73
Spener, Philip Jacob, 74

squatters, German, 111, 114, 115, 116, 118
state-building, 15–16, 18, 29
state churches, 53–54, 56–57, 58, 59–60, 69,
    95
Stedman, John, 93, 141, 142
Steel, James, 124, 126
Steitwald (contested forest), 32
Straub family, 78 n. 32

taxes
    colonies, 81–82, 131, 162–63
    Palatinate, 131, 158, 159–60, 162
Thirty Years' War, aftermath of, 13–14, 15,
    35, 54, 55
Thomas, Gabriel, 93
Thommen, Durst, 152
timber. *See* forests; wood
toleration, religious, 52–56, 59, 82–83, 84,
    96–97
Totenweg path (Waldhilsbach), 36 n. 21
trade networks, 6, 8, 9, 106, 177. *See also*
    commercial networks; German-
    Atlantic world; immigrants, trans-
    portation system of; import business,
    CW's
    transatlantic, 4, 93–94, 111, *143*, 147, 150,
    156, 173
Treaty of Ryswick (1697), 57, 58
Treaty of Westphalia (1648), *xvii, 54*
Tulpehocken Valley settlers, 105–6, 120–23,
    125, 129, 131
Turner, Robert, 98

Ulm, Johannes (CW's brother-in-law), 48
Ulrich, Philipp, 144
Umständige geographische Beschreibung
    (Pastorius), 73 n. 9, *80*
United Glass Company, 1, 5, 9, 155–71, 173,
    177

Venningen, Eberhard Friederich von, 17–18,
    21
Venningen, Karl von, 84, 159
voting rights. *See* elections, Philadelphia

Wägelis family, 78 n. 32
Wahl, Henrich van der, 157 n. 17

Waldhilsbach (Germany), 1–2, 29–42, 102,
    131–32, 176
    lack of schools in, 1–2, 28, 35, 66
    religion in, 35, 58, 61, *69*
Walking Purchase (Pennsylvania), 120
Wanner family, 78 n. 32
War of the Spanish Succession, 59
Welcker, Hans Georg, 147 n. 57
Welsh immigrants, *128*
Wentzel, Johann Christoph, 164
Wentzel, Johann Heinrich, 164
Wentzel, Johann Peter, 157–71
Wentzel, Johann Wilhelm, 165, 167
Wentzel, Leonhard Friederich, 164
Wistar, Caspar (CW)
    baptism, 39, 51, 58
    birth, 28, 36, 39
    childhood, 1–2, 4, 8, 13, 29, 35, 49
    death, 168, 170, 172, 173
    education, 1, 2 n. 10, 28, 35, 66–67
    emigration by, 3–4, 47, 70–85
    family of, 1, 3–4, 111, 175, 182
    legacy, 174–75
    letters from, 50, 51, 110, 134
    marriage, 102 n. 57, 107, 108
    memoir, 1–4, 12, 28, 70, 88, 89
    name change, 15 n. 4, 101, 147 n. 56
    as patriarch of birth family, 111, 135–36,
        144, 147–49, 153, 174
    wealth of, 1, 2–5, 9, 89, 123, 131, 144, 173
Wistar, Caspar (CW's son), 175
Wistar, Catharine Jansen (CW's wife), 1,
    107, 108, 111, 141, 155, 173, 174
Wistar, Katherine (CW's daughter), 175
Wistar, Margaret (CW's daughter), 175
Wistar, Mary Franklin (CW's daughter-
    in-law), 175, 176
Wistar, Rebecca (CW's daughter), 175–76
Wistar, Richard (CW's son), 155, 160–61,
    168, 175
Wistar, Sarah (CW's daughter), 175
Wistar, Sarah Wyatt (CW's daughter-in-
    law), 175
Wistarburg, New Jersey, 1, 9, 156, 163–64,
    168–71, 173
wood
    as commodity, 13–14, 16, 22–24, 30

wood (*cont'd*)
  for glass-making, 157, 158, 159, 160–61, 171
  stealing, 48
workers, glass-making, 155–59, 160, 163–64,
  165, 168–71, 177
Wüster, Albertina (CW's sister), 48, 66, 68
Wüster, Andreas (CW's grandfather), 12, 13
  n. 1, 15–25, 106, 173, 180
  religious affiliation, 53, 55, 65, 89
Wüster, Anna (CW's grandmother), 25–26
Wüster, Anna Barbara (CW's sister), 48,
  66, 140, 148
Wüster, Anna Catharina Müller (CW's
  mother), 4 n. 14, 12, 36
  death, 68, 134, 149
  marriage, 38–39
  religious affiliation, 51, 53, 54–55, 58, 61–62,
  65
  widowhood, 23 n. 36, 47–49, 111, 174
Wüster, Dorothea (CW's sister), 48, 49,
  58, 68
Wüster, Georg Bernhard (CW's brother),
  66
Wüster, Hans Caspar (CW's father), 12, 181
  death, 46–49, 68, 111, 136, 149 n. 69, 174
  as forester, 1, 13 n. 1, 26, 30 n. 2, *31*, 36–47,
  132, 173

marriage, 38–39, 107
political dispute with Andreas Ziegler, 4,
  40–47, 49, 82, 84
religious affiliation, 51, 53–55, 58–59,
  61–62, 65, 79
struggle for status, 4, 29–30, 89, 103, 106,
  124, 131–32, 173, 175–76
Wüster, Johannes (CW's brother), 47, 66,
  130, 136 n. 6, 140, 152
  name change, 15 n. 4, 147
Wüster, Johann Ludwig (CW's brother),
  48–49, 51, 66, 68
Wüster, Ludwig (CW's brother), 142
Wüster, Maria Barbara (CW's sister),
  47–48, 66, 140, 148
Wüster, Maria Margretha (CW's sister), 66

Ziegler, Andreas, 35–36, 48
  political dispute with Hans Wüster, 4,
  40–47, 49, 82, 84
Ziegler, Wilhelm, 140
Zimmerman, Andreas, 147 n. 57
Zimmerman, Heinrich, 140
Zuber, Hans Peter, 151
Zwengenberg, Johannes, 141 n. 32

CPSIA information can be obtained
at www.ICGtesting.com
Printed in the USA
FFOW03n1151170717
37864FF